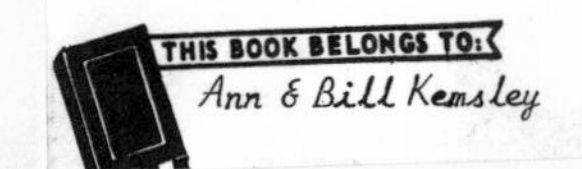
THIS BOOK BELONGS TO:
Ann & Bill Kemsley

D1159515

History of the

BROTHERHOOD OF MAINTENANCE OF WAY EMPLOYES

Its Birth and Growth • 1887-1955

D. W. HERTEL

RANSDELL INC., *Publishers,* WASHINGTON, D. C.

1955

Fulfillment

The publication of this history brings to fulfillment a project that has been attempted and abandoned many times during the past thirty years. It was written under the personal direction of President T. C. Carroll, who commissioned the author to prepare this history, approved the general format and collaborated step by step as the story of the Brotherhood evolved.

JOHN T. WILSON

Founder and First President of the Brotherhood

1887-1908

He laid the foundation and built strong thereon, dedicating his life to the service of his fellow men. His was the courage to undertake—the fidelity to continue—the fortitude to endure.

T. C. CARROLL
Eighth Grand Lodge President
(1947-)

A. SHOEMAKE
Grand Lodge Secretary-Treasurer
(1940-)

Dedication

Dedicated to the memory of the founding fathers whose faith in themselves and in their Brotherhood has been fulfilled.

INTERNATIONAL OFFICERS

1952 - 1955

T. C. CARROLL
President
Detroit, Mich.

A. SHOEMAKE
Secretary-Treasurer
Detroit, Mich.

VICE PRESIDENTS

W. ASPINALL
Winnipeg, Man.

GEO. HUDSON
Jefferson City, Mo.

J. H. HADLEY
Jacksonville, Fla.

T.L. JONES
Denver, Colo.

THOS. F. HOLLERAN
Wilkes-Barre, Pa.

LOUIS VOGLAND
Minneapolis, Minn.

EXECUTIVE BOARD MEMBERS

J. P. WILSON
New Hampton, Iowa

M. C. PLUNK
Jackson, Tenn.

R. FRECCIA
Brooklyn, N. Y.

C. L. LAMBERT
St. Louis, Mo.

J. A. HUNEAULT
Ottawa, Ont.

ADMINISTRATIVE STAFF

FRANK L. NOAKES
Statistician and Research Director
Detroit, Mich.

H. C. CROTTY
Assistant to President
Detroit, Mich.

D. W. HERTEL
Assistant to President
Detroit, Mich.

E. J. PLONDKE
Associate Editor and Director
of Public Relations
Detroit, Mich.

JOHN J. BERTA
Assistant to President
Chicago, Ill.

C. R. BARNES
Member, National Railroad
Adjustment Board,
Third Division
Chicago, Ill.

ERNEST H. BENSON
National Legislative
Representative
Washington, D. C.

Preface

This history of the Brotherhood of Maintenance of Way Employes is the story of the pioneer railroad workers who built our railroads' tracks and bridges, of the courageous men who founded the Brotherhood, and of those who brought it to its high place among labor organizations today. Inevitably, too, it is the story of the men who have worked at all times and in all places in the maintenance of way department of America's railroads.

No history of a labor organization, however, can be complete without at least a brief outline of the industry whose workers it represents. For the industry itself is the warp and woof of the fabric from which the organization has been created. The development of a labor union, its organizational set-up and its accomplishments depend in no small degree on the structure of the industry of which it is a part and the rise and fall of the fortunes of that industry. Thus, the story of America's railroads forms an integral part of this history of the Brotherhood.

The fabulous story of the railroad industry is more than a narrative of the development of transportation. It is the saga of man's restless urge to explore and develop new lands. At the turn of the nineteenth century, the restive colonial pioneers along the Atlantic seaboard looked longingly toward the vast tracts of virgin forests and the millions of acres of fertile land to the south and west. Here were rich new territories to be conquered and settled.

But man's slow and painful advance to the corners of the earth has been geared to his means of transportation. The modes of travel and shipping in that day—the sailing ship, the canal boat, the pony express, the pack horse, the stage coach, and the covered wagon—were slow and cumbersome, wholly unsuited to the needs of swift intercourse between widely separated communities. The mass exodus to the new lands had to await the development of faster and more adequate means of transportation.

In 1830, the inauguration of the first freight-and-passenger-train service in this country opened a new era of expansion and development. As the railroads began spinning their steel web across the continent, a horde of settlers followed, eager to cast their fortunes in the raw, uncharted lands. The track construction gang, the forerunner of today's maintenance of way crew, traveled in the vanguard of this conquering army, laboriously fashioning the right of way from earth and rock, blasting tunnels, laying track, erecting bridges, building trestles. Gradually they pushed the frontiers aside and spanned the continent by rail.

As the railroads established lines in all parts of the continent, maintenance of way crews became more an occupying army than a vanguard. They settled down along the right of ways to maintain the railroads' tracks, bridges, and structures and to raise their families. And as they became established members of their communities, they began to understand the need for collective action to protect and promote their mutual welfare as railroad workers. It was out of this first awareness that their organization, the Brotherhood of Maintenance of Way Employes, was born. And it is to trace the growth and development of that organization that this book is being written.

The writing of a book of this nature requires many decisions. The condensation within several hundred pages of the records of some sixty-eight years is in itself a task of no small magnitude. It means a constant choice between material to be included and that to be omitted, of persons to be named or left unnamed. It has not been possible, therefore, to give credit to all the individual officers and members who have contributed so much to the progress of the Brotherhood, nor to recount in detail all the happenings of these sixty-eight eventful years. A sincere effort has been made, however, to beam the spotlight of retrospection on the mileposts that have marked the growth of the Brotherhood and on the leaders who have made that growth possible.

Although it is difficult at times to keep personal opinion from intruding, one goal in writing this book has been to keep it as objective and as factual as possible.

Much of the material for the early history of the Brotherhood has been taken from the pages of the "Advance Advocate," the first official organ of the Brotherhood. Grand Chief John T. Wilson, founder of the Brotherhood, and those who assisted him in preparing the "Advocate" for publication wrote for the present and not for posterity. Minus the services of an editorial staff, they gleaned material wherever it could be found. The tiny force must have been hard pressed at times to maintain publication.

In view of these handicaps, it would be strange indeed if minor errors of fact and occasional inconsistencies did not appear in the "Advocate." Nevertheless, the "Advocate" was generally well prepared, and it gives us an authentic picture of the difficult but successful struggle of the young organization to establish itself. We hope that the use of this material has helped to recreate some of the aura of that day.

The preparation for a work of this kind requires not only the accumulation of a great deal of data but the collaboration of persons whose knowledge and personal experience form an invaluable source of insight into the significance of events over and beyond the mere recounting of facts. We are genuinely grateful to those who have assisted in the preparation of this book and whose helpful criticism has made the writing of this book easier.

Particular thanks are due President T. C. Carroll for his collaboration and cooperation, and members of his staff for their assistance in this arduous undertaking; Secretary-Treasurer A. Shoemake and his staff for making historical documents available and verifying certain portions of the manuscript; Vice President W. Aspinall for his history of the Central Committee of Canada and other data concerning the story of the Brotherhood in Canada; William Jewkes for his outline of conditions on Canadian railways many years ago; Statistician and Research Director Frank L. Noakes and members of his staff, who supplied the tables in the appendices and other statistical and historical data; Associate Editor E. J. Plondke and his editorial staff, who made their material sources available and supplied many of the photographs used in this history; the Public Relations Department of the Association of American Railroads for their cooperation in furnishing old and new photographs of the railroad industry; the various railroads whose photographs are a part of this history; Dr. William M. Leiserson for his careful reading of the manuscript and for his constructive comments and suggestions; and the secretaries who performed the tedious job of typing during the writing and revision of the manuscript.

Introduction

To those who are not familiar with the Brotherhood and its work, a formal outline of its objectives, its creed, and its organizational set-up is essential to a better understanding of this history.

The Brotherhood of Maintenance of Way Employes is a railroad labor organization representing some 300,000 railroad maintenance of way workers in the United States and Canada. Maintenance of way workers are often referred to as the "shock troops of the railroads," for it is their job to keep safe the tracks, trestles, and bridges over which freight and passenger trains move swiftly to all parts of the continent.

You have often seen them putt-putting down the track on a motor car or working in groups renewing ties, replacing rail, or refurbishing the right of way. You have seen them dangling from railway bridges and structures with paint brush or tool in hand, or repairing the thousands of buildings that make up our railroad system. They have no doubt often signaled you and your children safely across grade crossings with warning standard or red light. And you have seen them many times, I am sure, along the railroad right of way, operating cranes, ditchers, bull dozers, concrete mixers, and all the other modern machinery of present-day railroad maintenance.

The work of the maintenance of way man is hazardous. In addition to the ordinary dangers that beset the worker who uses tools and machines, he must often work in high places, on bridges, trestles, and structures. And usually his work is done under the hazards of train traffic, on the main line where he must keep a sharp lookout for trains, or in busy railroad yards where the switching of cars is constantly going on.

Our Brotherhood was formed in 1887 under the name of the Order of Railroad Trackmen. Organized first as a fraternal society, its objectives within the course of a few years became those of a labor organization, although fraternalism is still one of its basic principles. Amalgamation with other similar organizations of railroad workers in the years following resulted in the present form and name of our Brotherhood.

The Brotherhood is governed democratically by its members, who elect its officers, enact its laws, and decide its policies, either directly at subordinate lodge meetings or by electing delegates to represent them at conventions of the Brotherhood.

The primary purpose of our organization is to safeguard and promote the interests of its members and their families, and the Brotherhood holds contracts covering wages and working conditions with all the Class I railroads in the United States and Canada and with 98 per cent of the short lines. So well has the Brotherhood done its job, that approximately nine out of every ten workers it represents are members.

But we realize, too, that the welfare of our two countries is our welfare as their citizens, and we are vitally interested in the broad general problems that affect the lives of all citizens. The great majority of the railroad workers we represent are long-standing members of their communities who are helping to promote the general welfare of the community through active participation in church, educational, and civic work.

The objectives and beliefs of our Brotherhood are rooted deeply in the American tradition. We believe staunchly in our democratic form of government and in the principles upon which it is founded. We abhor subversive elements that would destroy our democratic self-government and the freedoms we enjoy, and for many years the constitution of our Brotherhood has specifically barred from membership any railroad worker otherwise eligible who is a member of the Communist party.

We believe in greater educational opportunities for our children, and we feel that if the American family is to enjoy all the opportunities that are possible under our free way of life, the progress already made toward raising the standard of living in every strata of our population to an adequate level must be continued.

We feel, too, that it is the duty of every citizen to take an active interest in government, whether it be on a local, state, or national level. We encourage our members to vote at every election, to vote as they please but to vote intelligently.

This, stated quite briefly, is the creed of our organization. Its general objectives are succinctly set forth in the preamble to our Grand Lodge Constitution:

Preamble

1. To exalt the character and increase the ability of its members.
2. To insure greater safety to the traveling public and effect economy in the departments in which our members are employed by interchanging ideas and adopting the best methods of performing our duties.
3. To benefit the general public by raising the standard of efficiency of our membership.
4. To alleviate distress and suffering caused by sickness or disability among our members.
5. To assist widows and orphans of deceased members.
6. To allow no person to remain a member of the Brotherhood unless he lives a sober, moral and honest life.
7. To require all members to faithfully and honestly perform their duties to the best of their ability for the Brotherhood and for their employers.
8. To use all honorable means to secure the passage of laws beneficial to our membership, and to improve labor conditions generally.
9. To stimulate the civic education of the members in their political rights; and to use the ballot intelligently to the end that the Government may not be perverted to the interest of the favored few, but that it may be a "Government of the people, by the people and for the people" in the fullest sense.

In organizational set-up, our Brotherhood is composed of three divisions: the Grand Lodge, the System Division or System Federation, and the Subordinate Lodge. Although the Grand Lodge is the supreme body of the Brotherhood, the System Division and the Subordinate Lodge are in many respects self-governing within the framework of our constitution.

Each System Division or Federation has under its jurisdiction one or more railroad systems and the Subordinate

Lodges located on those systems. Stemming from our Grand Lodge headquarters in Detroit, Michigan, our Brotherhood has 79 System Divisions or Federations and 1,446 Subordinate Lodges located in every state and the ten provinces of Canada on all major railroads and most of the smaller lines in both countries.

A better understanding of the functional set-up of the Brotherhood requires a brief detailing of the powers and responsibilities of these three major divisions.

GRAND LODGE

The fifteen Grand Lodge officers of the Brotherhood (the Grand Lodge President, the Grand Lodge Secretary-Treasurer, seven Grand Lodge Vice Presidents, a Grand Lodge Executive Board composed of five members, and a Grand Lodge Statistician) are, with the exception of the Statistician, who is appointed by the Grand Lodge President, elected at democratic triennial conventions of Grand Lodge. Each subordinate lodge is entitled to send a delegate to these conventions, who casts the numerical vote of his lodge membership in the election of Grand Lodge officers or in deciding questions affecting the policies, activities, or government of the Brotherhood. All matters properly brought before the convention are thoroughly discussed and decided by majority vote of the assembled delegates. The Grand Lodge convention adopts the Constitution and By-Laws for the general government of the Brotherhood. No delegate may represent more than 500 members unless they are all members of one lodge.

The duties of the Grand Lodge officers are prescribed by the Constitution and By-Laws. The Grand Lodge President exercises supervision over all affairs of the Brotherhood, presides at all sessions of the Grand Lodge, enforces the provisions of the Constitution and By-Laws, and works for the general welfare of the Brotherhood.

The Grand Lodge Secretary-Treasurer handles and disburses the funds of the Brotherhood, keeps and preserves its records, and serves as Superintendent of the Death Benefit Department.

The seven Grand Lodge Vice Presidents are assigned to specific territories, two in Canada and five in the United

States. They work under the direct supervision of the Grand Lodge President. Their primary function is to assist the committees of the Protective Department in carrying out their duties and to work for the general welfare of the Brotherhood.

The Grand Lodge Executive Board supervises the general welfare of the Brotherhood. One of its duties is to audit the accounts of Grand Lodge each quarter. A certified public accountant is employed by the Board for this purpose. Three members of the Grand Lodge Executive Board act as Trustees for the Brotherhood, and all real estate owned by the Brotherhood is held in the names of these Trustees.

In addition to the general departments maintained by the Grand Lodge President and the Grand Lodge Secretary-Treasurer in performing their duties, four distinct departments are maintained by Grand Lodge under the provisions of the Grand Lodge Constitution and By-Laws:

Editorial Department. By virtue of his office, the Grand Lodge President is the editor of the "Brotherhood of Maintenance of Way Employes' Journal," the official organ of the Brotherhood, but an associate editor is maintained to direct the preparation and publication of the "Journal." A non-partisan and non-sectarian publication, the "Journal" strives to advance the welfare of members of the Brotherhood from a literary, moral, and intellectual viewpoint. The "Journal" contains the official directory of officers of Grand Lodge and the Protective and Legislative Departments. It is mailed without charge to all members, but the subscription is $2.00 a year to non-members. Grand Lodge pays all costs of printing and mailing the "Journal."

Death Benefit Department. This department is maintained to pay to the beneficiary or estate of deceased members the death benefits provided by the Constitution. The Grand Lodge Secretary-Treasurer acts as Superintendent of this department.

Department of Statistics. Under the direct supervision of the Grand Lodge President, this department, headed by the Grand Lodge Statistician as Research Director, gathers and compiles statistics and material in the United States and Canada to be used in wage negotiations, conferences, or hearings before arbitration boards or other bodies that might be constituted to deal with matters pertaining to labor-management relations.

Legislative Department. This department works on national, state, and provincial levels, under the direct supervision of the Grand Lodge President, to promote the interests of railroad workers in legislative matters.

A national legislative representative appointed by the Grand Lodge President is stationed permanently in Washington, D. C., to look after the interests of railroad workers in connection with legislation coming before the United States Congress. A Canadian Grand Lodge officer, usually one of the Canadian Vice Presidents, is assigned by the Grand Lodge President to look after national legislative matters in Canada.

Under the laws of the Brotherhood's State and Provincial Legislative Department, a legislative representative is maintained on a part-time basis in each of the forty-eight states and the ten provinces of Canada. The legislative representatives are elected for three-year terms by local legislative delegates from subordinate lodges in their respective states or provinces. It is the primary duty of each legislative representative, as provided in the Grand Lodge constitution, "to work in conjunction with other legislative representatives in the state or province in the promotion of legislation favorable to organized labor or to oppose such legislation as may be detrimental to organized labor and the people." They are usually on active assignment during sessions of the state or provincial legislature.

PROTECTIVE DEPARTMENT

(System divisions and federations.)

The Protective Department functions on each railroad system, or group of federated railroad systems, with which our Brotherhood holds contracts, under the joint direct supervision of Grand Lodge and the subordinate lodges under the jurisdiction of the particular system division or federation.

Whenever the Brotherhood secures representation rights on a particular system, a Joint Protective Board is elected by delegates from subordinate lodges on that system. The Board consists of a General Chairman, other system officers (such as Assistant or Vice General Chairmen and a Secretary-Treasurer), an Executive Committee, and such additional members of the Joint Protective Board as may be provided for in the by-laws adopted by the lodge delegates. Two or more systems may join in forming a system federation having one Joint Protective Board and one set of system officers. On some systems or federations, the lodge delegates elect all Joint Protective Board officers and members. On others, the Joint Protective Board is elected directly by the lodges and the Board in turn elects its officers. Most system elections are held triennially.

The Protective Department on each system or group of federated systems negotiates and maintains agreements covering wages and working conditions on the individual railroad systems, polices these agreements, handles claims or grievances that may arise over the application of the agreement rules, and generally works to promote the welfare of railroad maintenance of way workers under its jurisdiction.

Five regions are created in the United States by the Grand Lodge constitution for the establishment of Regional Associations of system officers. A sixth region comprises all territory within the Dominion of Canada. The system officers comprising the Regional Association in each region meet regularly to discuss and take action on matters of mutual interest. The constitution also creates an International Association, consisting of all system and Grand Lodge officers, which also meets regularly for the purpose of carrying on concerted negotiations relating to wages and to take action on other important general conditions.

SUBORDINATE OR LOCAL LODGES

Subordinate lodges form the direct link between the individual member and his Brotherhood. They are actually the grass-roots segment of the organization. The subordinate lodge secretary-treasurer issues dues receipts to members of the Brotherhood covering payment of dues. Regular meetings are held by most lodges at which information is passed on to the membership and Brotherhood affairs are discussed and acted upon. Not only do the members of subordinate lodges elect their own officers annually, but they also select delegates to represent them at Brotherhood conventions to decide the policies of the Brotherhood, adopt laws to govern its activities, and elect system and Grand Lodge officers and state legislative representatives.

DUES

The delegates assembled in triennial conventions of Grand Lodge determine the initiation fees to be charged new members, the amount of Grand Lodge dues, and the minimum dues to be charged by system divisions (or federations) and subordinate lodges. Individual system divisions (or federations) and subordinate lodges can establish dues exceeding this minimum if they wish.

Although the Grand Lodge Executive Board is authorized to levy special assessments upon all members of the Brotherhood, such assessments are rare. Only one assessment of 50c has been made in the past thirty-three years. The activities of the Brotherhood are financed entirely by the dues collected quarterly from its members.

Dues are payable in advance on or before the first day of January, April, July, and October, but they may be paid six months or more in advance. Each time he pays dues, a member must pay combined Grand Lodge, system division, and subordinate lodge dues, plus initiation fee if he is a new member. As evidence of the dues payment, he receives an official serially-numbered dues receipt from the lodge secretary or other Brotherhood representative to whom the dues were paid. The lodge secretary must remit all dues and initiation fees which he collects to the Grand Lodge Secretary-Treasurer (or to the System Secretary-Treasurer where a system office handles its own funds and is qualified to receive remittances), except that he retains in the lodge treasury that portion of the dues collected which belongs to his lodge. Representatives other than lodge secretaries must remit full dues and initiation fees. Regardless of whether remittance is made to Grand Lodge or a system office, distribution is made so that each of the three divisions of the Brotherhood (the Grand Lodge, the system on which the member is employed, and the lodge in which he holds membership) receives its portion of the dues and initiation fees.

The present initiation fee of $5.00 is divided among the three divisions of the Brotherhood. Three dollars of the fee goes either to Grand Lodge, the system, or the subordinate lodge, depending on which of these three divisions is represented by the person who issued the dues receipt to the new member. One dollar each is then credited to the two remaining divisions.

Current Grand Lodge dues are $3.50 each quarter (except for retired members who pay $2.50 each quarter and, incidentally, are exempt from payment of system or subordinate lodge dues). Of this amount, $1.00 is credited to the death benefit fund and 10c is credited to the state and provincial legislative account to defray the expenses of that department. The remainder is placed in the general fund, a portion to be used to pay the cost of a subscription to the newspaper "Labor" for each member and the remainder to pay the general expenses of Grand Lodge.

The dues charged by individual systems and subordinate lodges vary, but under the Grand Lodge constitution, system dues cannot be less than $1.50 a quarter and subordinate lodge dues cannot be less than 25c a quarter.

Revenue from dues and initiation fees is used to defray necessary legitimate expenses of the Brotherhood. Surplus funds may be invested upon approval of the appropriate body; i.e., the Grand Lodge Executive Board for Grand Lodge, the System Joint Protective Board or Executive Board for the system, and the subordinate lodge members in regular session for the lodge.

All financial transactions of Grand Lodge must be made in accordance with the provisions of the Grand Lodge constitution or under the express authorization of the Grand Lodge Executive Board. The accounts of Grand Lodge are audited regularly by a certified public accountant, who furnishes each member of the Executive Board with a quarterly audit report and prepares a three-year comparative report for the delegates at each triennial convention. The salaries of elected Grand Lodge officers are fixed by subordinate lodge delegates at triennial conventions of the Grand Lodge.

All representatives of the Brotherhood handling funds of the organization are bonded and are held accountable for all money or other assets belonging to the Brotherhood coming into their possession.

Lodge secretaries must keep an account of all funds received and disbursed and must furnish quarterly audit reports of receipts and disbursements to Grand Lodge. Disbursements from lodge funds must be for legitimate expenses or other transactions approved by the lodge.

Systems or federations handling their own funds are similarly obliged to account for funds of the Brotherhood coming into their possession. In most instances, Grand Lodge handles the funds of the system, crediting the system account with system dues and fees and making disbursements from the account on authorization by the system. System funds are handled by Grand Lodge only at the request of the individual systems and entirely for their convenience.

LADIES' AUXILIARY

The Ladies' Auxiliary is an adjunct of the Brotherhood. The first local chapter was organized at Macon, Georgia, in 1898. A Grand Lodge of the Ladies' Auxiliary was formed at the 1902 convention of the Brotherhood and local auxiliary units were established throughout the United States and Canada. Although the Auxiliary was inactive for a few years during World War I, it was later re-established and is quite active today.

The Ladies' Auxiliary is composed of the womenfolk of maintenance of way families. Members of the Auxiliary have no official standing in the Brotherhood and take no direct part in its work. They serve instead in a supporting role, helping at meetings and conventions of the Auxiliary and in their respective communities to promote the broad objectives of the Brotherhood to improve the lot of the maintenance of way family. They realize that they have as great a stake in the welfare of the Brotherhood as does the breadwinner of the family.

It will be seen from the foregoing that the Brotherhood in all its activities strives to maintain and perpetuate the principle that the majority vote of the individual members, or the representatives they have selected to speak and act for them, shall govern. It is, I believe, an organization founded, operated, and controlled on the basis of true democracy.

What does the maintenance of way worker receive in return for the dues he pays to the Brotherhood? For the few pennies a day he contributes to maintain the Brotherhood, he receives skilled, specialized representation to protect his job, his earning powers, and his family's happiness and welfare. As will be amply illustrated by this story of the Brotherhood, these are some of the important benefits obtained and services provided for its members:

Higher wages; improved working conditions; an old-age and disability retirement system; unemployment and sickness benefits; a forty-hour week with forty-eight hours' pay; vacations with pay; a health and welfare plan; the monthly Brotherhood "Journal" and the railroad workers' weekly newspaper "Labor," without extra cost; the handling of claims or grievances; participation in the Brotherhood's Death Benefit Department without extra cost; protection in the legislative field.

Although the primary purpose of maintenance of way workers in supporting the Brotherhood is to better their conditions, they realize that they are an integral part of an industry that is indispensable to the healthy economic life of their two nations, the United States and Canada. They understand, too, that their welfare as railroad workers is inextricably interwoven with the welfare of the industry in which they are employed. One of the general objectives of the Brotherhood and its members, therefore, is constantly to improve efficiency and productivity in the maintenance of way department and to maintain railroad facilities in the safest possible condition, to the end that the carriers may best serve the traveling public and the shippers who use rail lines.

It is in accordance with the general procedures and the principles outlined in this introduction that our Brotherhood functions today as a labor organization in protecting and promoting the welfare of maintenance of way workers and their families.

T. C. Carroll,
President.

March, 1955.

History

Appendices

Illustrations

SECTION FOUR between pages 196 and 197

SECTION FIVE between pages 260 and 261

"Conceived in want and born of necessity"

I can remember vividly hearing John T. Wilson tell in conversation with my father when I was a small boy of how the idea of forming an organization of railroad maintenance of way workers first germinated in his mind. In those days, the portion of the railroad on which Wilson worked was located in isolated country, and the sections were quite long. In walking track, the foremen of adjoining sections would each start from a designated point and walk toward each other. When they met, they would turn around and return to their headquarters.

On this particular day, the foreman of the adjoining section was not at the appointed meeting place, and Wilson continued walking until he reached the foreman's house, located in a desolate and inaccessible region. There he found the foreman's wife with her small children huddled about her. The foreman had died unexpectedly. His wife had wrapped the body in a sheet and waited for hours for someone to come along to help them.

Wilson built a crude coffin and buried the foreman. He gave the widow and her children what aid he could from his own meager funds. For weeks afterwards the pitiable plight of this destitute family continued to haunt Wilson, and it was then he decided to form a fraternal order that could assist maintenance of way families in similar circumstances. As time passed the idea grew. Wilson sought the aid of other foremen, and in the spring and summer of 1887 the plan reached fruition in the formation of the Order of Railroad Trackmen.

It was from this humble and inauspicious beginning that the Brotherhood has grown to its high place among labor organizations today.

T. C. C.

History of the

BROTHERHOOD OF MAINTENANCE OF WAY EMPLOYES

CHAPTER I

THE BEGINNING

EVERY EVENT in history has a beginning, a time when it is first conceived in the mind of man. But trying to trace that event through the tortuous channels of men's thoughts to its pristine source is much like attempting to seek out the myriad springs and underground streams that feed a broad river. Thus, a day set down in the pages of history to commemorate a particular happening is not always the beginning but often merely a focal point well along the way.

Such a day was a Sunday afternoon in the spring of 1887 when a small group of railroad section foremen gathered together on a river bank near Demopolis, Alabama. The day was warm and they stood in the shade of a huge oak tree. They had met to discuss mutual problems of low wages, the hazards of their work, and the insecurity of their families.

Their thoughts, however, were vague and exploratory. The idea of unionism had not as yet fully crystallized. The organization they decided to form, the Order of Railroad Trackmen, was to be established to assist fellow railroad workers in times of sickness and financial trouble. They had no way of knowing when this order was chartered in July, 1887, under the laws of the State of Alabama for benevolent and charitable societies, that eventually it would become one of the largest railroad Brotherhoods in America.

The leader of this group was a young foreman named John T. Wilson. In his mind a profound understanding, as yet ill-defined, was beginning to develop: a conviction that group action by maintenance of way workers was needed to promote their welfare. Even then he must have visualized in a vague way the growth of this new-born order into a powerful organization capable of becoming the collective voice of the thousands of workers who build and maintain the tracks, bridges, and structures of America's railroads.

This visionary young worker, however, was not alone in his prophetic thinking. At almost the same time, other groups of maintenance of way workers in the United States and Canada were grappling with the same problem, and similar organizations were in the process of formation at several points.

A concerted movement of this kind does not grow overnight. It has its roots planted deeply in the soil of human needs long before the bud of action breaks through. To better understand why this organization was founded, it is necessary to know something of the background against which it was conceived—the fabulous rise of the railroad industry and the turbulent labor-management relations of the 1870's and the 80's—and the basic needs out of which it arose.

The remarkable growth of America's railroads during the nineteenth century is in itself a fascinating story. No nation has needed railroads more than the United States, and none has done such an outstanding job of meeting the need. Starting with 23 miles of track in 1830, the railroads in the United States had a total mileage of 193,346 by 1900. This amazing record grew out of the critical need of a new nation to develop its vast territories.

The American colonists had emerged from the Revolutionary War owning the entire country, except Florida, from the Gulf of Mexico to the Great Lakes as far west as the Mississippi River. The blood of many a colonist must have surged at the thought of the rich new lands to the west, but all but the hardiest pioneers were held mired in the mud of primitive roads to a comparatively narrow strip of territory along the Atlantic Coast.

The primitive methods of transportation available to the colonists—the stagecoach, the pack horse, the pony express, the flat boat, the sailing ship—were wholly inadequate. If you lived in the middle west, for instance, and wanted to ship products to the east, you could send them down the Mississippi to New Orleans and thence by ship. The new country, straining to break its geographical bonds and exploit its rich possessions, needed a cheap and fast means of transportation if the seaboard states and the scattered settlements to the west were to be held together.

In 1802, the Federal government passed an act financing the building of a national highway to the west, which was constructed some years later through Cumberland, Maryland, to Wheeling, Virginia, and finally on through Ohio and Indiana to Illinois. To the north, the Erie Canal, running from Albany to Buffalo, New York, was completed in 1825. These palliative measures were not enough, however, and as men searched feverishly for new and better means of transportation and communication, the advent of the railroad became inevitable.

Actually, the steam railroad was not something entirely new, but a combination of old ideas. Wagon- or tramways had been used in England since as early as the sixteenth century to haul minerals from mines to rivers or ports. The earliest forms consisted of rails of wood or flat stones over which vehicles were drawn by horses. The steam engine had already been invented, and only man's ingenuity was needed to fit the component parts together. By the end of the eighteenth century, inventors in England were already experimenting with the steam locomotive.

On February 6, 1815, John Stevens, an American inventor called in the United States "the father of railroads", obtained the first American railroad charter from the State of New Jersey, although he did not complete the first railroad across the state until 1832. The Charleston and Hamburg, later to be known as the South Carolina Railroad, began formal operation of a steam railroad in January, 1831, over a few miles of track. It is considered to have been America's first railroad in the ordinarily accepted sense of the word. When its 135 miles of track had been laid in 1833 from Charleston to Hamburg, South Carolina, it was then the longest railroad in the world.

To the Baltimore and Ohio Railroad, however, goes the distinction of building the first railroad in the United States for the specific purpose of carrying passengers and freight.

On May 24, 1830, the company began the operation of horse-drawn carriages over thirteen miles of track from Baltimore to Ellicott's Mills. It was not until sometime later, however, after the company had experimented with horse power by treadmill and with wind power, that it converted to the steam locomotive.

The first trains were crude affairs. Their inventors drew heavily on existing designs. Some of the earlier locomotives appear to have been little more than steam engines mounted on platforms. The coaches, some of them double-deckers, were replicas of stagecoaches with flanged wheels to fit the rails.

A ride on one of the early trains, although it must have been a unique experience, was not entirely a pleasure trip. The cars were coupled together with chains almost three feet long. The resulting jerks and jolts when the train started or stopped were likely to throw the unwary passenger from his seat. And when the train crew raised steam, the passengers would be showered with sparks and burning embers.

The rails of some of the earlier trains were laid on slabs of stone or over wood piling sunk in the ground. The stone proved to be too rigid and the piling soon rotted. It was not long until the familiar wooden crosstie had been adopted and put into general use.

The first rails had stone or wood sills with an iron strap for a surface. Sometimes the strap would become loose, curl up, and break through the floor of the coach. In 1830, Robert L. Stevens, son of John Stevens, while on a trip to England to inspect equipment in use there, decided that a rail made entirely of iron would be feasible. From a piece of wood he fashioned a model of the T-shaped iron rail which was eventually accepted and is still in use.

In spite of their many shortcomings, however, the railroads were rapidly revolutionizing transportation. Even on the earlier trains, a trip that would take all day in a stagecoach could be made in a few hours by rail. By 1850, 8,683 miles of track had been laid, most of it in the eastern states. The settlers in the middle western states, meantime, were clamoring for the construction of railroads, but sufficient money to build rail lines could not be raised in these sparsely-settled regions.

Stephen A. Douglas, United States Senator from Illinois, took up the cudgel for the people in these isolated regions. He proposed that the Federal government turn over public lands to the states, who would in turn give it to the railroads. By selling the land, the railroads could raise money to carry on construction. Congress passed a land-grant law on September 20, 1850. It is estimated that eventually the government gave more than 131 million acres of land to the railroads in land grants.

By 1860, the railroad mileage in the United States had soared to 30,283. Wherever the railroads laid their tracks, prosperity followed. New towns were built, new farming lands were opened to cultivation, the value of land increased, cities grew larger, and industry poured its products into the new territories. The development of the railroads completely changed the economic conditions of the nation.

Although lagging behind the United States in railroad construction in the first half of the nineteenth century, Canada began building its rail lines on an extensive scale after 1850. The first railway in Canada, a horse-traction line at St. Johns, Quebec, was converted to steam engines the year following its opening in 1836. Railway construction during the next few years proceeded slowly. In 1850, there were only 66 miles of railway in Canada.

The railway era in Canada actually began with the construction of the Grand Trunk Railway, the first large railway in Canada. In 1856, the company completed its line from Montreal to Toronto. By the 1880's, it had a line running from Portland, Maine, through Montreal, Toronto, and Sarnia to Chicago.

During the next ten years, the Grand Trunk added numerous smaller lines to its system. By 1890, the company had 3,122 miles of line in Canada and a considerable mileage in the United States. The Grand Trunk later became a part of the huge Canadian National system.

It was not until 1885, however, that a Canadian rail line reached the Pacific Coast. When British Columbia entered the Confederation in 1871, one of the conditions was that a railway would be constructed to connect the province with the rest of the Dominion. The Canadian government began construction of the line in 1874. In 1880, after a few hundred miles of track had been laid, the government turned the project over to the Canadian Pacific Railway syndicate.

The Canadian Pacific was to complete construction of the line from Montreal to Vancouver. In return, the Canadian government agreed to give the company certain assistance, including $25 million and 25 million acres of land. The railway was also granted protection from competing lines for 20 years. On the morning of November 7, 1885, the driving of a golden spike at Craigellachie, British Columbia, completed the rail line to the Pacific Coast. Other transcontinental lines soon followed.

The following table shows the growth of Canada's rail lines over a period of 100 years:

	Number of Miles of Railway
1836	16
1856	1,414
1866	2,278
1876	5,218
1886	11,793
1896	16,270
1906	21,423
1916	36,985
1926	40,353
1936	42,552

Like the United States, Canada's growth and prosperity have been related to the development of its railways. Before the advent of the steam railway, practically all of Canada's population was concentrated along the seacoast and along rivers and lakes. After the construction of rail lines across the western provinces, settlers began to flock into the country. In the 30-year period between 1881 and 1911, the population of the prairie provinces increased from 118,000 to 1,328,000.

As the rail network in the United States penetrated further and further into the frontiers to the west, the idea of a continuous line of rail from the Atlantic to the Pacific became inevitable. On July 1, 1862, President Lincoln signed the Pacific Railroad Act authorizing the Central Pacific and the Union Pacific Railroads to build a railroad between Sacramento, California, and Omaha, Nebraska.

The United States government agreed to lend the two railroads $16,000 a mile for track laid on level ground, double that amount for track laid on more difficult terrain, and three times that amount for track laid in mountainous country. In addition, the two railroads were to receive 20 sections of land for each mile of railroad.

The difficulties in constructing the transcontinental railroad were tremendous. Materials and supplies had to be hauled long distances by roundabout routes—and labor was scarce. The able-bodied men who were not fighting in the Civil War were not to be lured from more lucrative employment in mines and factories and on farms. The Central Pacific, starting eastward from California, could recruit only a few hundred men in its initial labor force. It solved the labor problem by importing coolies from China.

The Union Pacific, too, encountered trouble in starting its line westward from Omaha. Because of the labor shortage and the difficulty in raising money, its progress during the first two years was extremely slow. Eventually it was able to recruit in its labor force ex-soldiers, Irish workers from the east, and nondescripts from wherever they could be found.

Crossing the Sierra Nevada range, the crews of the Central Pacific fought their way through rock and heavy snowdrifts. The Union Pacific, working through Indian territory, had to be constantly on the lookout for raiding parties.

The government had specified no point at which the two lines were to meet, and each of the roads worked feverishly to lay the most track and dig deeper into the government subsidy. By using speed-up methods, the Union Pacific was able to lay a record ten miles of track in a day. Even after they had met and passed each other, the two roads continued to lay parallel track, the Central Pacific eastward, and the Union Pacific westward. At this point the government stepped in and designated Promontory Point, Utah, as the meeting place. On May 10, 1869, the driving of the golden spike signalized the completion of the coast-to-coast line.

Building the grade of America's railroads was a backbreaking job. Except in clear and comparatively flat regions, trees and undergrowth had to be removed, hills cut away, tunnels bored, and low places filled in. This involved the moving of immense quantities of dirt from one place to another. Much of this work had to be done by hand. Such primitive devices as the pick, the shovel, the hoe, the scraper, the wheelbarrow, the wagon, and the mule cart were the only tools and "machinery" then available.

Labor was secured wherever it could be recruited. Slaves were pressed into service when they were available. The contractors who built America's railroads were, to say the least, aggressive men who drove themselves and their men unmercifully. Certain it is that life in the construction crews was not easy. Riots among the crews were no rarity, and occasional skirmishes with the populace took place as the shining rails crept slowly across the land.

The builders of the early railroads had not been overly concerned with the niceties and precisions of the engineering science. Many of the tracks were hastily laid. Little attention had been paid to the stress and strain on track and equipment as trains rounded curves. Trestles had been hurriedly erected. As the speed of trains increased and the number of accidents mounted, the railroads began putting their right of ways in better order. Roadbeds were improved, lines relocated, curves widened, makeshift bridges and trestles replaced with sturdier structures, and tunnels bored to run a train through a hill rather than over the top of it.

From the constant necessity to keep the tracks and bridges in safe condition, a new and more stable class of railroad workers evolved from the early construction crews. It became the duty of the employes of the maintenance of way department to build, rebuild, repair, and maintain the railroads' tracks, bridges, trestles, and the thousand and one other structures and buildings along the right of way.

With the close of the Civil War, a new and even more frantic era of railroad building began. By 1870, the railroad mileage in the United States had increased to 53,878, and in the ensuing thirty years, almost 140,000 miles of track were laid.

But as the railroads spread their web of rails and crossties throughout the nation, as business expanded and flourished, the problems of the worker increased. With growing industrialization came the inevitable clash between worker and employer. As workers attempted to band together for their mutual welfare, a bitter anti-union attitude crystallized among employers. Company agents were used to discourage union activity. Employers secretly circulated "whitelists" of persons to be hired and "blacklists" of those to be rejected. Eventually, the "yellow dog" contract made its appearance and became a potent weapon against unionism. In signing such a contract, the employe agreed that so long as he was employed he would not join or support a labor union. Such a contract was entirely unilateral, the employer reserving the right to discharge an employe at will.

It was not unusual for union leaders and organizers to be beaten by company agents and even forced to leave the community. Public officials frequently refused to permit unions to hold outdoor meetings or parades. The distribution of union pamphlets or papers was often prohibited by ordinance. Business and professional people campaigned against unions, and employers sought the passage of laws to curb their activities.

By 1873, three railroad Brotherhoods had been organized: the engineers (1863), the conductors (1868), and the firemen and enginemen (1873). These organizations had been formed not as collective-bargaining agencies to improve the wages and working conditions of their constituents, but primarily to furnish insurance benefits to the families of injured or deceased workers. So hazardous was their work in those days that many railroad workers were unable to secure insurance protection from the standard companies. Railroad owners opposed these fraternal societies, fearful that they contained the seed of a union movement on the railroads. The transition of these organizations from purely fraternal and benevolent Brotherhoods to bona fide labor unions did not begin until 1877, after the first and biggest railroad strike.

This bloody strike resulted from wage cuts ordered by the railroads during the business depression which began in 1873. The high cost of the Civil War, excessive railroad building, inflated credit, and other related economic problems had brought on the 1873 panic. Times were bad and became worse as the panic continued. The ranks of the unemployed grew larger. In the early years of the depression, workers on the railroads and in other industries accepted wage cuts with little protest. In 1877, the railroads began to feel the severe pinch of reduced income. Their owners decided that in order to continue to pay dividends and maintain their credit standing they must make further wage reductions. In June and July, 1877, the Pennsylvania, Erie, Michigan Southern, Lake Shore, New York Central, and other railroads, put wage cuts of 10 per cent into effect. Effective July 16, the Baltimore and Ohio ordered a 10 per cent wage cut in all wages of more than $1.00 a day.

This was the coup de grace that released the pent-up emotions that had simmered in the minds of the workers during the difficult years of the panic. They had already accepted several wage reductions, although many of the railroads had continued to pay substantial dividends to their stockholders. They could barely support their families on the meager wages being paid for dangerous and responsible work. When the company rejected their protest, Baltimore and Ohio firemen and brakemen at Martinsburg, West Virginia, walked off the job. The strike spread rapidly and sporadically across the country, from road to road, from point to point, to Chicago, to St. Louis, and finally to California.

Several states mustered their militia. Federal troops were called out to settle a strike for the first time in American history. Riots and bloodshed followed. The strike was broken, but it is estimated that in the process more than one hundred men lost their lives and some five hundred persons, including women and children, had been wounded. Untold damage had been done to railroad property.

Although railroad workers lost the strike, they had still gained a victory. For out of the bloody disaster came the realization that the strike had been lost through lack of unity. A new feeling of solidarity grew between the Brotherhoods and they emerged from the phase of pure fraternalism to turn resolutely toward the goals of collective bargaining.

The nation recovered slowly from the depression and business activity did not return to normalcy until 1879. Meanwhile, the fortunes of labor unions had waned. The hard years of the depression and the merciless determination of employers to smash the unions had combined to reduce union membership to a low level. But a new champion of labor had appeared on the scene and was rapidly gaining national prominence.

Started modestly by a few garment workers in Philadelphia in 1869, the Knights of Labor, as this incredible organization was called, had profited by defections from the ranks of the craft unions. On the principle of one great union for all workers, the sprawling, unwieldy giant rapidly gained strength, encompassing within its ranks workers in all crafts and industries, regardless of creed or color, and persons in many professions. Impetus had been given to its drive for members by its victories in a series of railroad strikes, particularly in its conflicts on one of the roads controlled by Jay Gould, then a powerful figure in railroad circles. By 1886, it had a membership of almost 700,000. But a process of disintegration had already begun. Organizational weaknesses, the dissimilar nature of its membership, its attempts to dabble in cooperative schemes, the inevitable conflict with craft unions, and unsuccessful strikes which drained its financial resources, all contributed to its downfall. By 1890, its membership had dwindled to an estimated 100,000, and the American Federation of Labor, formed in Pittsburgh in 1881, was rapidly usurping its place as the champion of labor in America.

In 1894, seventeen years after the great strike of 1877, another widespread railroad strike took place. The American Railway Union, a newly-formed railroad labor organization soliciting membership among workers of all classes, with Eugene V. Debs as president, called a strike against the Pullman Company to secure a living wage for the employes of that concern. Members of the American Railway Union not directly involved in the strike immediately began a boycott against the handling of Pullman cars.

The General Managers' Association, a group of railroad officials, retaliated by having strike breakers attach United States mail cars to trains made up of Pullman cars. Thus, if the strikers attempted to interfere with the passage of trains in any way, they could be accused of obstructing the mails. In a second move to break the strike, the Association called on the United States government for Federal troops. Thousands of Federal troops, state militia, or special deputies were soon guarding the movement of trains. Riots and street fighting followed. Finally, the General Managers played their trump card by securing a sweeping injunction from the attorney general of the United States against the strike and the boycott.

Thus, for the second time in less than twenty years a major strike had been lost by railroad workers. But out of these unsuccessful battles emerged a stronger and more aggressive group of railroad Brotherhoods. Important, too, was the growing conviction, accentuated by experience, that the craft union was the better type for railroad workers and that the industrial type of union could not survive under existing conditions.

It was during this period of turmoil and in this atmosphere of bitter labor-management strife that John T. Wilson and the small group of his fellow foremen met in 1887 to form the Order of Railway Trackmen.

CHAPTER II

THE UNIFICATION

THE STORY of the Brotherhood in its early years is the story of John T. Wilson. For it was Wilson's spirit that imbued its members with hope, his energy that spread its message in an ever-widening circle, and his confidence that kept the young order alive in the days of crisis. As the years passed, the name of John T. Wilson became more and more a symbol of the Brotherhood.

The available facts about Wilson's early life are meager. Born in Riceville, Tennessee, on January 29, 1861, and raised on a farm, he must have entered railroad service when he was quite young, for he was already a railroad section foreman on the East Tennessee, Virginia & Georgia Railway at Childersburg, Alabama, when he became head of the new order at the early age of twenty-six. Wilson has been described by those who knew him as a dynamic leader. A large man, over six feet tall, robust and well-proportioned, with heavy moustache and thick brown hair, and emanating superabundant vigor, he made a striking appearance in the meeting hall or on the convention rostrum. Moreover, his genuine sincerity quickly gained the confidence of the men. In describing Wilson, A. B. Lowe, who succeeded Wilson as president of the Brotherhood in 1908, said: "In the presence of Wilson you feel you are in the presence of a big man, a man that has the paramount interest of the working man at heart and one that you can respect and admire."

What motives impel a man to undergo privation and self-sacrifice, risk discharge, and submit to the calumny so often directed against union leaders, in order to crusade in behalf of his fellow workers? Wilson gave at least a partial answer to this question. In his book "The Calcium Light," published after the successful settlement of the Canadian Pacific strike in 1901, he said:

"My first thought of organizing the maintenance-of-way men was entertained in the spring of 1887. Having given the subject much consideration; having weighed the hardships, sacrifices, expenses to be met, and the ends to be gained, I decided, notwithstanding all these, that an organization of maintenance-of-way men was not only possible but necessary to their personal welfare as regards wages, advancement and freedom."

But there is a vast difference between the plan and the execution, Wilson found. "It is easier to suggest plans of relief than to operate them," Wilson continued. "The reader can readily see the many difficulties—inability, poverty, jealousy, prejudice, and opposition from within and without—that would naturally rise to the view of a thinking mind. But, fortunately for the maintenance-of-way men, the writer's foresight was not so fully developed as to disclose all the drawbacks that existed."

A crude draft of a constitution and by-laws for the new order was prepared and adopted. "Everything seemed to be in fair shape to proceed with the work," Wilson related, "when the enterprise was suddenly paralyzed by the most trivial causes—but causes which were at such a time and under such conditions sufficient to scatter the little sentiment that had been created in favor of organization." Personal jealousies, a desire for self gain, unwillingness to undergo the necessary sacrifices—all these familiar human weaknesses caused the new order to languish and almost expire even before it had been fully organized.

In the spring and summer of 1888, however, the organization was revitalized. Wilson gave up his work on the railroad, and from the newly-established headquarters at Demopolis, Alabama, and later from Birmingham, Alabama, where the headquarters were moved in the fall of 1889, he carried on an active crusade, tramping thousands of miles to see maintenance of way men and tell them the story of the order. It was a difficult undertaking, but there was no other way. The majority of the men he interviewed understood the dire need to remedy existing conditions, but to persuade them to take positive action was another matter. Others appeared to entertain no hope for the future and had resigned themselves to an acceptance of existing conditions. And quite early in the life of the order, Wilson found that there were Judases among his followers.

But Wilson was philosophical about it all. "Look at the trees of the forest!" he said. "Consider their ages; count the storms they have passed through; see how every opposition has tended to make them strong, and the observation ought to be significant." Gradually, through the force of his character and his utter sincerity, and by sheer hard work, Wilson was able to overcome much of the mass inertia that gripped many of the men he interviewed, and to allay their fears. The new order began to grow.

In later years, Wilson was able to analyze from the rich experience of his years as an organizer for the Brotherhood the basic qualities of character which he decided maintenance of way workers must possess if they are to carry on successfully group action to better their welfare. In the introduction to "The Calcium Light" he said:

"If [maintenance of way employes] wish to have their burdens made lighter and their lives made brighter—if they wish to have their many grievances properly adjusted—the remedy lies within themselves. Whining will not help them. Prayers and petitions will be alike in vain. The *only* source of relief is *organization.* The *only* remedy is *united,* persistent *action.* Such action can only be had where the men engaged in it are possessed of three sterling traits of character, to wit: *courage, fidelity* and *fortitude*—courage to undertake, fidelity to continue, and fortitude to endure without murmuring the trials and deprivations incident to all great movements for the establishment of better conditions, higher ideals and greater liberties for the mass of mankind."

It is quite evident that Wilson was abundantly endowed with the three basic requisites of character which he described. In the concluding pages of his book, Wilson enunciated his steadfast determination to continue the work of the Brotherhood. "Do you think for a moment," he asked, "that we are going to lay down our organizing armor? We are equipped for a successful journey, and success will surely crown our efforts if we use our opportunities aright." And in assaying the Brotherhood's future, he said:

"Having passed some of the most dangerous breakers in our infancy; having passed an army of complainers and fault-finders from within and without; having struggled through the most trying financial crisis our nation has ever witnessed; having emerged from the demoralizing effects of rival organizations and withstood the crucial test of the winnowing of our membership, what, then, may we not accomplish in the future?"

And, indeed, it could well be asked at the turn of the twentieth century what this young organization, which had literally pulled itself up by its bootstraps, might not accomplish in the future.

These revealing fragments of thought are taken from the book written by Wilson in 1901, at a time when both he and the Brotherhood had reached a comparative state of maturity, and just after the successful strike which led to the negotiation with the Canadian Pacific Railway of the first agreement covering wages and working conditions ever secured by the Brotherhood. Between the inception of the order in 1887 and the beginning of this halcyon season, however, lay a period of fourteen years of struggle, often mixed with discouragement; but it had been, too, a time of important unification and preparation.

The founders of the order in 1887 had developed no well-defined idea of the scope of its activities. Although it was intended primarily to be a fraternal and insurance society, it is clear from Wilson's later writings that over and beyond this basic purpose was the latent thought that eventually it could provide security and protection for maintenance of way workers and help to improve their low wages and poor working conditions.

The need to improve wages and working conditions was indeed acute. In writing about the conditions on the railroads in those days, a member of the order said that when he entered the service of a southern railroad as an extra gang man in 1884, he received 70¢ a day. At that time, he reported, section men received 95¢ a day, and section foremen $35.00 a month. For these wages, the men worked from sunrise to sunset. The June, 1895, issue of "The Foremen's Advance

Advocate," the official organ of the Brotherhood, quoted the following among the rules it listed as having been adopted by a southern railroad for the guidance of its trackmen: "Working hours are from sunrise until sunset, with one hour and a half for dinner, between May 15 and October 15, and one hour between October 15 and May 15." Obviously the company had generously conceded that even trackmen needed a little more time for relaxation during the summer months.

In this same issue, the "Advocate" listed some of the perpetual problems that have confronted maintenance of way workers throughout the years. "When reductions in the expenses of the operating railways are necessary," it quoted the President of the American Railway Association as saying, "the reduction must fall on the unorganized classes." The "Advocate" estimated that trackmen lost $2 million in wages annually for this reason alone.

"The loss in wages is only one of the sacrifices trackmen are compelled to make for remaining in disunion," the "Advocate" continued. "Many of them are required to work at nights and on Sundays, whenever called upon, without compensation; others are compelled to work an inhuman number of hours, the old slave standard being re-established in their case; they begin to labor at 4:30 a.m. and quit at 7:00 p.m. . . . While forced to labor in order that they may live, their jobs may be snatched from them at any time, with or without just cause, this being part of the price they pay for remaining in disunion."

In its issue for December, 1893, the "Advocate" listed the wage rates being paid to track foremen and trackmen by nine southern railroads:

Name of Road	*Foremen per month*	*Men per day*
Richmond & Danville	$40.00	$ .75
Eastern Tennessee, Virginia & Georgia	45.00	.90
Central of Georgia	40.00	.75
Georgia Railroad	35.00	.95
Nashville, Chattanooga & St. Louis	45.00	1.00
Atlanta & West Point	45.00	.80
Georgia Pacific	40.00	.90
Seaboard Air Line	38.00	.70
Atlanta & Florida	40.00	.80

As sorely as maintenance of way workers needed its services as a collective-bargaining agency, however, the new order was faced with the immediate and practical problem of organization. This proved to be a discouraging undertaking. Some workers were apathetic toward unionism. Others feared to join because many railroad officials were opposed to labor unions, and any organization of workers, no matter what its stated purpose, was looked upon with suspicion by employers. Many workers faced possible discharge if they affiliated with the order merely to obtain insurance protection.

Organized as a benevolent and fraternal society, the order depended on its insurance feature to attract members. But this inducement in itself was not enough. In spite of Wilson's valiant efforts, the growth of the order was disappointingly slow in the first few years of its existence. In 1890, the membership numbered only 628.

One of its major handicaps was the fact that it restricted membership to white foremen with six months' experience although white apprentices were to be admitted if six months' trial had shown that they were worthy. A similar restriction on membership had seriously hampered the growth of another organization of maintenance of way workers, the Brotherhood of Railway Section Foremen of North America, founded in an old demounted box-car at La Porte City, Iowa. No record exists of the name of the president of this organization in the beginning, but Samuel J. Pegg succeeded James Sweeney and was its president in 1891 when plans for amalgamation with the Alabama Brotherhood were under way.

It had become apparent that two organizations representing the same class of railroad workers could not succeed, and amalgamation committees were formed. At a joint meeting in St. Louis, beginning on October 13, 1891, the amalgamation was completed, to become effective January 1, 1892, and the name of the unified organization became the "International Brotherhood of Railway Track Foremen of America." The first ballots to elect a Grand Chief Foreman resulted in a tie between Wilson and Pegg. Wilson became Grand Chief Foreman when he drew the long straw. The convention elected M. O'Dowd Grand Secretary and Treasurer and moved the headquarters from Birmingham to St. Louis, Missouri, where they remained until they were transferred to Detroit, Michigan, in 1913.

The two organizations had a combined membership of only 863 at the time of amalgamation, and the need to venture beyond the realm of fraternalism was acutely apparent. The convention decided to set up for the first time a procedure for handling grievances. The officers of the subordinate divisions (local lodges) were to act as grievance committees. If they could not settle a grievance with the railroad officials, it would be referred to the Grand Chief Foreman. Thus, Wilson became not only the chief organizer and administrative head of the Brotherhood, but the adjudicator of serious grievances as well. Another move of the Brotherhood to increase its membership was the expansion of its jurisdiction by enrolling track laborers in "The Trackmen's Protective Association," established as an adjunct to the parent organization.

Pegg returned to railroad work following his defeat at the convention. His Iowa organization had had no effective insurance program, nor had it established any machinery for collective bargaining. One of its declared "objectives" was "to censure in the fullest measure the inauguration of strikes." Although the Wilson organization likewise had established no grievance machinery, its condemnation of strikes had not been so sweeping. Strikes were to be censured "in the fullest measure," it declared, except as a last resort when all reasonable requests for justice were refused.

This attitude of the two young organizations toward strikes is readily understandable. Representing only a few hundred of the thousands of maintenance of way workers in the United States at that time, any attempt to enforce their demands through strikes would have been disastrous. Wilson's early policies were conservative. He tried to educate maintenance of way workers as to "justice" and the "sources of oppression." In May, 1893, he declared that the order was not a fighting or striking organization. By December of that year, however, wage reductions and layoffs had modified his opinion to such an extent that he declared in the "Advocate": "Strikes are certainly to be deprecated but efforts to treat employes as dumb animals must be met at any price." The next issue of the "Advocate" reported that the monthly wages of some foremen had been cut from $40.00 to $36.00, and that on at least one road track laborers had had their wages reduced to 67½¢ a day.

In commenting on the unsuccessful Pullman strike (in 1894) of the American Railway Union, an organization formed by Eugene V. Debs in 1893 to enroll railroad workers of all crafts, Wilson said: "It is impossible for labor to organize successfully except on class lines, and organizations such as the American Railway Union are like mobs, which . . . accomplish nothing but destruction." Again, in December, 1895, Wilson said: "That strikes are sometimes justifiable we do not dispute; but we cannot believe that any organization which is built and equipped for striking, and for no other purpose, can long maintain existence or render substantial benefits to the cause of labor."

But if Wilson had learned the valuable lesson that there is a time when strikes are not to be called, he also knew that the time would inevitably come when maintenance of way workers must use their collective strength, if necessary, to improve their conditions. For the railways were strongly opposing efforts of the Brotherhood to organize the trackmen. Their attitude is succinctly illustrated in a circular issued by the superintendent of a midwestern railroad to section foremen on one of its divisions in 1893:

"I find that J. Craiglow is organizing a trackmen's protective association with subdivisions along the line," the superintendent wrote. "This will result in nothing but expense and loss to yourself and trouble for the railway company, and we do not want it. We desire the employes on this division of maintenance of way department to stay out of the organization. Let me know by return mail if you or your men belong to it and what you propose to do. We pay as good wages as other roads and there is no need for the so-called protection. . . . If you feel in any other way about this matter it will be better for both parties to make a change."

The "good wages" mentioned in the circular amounted to $1.10 a day. The May, 1893, issue of the "Advocate" reported, rather sketchily, a sequel to this circular. Apparently the company discharged several of the foremen to whom the circular was addressed, probably because of organization activities. After a strike of track gangs in the territory, which lasted a week, the company restored the discharged men to the service, thus considerably modifying its arbitrary stand toward unionism.

In 1892, a wave of railroad prosperity and a spreading unrest among workers throughout the country brought hundreds of members into the Brotherhood. By October, 1892, the membership of the Brotherhood had increased to 2,000. Seven organizers were at work and new members were being enrolled at the rate of 250 a month. The period of expansion continued on into 1893, and the Brotherhood began to meet with some success in improving wage rates in isolated cases. In July, 1893, a committee headed by Wilson secured a wage increase for track employes of the Ohio & Mississippi Railway amounting to $2.00 a month for foremen and 10¢ a day for laborers. But the order's bright prospects were dimmed and its organizing activities gradually stifled by the business panic which began in 1893 and continued for four more years.

The election of 1892 had returned the Democrats under Cleveland to power with a Democratic majority in both Houses of Congress. But hardly had President Cleveland embarked on his second term than serious economic maladjustments, brought into focus by business failures in the spring of 1893, including that of the Reading Railroad, engulfed his administration. The financial situation became critical and business failures were common. Eventually, some 22,000 miles of railroad were in the hands of receivers and new construction had virtually ceased.

By the spring of 1894, the flow of new members into the Brotherhood had dwindled, and a special assessment was levied to keep organizers in the field. Many of the new members enrolled the year before were lost through force reductions. In a letter appearing in the December, 1893, issue of the "Advocate," a member reported that of nine roads running into Atlanta, Georgia, only one or two were working more than four men to the section. In addition, the American Railway Union, under Debs, was making heavy inroads on the Brotherhood's membership. Wilson later estimated that two-thirds of the order's members had deserted to the Debs organization.

The raid of the Debs organization on its membership was the Brotherhood's first experience with a long list of rival organizations that have tried unsuccessfully to wean away its membership. In an effort to stem the flow of members to the rival organization, Wilson said in a circular to his membership on May 17, 1894:

"The whole country is still in the throes of a great business depression. Trade is paralyzed, and the wheels of progress have to a serious extent ceased to revolve. . . . New-fangled ideas of organization are being sprung upon railway employes and advocated in sensational speeches as cures for all the ills from which we suffer. The natural result is that a wider breach than ever is being formed between organized capital and organized labor, between employer and employe. . . .

"An organization that, like a mushroom, springs up in a night cannot be depended upon for practical and beneficial results. . . . Class organizations have been maintained by railroad employes, and through their wise, conservative and moderate methods they have secured unnumbered concessions from railway managements in the way of wages and rules and regulations. These organizations have maintained friendly relations with the railway companies, have won the esteem and respect of the public, and have been recognized and commended by the courts as legal and useful institutions."

Wilson urged his membership to "stand by their employers" until prosperity had returned to the country. This, he felt, would be the wisest course to pursue and would "pay best in the long run."

The loss of the Pullman strike in 1894 brought about a rapid disintegration of the Debs organization. But another problem of long standing had now become acute. The amalgamated organization had continued the insurance program inaugurated by the Wilson organization, and the state of the insurance fund was becoming precarious.

Complete information is lacking on the early dues of the Brotherhood. A notice issued in December, 1893, reminded all members that grand dues of $1.50 for the half-year ending June 30, 1894, were payable January 1. Effective January 1, 1895, the 1894 convention reduced dues to $2.00 a year payable each six months in advance. For odd months, dues of 17¢ a month were collected from the date of application for membership. The dues included a subscription to the "Advocate." Additional assessments, however, were levied to cover insurance.

The early records of the Brotherhood likewise do not furnish much information about the laws of the Insurance Department. It appears that in the beginning a maximum of $1,000.00 was paid in the event of death or total disability, and lesser amounts for partial disability. The 1893 Convention defined the term "partial disability," for which $500.00 would be paid, and decided that $250.00 should be paid for the loss of one eye. Assessments were levied as claims were paid and the fund became depleted. An appeal to members to pay their insurance assessments, accompanying an assessment notice dated March 1, 1893, stated that the assessment fund contained a balance of only $700.00. Writing to the "Advocate" in November, 1893, a member reported that he had been assessed only $17.00 in two years to cover his insurance of $1,000.00. A review of the Insurance Department's records made in 1897 for the five-year period January 1, 1892, to January 1, 1897, showed that the Brotherhood had furnished insurance against partial disability, total disability, and death at an average rate of $12.00 a year.

During 1892 and 1893, the carrying of insurance was compulsory. In 1893, however, the convention decided that the policy of compulsory insurance might be a deterrent to the enrolling of new members and placed the insurance plan on an optional basis during 1894. The expected influx of new members did not materialize, however, and at the 1894 convention the laws were changed to make it compulsory for all applicants for membership between age 20 and 50 in good health to carry not less than $500.00 in insurance. In later years, a minimum coverage of $250.00 was reestablished.

The condition of the insurance fund continued to be serious, and the August, 1895, issue of the "Advocate" carried a notice that for the second time in the history of the Brotherhood, members were being asked to pay a double insurance assessment two months in succession. At the 1896 convention, membership in the Insurance Department was made optional with applicants for membership.

By the time it held its second annual convention (in 1893), following amalgamation, the Brotherhood had already begun to expand its activities and to look toward the improvement of working conditions for its members. "The Foremen's Advance Advocate," which began publication in 1892, was being sent to the membership. It contained reviews of the union's activities, reprints of articles from other labor magazines, items of general interest, discourses on track work, letters from members, and a "Woman's Department."

If the pen is mightier than the sword, then truly Wilson stood in need of a fluent and persuasive pen to serve as both. For the sword of collective strength with which the Brotherhood was to hew out its place among American labor organizations had not yet been forged, and even though it had been, the young order would not have had the strength to wield it. In the "Advocate," Wilson found a powerful medium for carrying on his educational campaign in unionism among trackmen, and the comparatively new magazine had already become an important force for organization when the delegates representing 83 subordinate divisions met in Atlanta, Georgia, in October, 1893.

Reports of committees on track work usually consumed a considerable portion of the session at the early conventions, and the 1893 convention was no exception. But the delegates at last began to turn their thoughts toward questions more directly affecting the welfare of the workers. The convention unanimously adopted a resolution calling for extra pay for work in excess of 10 hours a day or on Sunday; declared that it was the purpose of the organization to bring about the moral and material improvement of trackmen of America, irrespective of creed or party; decided that its members should act in concert with the wishes of the majority; suggested a closer inter-relationship with other labor organizations; and took action to place the Insurance Department on an optional basis. M. O'Dowd had resigned as Grand Secretary and Treasurer in April, 1893, and the Grand Executive Committee had appointed W. W. Allen to fill his unexpired term. The convention continued Allen in this office and re-elected Wilson Grand Chief Foreman by acclamation.

When it held its next convention in St. Louis, Missouri, beginning October 1, 1894, the directory in the "Advocate" showed that the Brotherhood had subordinate divisions in thirty states and in Indian Territory. The delegates voted to hold future conventions biennially instead of annually, reduced dues to $2.00 a year, made the carrying of insurance compulsory, elected J. R. Ice Grand Secretary and Treasurer, and again re-elected Wilson Chief Foreman by acclamation.

As an interesting sidelight on the financial worth of the Brotherhood following the 1894 convention, the report of the auditing committee for the last six months of 1894 showed a cash balance of $2,716.92 on hand at the close of the year. An inventory of fixed assets listed a printing plant valued at $1,000.00 and furniture and fixtures worth $575.00 This balance sheet of the Brotherhood's assets clearly reflected the Brotherhood's comparatively dormant state, and soon its financial condition grew worse.

Two serious problems had prevented the expected growth of the Brotherhood following the merging of the Alabama and Iowa organizations in 1891: (1) The lack of the necessary machinery for handling and settling grievances; and (2) the exclusion of track laborers from membership. The delegates attending the first biennial convention, held in St. Louis, Missouri, beginning October 5, 1896, set about promptly to correct these deficiencies. For the first time, system grievance committees, to be composed of one member from each lodge, were established. With this change, the convention voted to modify an old clause in the preamble of the constitution in opposition to strikes.

The Trackmen's Protective Association, established as an addition to the Brotherhood to permit the admission of track laborers to membership, had not proved satisfactory. The convention thereupon changed the laws of the organization to admit both track foremen and white track laborers to membership. By this action, the convention took one of the most important steps in its history, for by making membership in the Brotherhood available to track laborers on the same basis as for foremen, it increased its potential strength immeasurably. Gradually, the unrealistic distinction between groups or classes of workers was being eliminated. Along with this amendment to the constitution, the convention changed the name of the organization to the "Brotherhood of Railway Trackmen of America," and the name of "The Foremen's Advance Advocate" to "The Trackmen's Advance Advocate."

Annual dues were established as follows: foremen $3.00, laborers $2.00. In addition, because of the Brotherhood's poor financial condition, the delegates abolished the office of

Grand Secretary and Treasurer, assigning the duties of this office to the Grand Chief Foreman, made membership in the Insurance Department optional, and re-elected Wilson Chief Foreman.

But this did not end the business of this important convention. Early in the 1890's another organization, known as "The Independent Order of Railway Trackmen," had been formed with headquarters at Wheeling, West Virginia. After struggling along ineffectively for several years, the officers of this order decided to seek amalgamation with the Wilson order. A joint committee composed of delegates from the two organizations completed the amalgamation at the 1896 convention.

The effects of the business depression were still being felt in 1898, and despite Wilson's hard work the Brotherhood continued to lose ground in membership. Apparently the order had not yet been able to recoup its losses to Debs' American Railway Union nor to recover from the heavy force reductions made by the railroads during the panic. Probably some men remained in the Brotherhood during this period of time because of its insurance protection, but it seems evident that many others paid their dues because they had confidence in Wilson and in the Brotherhood.

In an effort to stimulate organization, the Brotherhood had prepared a crude model agreement in 1897. Drafted as a modest prospectus of future objectives, this agreement proposed rules requiring investigation in discipline cases; a ten-hour day with time and one-half for overtime; the granting of periodic passes; promotion on capacity and seniority; leave af absence, passes, and protection against discrimination for members of committees; and notices of change in agreements. Other proposals also contained in this model agreement were soon abandoned as being impractical: thirty days' notice by employer and employe before separation from the service; houses for all foremen at convenient places; and a provision establishing the maximum length of sections and the minimum size of gangs.

Although the Brotherhood could set its goals for the future, it was not yet able to take any definite action toward achieving these goals. Perhaps one of Wilson's greatest assets was his instinctive knowledge of human nature. He realized that until the Brotherhood could offer to its membership immediate benefits in a tangible form, it must maintain a constant focus on the achievements which could eventually be possible through organization.

Through the pages of the "Advocate," Wilson continued to stress the value of unionism. It must be assumed that Wilson wrote most or all of the articles originating in the "Advocate" in those days. If any were prepared by other members of his small staff, it must have been under Wilson's careful scrutiny, judging from the consistency of approach and treatment that characterized the writing in the early issues of the "Advocate." In fact, from 1896 to 1902, Wilson was a veritable major-domo for the Brotherhood. Not only did he look after the administrative duties of the Grand Chief Foreman and the financial responsibilities of the Grand Secretary and Treasurer, but he served as editor and manager of the "Advocate" as well.

The "Advocate" stressed, too, the need for activity in the political field. "Labor is learning the value of the ballot," the "Advocate" said in 1895, "and despite all obstacles will use it, and the time is coming when, through the efforts of organized labor, laws will be enacted which will bear equally on all the people, and not favor the few at the expense of the masses, as is now too frequently the case." In September, 1896, the "Advocate" condemned the reported action of railroad officials in telling some section foremen and their men how they should vote at the coming election.

It was through reading the "Advocate" that A. B. Lowe, at that time Grand Organizer for the United Brotherhood of Railroad Trackmen in Canada, became acquainted with the work Wilson and his organization were doing in the United States, and it was because of the influence of Wilson's writings that Lowe began to work toward the amalgamation of the two organizations.

In his memoirs written in 1902, Lowe gave a concise account of the development of the labor movement among Canadian maintenance of way workers. Their earliest attempts to act collectively in protest against low wages or intolerable working conditions, he related, consisted of petitions or "round robins" sent to the company. Strikes frequently followed the ignoring of these "round robins" by the company, and the strikes were often successful. These protests, however, were of a localized nature, seldom affecting more than a few gangs or a division at most. No attempt was made for unified action on a system or nation-wide basis. Nevertheless, these isolated strikes were of concern to railroad officials, for without the stabilizing effect of a labor organization through which the workers could present their grievances formally, there was always the possibility that a strike would spread and get completely out of hand.

The first organization bearing any resemblance to a bona fide union for Canadian maintenance of way workers was called the "Order of Section Foremen." No record exists as to when or by whom it was formed. This order, however, had the same constitutional defect that had so seriously retarded the growth of the Iowa and Alabama organizations in the United States, for it restricted membership to section foremen. Undoubtedly this is the reason it met with little success and was soon abandoned.

In 1892, Canadian railroad workers formed the "United Brotherhood of Railroad Trackmen" with headquarters in Ottawa, Ontario. Unlike its predecessor, which had restricted membership to foremen, the new organization threw its ranks open to both track foremen and their men; consequently, it achieved much greater success. In the same year, railway workers in the vicinity of Battle Creek, Michigan, formed a similar organization. The Battle Creek order passed out of existence the following year, however, when practically all its members joined the Ottawa organization.

On June 10, 1893, the U. B. of R. T. held its first convention in Ottawa and elected J. P. Kelly Grand President, but it was Lowe as organizer who became the driving force of the Canadian organization, who covered the railway lines in Canada from one end to the other soliciting membership in the order, and who in 1893 brought about the amalgamation with the U. B. of R. T. of another organization of maintenance of way workers in the vicinity of Truro, Nova Scotia.

William Jewkes, who joined the Canadian order in August, 1892, and who was the oldest living member of the Brotherhood when this history was written (1954), has given a vivid account of wages and working conditions on Canadian railroads in those early days. At that time, trackmen on the

Canadian Pacific Railway at Spragge, Ontario, where he worked, received from $1.00 to $1.15 a day to cover ten hours' work, with no extra pay for overtime. After paying $15.00 a month for board, Jewkes actually had only $11.00 left for clothing and other expenses out of monthly earnings of approximately $26.00. When he got married, his fortunes had improved somewhat—he earned $32.50 a month and received free fuel and a house in which to live.

The company resisted efforts of the employes to organize for the improvement of their conditions. Until the company recognized the union in 1901, members had to attend meetings of the order in secret. Although he had worked for the company six years, on one occasion Jewkes was denied a pass to attend a convention of the Brotherhood. When A. B. Lowe traveled from coast to coast organizing workers in the Canadian Brotherhood, Jewkes related, the men often risked discharge by taking him from one point to another on their hand cars.

In the early 1890's, the employes sent a committee to Montreal to secure a wage increase. The committeeman from Jewkes' district reported upon his return that the officials had painted a gloomy picture of the company's financial condition. They could not afford to grant any wage increase to the trackmen, but they would make some concession to the foremen. The section foremen could have the hay along the right of way if they would cut it on their own time. Hay at that time was worth about $5.00 a ton.

The wages of trackmen, Jewkes reported, were eventually increased to $1.10 and $1.25 a day, but before the 1901 strike on the Canadian Pacific, other concessions were minor. The company agreed to furnish houses to foremen without charge, to supply water by train where it could not be obtained by digging wells, and to ship fresh meat twice a week to isolated regions. The basic protection of an agreement containing essential rules covering working conditions, however, was still in the future.

But even though the Canadian order had not attained the full status of a bona fide union, it was able to bring about the improvement of conditions on some Canadian railways. The memoirs of A. B. Lowe contain a summary of its early progress:

"On the Canadian Pacific Railway, in 1897, on the Eastern Division, we got an increase of 10 cents per day or $30 per year for all hands, and at the same time 20 cents per day for foremen and 10 cents for men on the Ontario and Quebec Division and a cut of $5 per month for foremen and 10 cents per day per man, restored to our men on the Western Division from Fort William to Laggan. The previous winter I had made a trip from Ottawa to Winnipeg, arriving there Christmas Eve. The same year the Canada Atlantic Railway boys quit work for four days and gained a 10 cent increase. Next year the Ontario & Quebec and Eastern Division to Fort William received a 5 cent increase (in some parts for foremen), and the Atlantic Division foremen in New Brunswick were increased in pay to $1.70 per day on main line and $1.60 on branch lines, the previous rate being $1.45. The following year the Canada Atlantic men were increased to $1.75 and $1.15 per day, and the Intercolonial Railway men to $1.65 and $1.20 per day."

Beginning in 1897, Wilson had worked to bring about a consolidation of the two organizations in the belief that an international organization would be much to the advantage of maintenance of way workers in both countries. He accepted an invitation to visit the convention of the Canadian order in Toronto in September, 1897, and received a cordial welcome from the delegates. He again attended the Canadian convention in 1898 and discussed with the delegates many of the problems pertaining to the consolidation of the two orders. In spite of the widespread dissatisfaction over the manner in which the Grand officers were conducting the affairs of the order, however, and the general inertia that had gripped its membership, the Canadian Brotherhood was not yet ready to take the final step toward amalgamation.

In commenting on the condition of the Canadian order following his visit to the 1898 convention, Wilson said: "Their by-laws are imperfect and ambiguous, and their plan of organization is not at all practical. . . . At their convention in 1897 it seemed that a lack of proper understanding as to what is best for the trackmen of the country, and how to go about getting it in a practical way, was the only obstacle in the way of consolidation. . . ." He said that at the convention held in Hamilton, Ontario, in 1898, however, some of the Grand officers of the Canadian Brotherhood were influenced by men who opposed the trade union movement and who were in fact urging railroad workers in other crafts to withdraw from international unions and form separate unions of Canadian workers. Wilson had stressed to the Canadian delegates the advantages of amalgamation and the weakness of disunity, but one of these opponents of amalgamation, he said, who had been present in the guise of a delegate, had so aroused the prejudices of the delegates and paralyzed their reasoning faculties that for the time being they would not listen to reason.

In a letter to the 1898 convention of the Wilson organization, A. B. Lowe said: "I am sorry our men could not see their way to immediate amalgamation of the two orders, but I think a forward step was taken in declaring most heartily for closest cooperation, and I think the stern logic of events will yet bring about the union."

Meanwhile, members of the Canadian order who had not been present at the convention were anxious to know why the consolidation had not taken place. The 1898 convention of the Wilson order passed a motion authorizing the Grand Executive Committee to confer with a legally constituted committee of the Canadian Brotherhood to agree upon terms to bring the members of the two orders together. This action, coupled with the increasing pressure being exerted on their officers by the Canadian membership, made eventual unification only a matter of time. At the next convention of the U. B. of R. T., held in Ottawa in September, 1899, the delegates instructed an amalgamation committee to proceed with negotiations to complete the consolidation of the two Brotherhoods. But one final obstacle in the way of unification had yet to be cleared: the uncompromising attitude of the Canadian amalgamation committee.

Although a special assessment had been levied by the Canadian Brotherhood to defray the expense of amalgamation, and in spite of repeated attempts by Wilson and Lowe to arrange a meeting of the two committees, for some inexplicable reason the Canadian committee failed to respond or to carry out the instructions of the convention to proceed with the consolidation. Upon the death of J. P. Kelly, the first president of the U. B. of R. T., James Logan had been elected

Grand President, and when plans for consolidation were approved at the 1899 convention, he became chairman of the amalgamation committee. In a letter dated July 15, 1900, addressed "To The Trackmen of Canada," the secretary of the Canadian Committee on Amalgamation said:

"I have no desire to criticize Bro. J. Logan, our Grand President, who was chairman of our committee; but at the same time I consider it was his duty as chairman of committee to do all in his power to bring about amalgamation, and of course it is quite plain that he did not desire to carry out the expressed wishes of the delegates in convention assembled in regard to amalgamation."

In commenting on the conditions that led him to resign as Grand Organizer for the Canadian order in the latter part of 1899 and to urge immediate consolidation with the B. of R. T. of A., Lowe stated that he could receive no reply to letters he had written to Grand officers of the Canadian organization concerning consolidation. He said: "I found that the men had absolutely lost confidence in our Grand officers at Ottawa, and the only way to secure their co-operation and support was by guaranteeing that we would have amalgamation with the B. R. T. of A."

For if the Grand officers and the amalgamation committee of the Canadian order were disinclined to take positive action toward consolidation, the rank and file members were not, and the amalgamation eventually became effective as they transferred their membership to the B. of R. T. of A. in large numbers. It is estimated that between 1,500 and 2,000 Canadian workers joined the international order (the B. of R. T. of A.) in 1899 and early 1900. The wisdom of their decision to form an international Brotherhood was to be convincingly demonstrated within the next eighteen months.

Meantime, the Wilson organization in the United States had continued its efforts to build a substantial foundation for future collective action. In its May, 1895, issue the "Advocate" reported that the Burlington System had increased the wages of its foremen by 10 per cent from $50.00 to $55.00 a month. At the close of 1897, in summarizing the progress of the Brotherhood since the uniting of the Alabama and the Iowa orders in 1891, Wilson said: "Although the past six years have been a very unfavorable time to keep alive and increase the strength and usefulness of a young labor organization, and we have had some opposition without and dissension within, we are proud of the history made by our young and growing Order. . . . The few trackmen who have banded themselves together have accomplished a great deal during the past six years, that they should be proud of. . . . We have made a good start in the right direction. . . . The foundation for a great and grand Brotherhood is well laid. . . . Let us proceed to build upon it."

To illustrate one way in which this could be done, on March 15, 1898, Wilson addressed a circular to the membership urging that the members on each system decide on the kind of rules agreement they would like to have, put the agreement in writing, and send it to him. It would then be reproduced and circulated on the system as a goal toward which to work. It is apparent that in this way Wilson laid the groundwork for the important change to be made at the coming convention in the laws governing the handling of grievances and the negotiation of agreements.

On June 19, 1898, the wives of members of the Brotherhood met at Macon, Georgia, organized the first chapter of the Ladies' Auxiliary of the Brotherhood of Railway Trackmen of America and elected Mrs. Lizzie Shirah president. They approved an outline of the objectives of the newly-formed auxiliary, reading in part: "Realizing the great responsibility that devolves upon us as members of trackmen's families, and knowing that what affects them also affects us, we deem it our duty and in justice to them and to ourselves to place ourselves in a position which will enable us to aid in promoting the interests of the B. of R. T. of A. and in protecting its members and their families against the many misfortunes that have made the homes of so many trackmen desolate."

As the date (October 3) for the 1898 convention in Macon, Georgia, approached, an epidemic of yellow fever in the south forced its postponement until December of that year. When the delegates assembled in Macon on December 5, Wilson's program to educate the trackmen in trade unionism had begun to bear fruit. The convention followed Wilson's recommendations in establishing the first Protective Department providing for the election of a General Chairman, system officers, and

Joint Protective Board members by delegates from lodges on each railroad system in much the same manner as they are elected today.

Formerly, grievances which could not be settled by local lodge grievance committees were referred directly to the Grand Chief Foreman for handling. Under the new system, unsettled grievances were to be referred by the local committees to their respective system Joint Protective Boards for further handling. A Joint Protective Board consisting of a General Chairman and other system officers and members of the Board was to be established on each railroad system, and in addition to handling grievances they had the power to enter into agreement with the managements of their respective roads, with the approval of the Grand Chief Foreman. Thus the General Chairman and his Joint Protective Board were given an important part not only in the handling of grievances, but in negotiating agreements covering wages and working conditions. Previously, negotiations on rules agreements were conducted by the Grand Chief Foreman or his authorized representative.

The new laws required that grievances were to be started locally and progressed on the system. The Grand Chief was to be called on only as a last resort. Unauthorized strikes were to be dealt with severely. If "all honorable means of peaceful and satisfactory settlement" proved futile, the Grand Chief and the Joint Protective Board could call a strike if two-thirds of the members involved agreed to this extreme measure. The new provisions of the constitution authorized strike benefits of $20.00 a month when the strike lasted more than two weeks, but no member could receive more than three months' benefits, nor benefits while he was employed or after the strike. The revised laws required each member to pay 50¢ quarterly to finance this new Protective Department.

The convention also attempted to find some solution to the perpetual problems of the Insurance Department. A new plan providing insurance benefits of either $500 or $1,000 and premiums on a step-rate basis increasing as the insured member grew older was to be publicized in each issue of the "Advocate" until June, 1899, and voted upon at that time by the membership at meetings of subordinate divisions. Apparently the plan failed to receive the necessary majority vote

The locomotive "Atlantic," placed in service in 1832 by the Baltimore & Ohio Railroad. The first train to enter Washington, D. C., it is still in operating condition and is shown here pulling two double-decked Imlay coaches.

This early painting captures the carnival air which accompanied the arrival of a train when the chugging steamers were still novelties. The painting was inspired by a scene in a typical Canadian frontier town.

The driving of the golden spike at Promontory, Utah, on May 10, 1869, joined the last rails of the Union Pacific and the Central Pacific (now the Southern Pacific) to complete the first transcontinental railroad.

The Tehachapi loop on the Southern Pacific in South Central California was a rigid test for the old wood-burning locomotive in 1876. Here the tracks looped the loop to gain seventy-seven feet elevation.

→

Construction crew at work on a "bean-pole" bridge over Running Water Creek on the Nashville, Chattanooga & St. Louis Railway during the war between the states (1861-1865).

←

These "skyscraper" cars were used as dormitories for railroad construction forces in the 1880's.

Track on the old Camden and South Amboy Railroad at Jamesburg, New Jersey. The steel rails were manufactured in England. They weighed forty pounds to the yard and were attached to stone ties by hooked-head spikes.

A section of double track dressed and conditioned by maintenance of way workers for today's highspeed traffic.

for adoption, for there is no evidence that it was ever put into effect, but a similar plan was adopted at the next convention.

The convention voted to discontinue the printing of the division directory and financial statements of the Brotherhood in the "Advocate," and concluded the meeting by again re-electing Wilson Grand Chief by acclamation.

As the business depression subsided and railroad prosperity returned, the organization began to grow again. In 1899, it had regained its numerical strength of 1893, and its officers were becoming more skilled in labor relations. At last, too, the order was obtaining public recognition. Legislation enacted by Congress in 1898 authorized the appointment of an Industrial Commission to collect information and to consider and recommend legislation to meet the problems presented by labor, agriculture, and capital. On March 1, 1899, Wilson appeared before the Commission and testified as to the conditions under which trackmen worked.

He estimated that the railroads in the United States employed approximately 180,000 trackmen. About 30,000 of these men were section foremen who received from $1.05 to $2.00 a day, depending on locality, and who received no extra pay for Sunday or night work. Track laborers numbered approximately 150,000, but he doubted that more than half this number were employed during the winter months because of the railroads' practice of concentrating their track work during the months of most favorable weather. Thus, many track laborers were forced to become transients, moving from job to job as forces were reduced. The wages of trackmen ranged from a low of 47½¢ to a high of $1.25 a day, he testified, according to locality. On some roads laborers worked ten or eleven hours a day; on others from daylight until dark. Unlike the foremen, who worked on an all-service-rendered basis, track laborers received extra pay for work at night or on Sunday.

Wilson presented a convincing case in behalf of trackmen, but there is no evidence of any tangible action taken by the government to correct their substandard wages and working conditions. The Brotherhood, however, was beginning to make substantial progress of its own in settling accumulated grievances on various systems. Wage increases were obtained on several roads in 1899. The Boston & Maine increased the wages of foremen 10¢ a day and those of laborers 5¢ a day. The Baltimore & Ohio increased wages in some districts $5.00 a month for foremen and 5¢ and 10¢ a day for laborers.

Trackmen on the Southern Railway had traditionally been required to work from daylight until dark, often as long as 14 or 15 hours during the summer months. Their repeated protests resulted in a change in the work schedule by the company: Effective July 1, 1899, their working day was reduced to 11 hours from April 1 to November 1 and to 9 hours from November 1 to April 1. The following year, effective June 1, 1900, the Chesapeake & Ohio Railway reduced the working day of its trackmen from 11 to 10 hours.

But the railroads still resisted efforts of trackmen to organize. The May, 1900, issue of the "Advocate" quoted a telegram purportedly sent by the general superintendent of a southern railroad to all division superintendents, reading in part: "You had better take up with your roadmasters and have them watch the trackmen for fear they will organize; such a movement should be headed off at once."

Whether trackmen were organized or not, however, the railroads could not prevent the outbreak of spontaneous protests against their low wage rates. In the summer of 1900, trackmen in section and extra gangs in various localities on five or more railroads in central Illinois went on strike to obtain a wage increase. So far as was known, none of these men was a member of the Brotherhood. In commenting on this fact, Wilson pointed out that during the preceding ninety days the Brotherhood had been able to secure wage increases for its members amounting to approximately $200,000 a year without the necessity of their losing any wages through strikes.

In February, 1900, the Brotherhood affiliated with the American Federation of Labor. Information accompanying the application showed that the organization had a paid-up membership of 1,500, and the jurisdiction of the order was outlined by the following quotation from the constitution:

"GRAND LODGE—ARTICLE XII—Membership.

"Section 1. Any employe born of white parents, who can read and write, who is sober, moral and otherwise of good character, and has served in the maintenance-of-way department for one year or more, is eligible to membership in the Brotherhood. Any person gaining admission under false representation shall not be entitled to any benefits from the Brotherhood.

Note: By maintenance-of-way employes is meant persons employed in the Track, Bridge and Building, Water Supply and Fuel Departments, and Signal and Interlocking Service on all Railways of America."

When the third biennial convention of the Brotherhood was called to order in St. Louis, Missouri on December 3, 1900, Wilson indicated plainly the drastic policy that would be followed in dealing with violations of the organization's laws pertaining to strikes. He reported that the charter of a subordinate division located at Baltimore, Maryland, on the Baltimore & Ohio System had been revoked for engaging in an unauthorized strike. On the question of insurance benefits, the delegates voted to amend the laws to provide that the premiums on insurance benefits of $500 would range on a step basis from 50¢ to $1.00 a month, depending on the applicant's age (18 to 55), and on insurance benefits of $1,000, from $1.00 to $1.75 a month, also depending on the applicant's age.

The convention made dues payable quarterly, semi-annually, or annually, in advance, voted to change the language in the constitution to make it clear that bridge men and others employed in the maintenance of way department were eligible to membership in the order, and changed the title "Grand Chief" to "Grand President." A Canadian delegate from British Columbia nominated Wilson for the office of Grand President, and he was re-elected without opposition.

"The tide has certainly turned in our direction," Wilson said as the nineteenth century waned, and indeed it had. The Brotherhood had become an international order and at that time was the sole organization representing maintenance of way workers in the United States and Canada (a new order called "The Western Brotherhood of Railroad Trackmen" had sprung up in western Canada in 1899 but had been short-lived). Its membership was growing larger. It had gained added prestige through its affiliation with the American Federation of Labor. And with the adoption of a practical and effective method for negotiating agreements and handling grievances, it was prepared to move into new fields of conquest. Wilson undoubtedly knew that the time was soon to come when the young organization, if it were to survive and grow, must throw down the gauntlet and meet the railroads in mortal combat to obtain the concessions in the way of higher wages and improved conditions so sorely needed by maintenance of way workers. Like a general preparing to do battle with an unknown foe, Wilson built his fortifications and marshalled his forces in preparation for the first skirmish. And as the new century began, he had not long to wait.

CHAPTER III

THE GROWTH

THE early years of the new century witnessed a distinct upturn in the general prosperity of the United States. By 1900 recovery from the low points of the depression years had been substantial. Exports of food and merchandise had increased greatly and pig-iron production was nearly twice that of 1893. Bank clearings in 1901 amounted to more than two and one-half times those in 1894. The depression years and the period of economic prosperity that followed, however, had been favorable to the growth of huge business monopolies, and at the century's turn the public viewed with concern the dangerous concentration of business and financial control in the hands of a few. The time for reform was ripe.

Shot by an assassin on September 6, 1901, President William McKinley died eight days later. Vice President Theodore Roosevelt succeeded him to office, and in response to a sweeping protest from all parts of the nation against organized wealth and its abuses, he began a movement of reform. The strength of labor unions increased considerably during this period of recovery and progressive reform. By 1905 the total membership of unions in the United States had increased to more than 2 million. Political leaders, too, were becoming increasingly aware of the growing strength of labor and the need to work out some of the critical labor-management problems. State legislatures gave more consideration to labor legislation and in 1903 Congress established a department of Commerce and Labor and made the Secretary a member of the cabinet. But as the power of labor unions grew, alarmed employers set about to form organizations to combat the movement.

The upturn in general business conditions brought with it a corresponding improvement in the fortunes of the Brotherhood. The membership continued to increase, and the Brotherhood obtained wage increases on several railroads. As yet, however, the order had not had either the opportunity or the inclination to test its economic strength through a strike. This was in fact a period of preparation. Sailing an unknown and uncharted sea, Wilson set his course cautiously, sounding the dangerous shoals and reefs upon which the not too sturdy Brotherhood craft he was piloting could quickly be battered and broken.

The establishment of the new Protective Department had stimulated the movement to obtain agreements from the railroads covering wages and working conditions, but the first agreement was yet to be signed. It is quite evident, however, that the activities of the Brotherhood were now definitely concentrated toward this goal. But Wilson wisely understood the need for strength and unity. It would be a great mistake, he felt, to attempt to secure increased wages and better conditions of employment until the majority of the trackmen on a railroad were members of the Brotherhood and had authorized the organization to represent them. In addition to stressing continually the advantages of membership, he suggested that trackmen sign certificates of authority empowering the general grievance committee to confer with officials of the railroad company and to enter into an agreement with them covering wages and working conditions.

In the early part of 1901, a southern railroad issued instructions on one division changing the working hours of track employes. The "Advocate" estimated that this order added 117 hours a year to the old work schedule without a corresponding increase in pay, and pointed out the necessity for organization to combat such moves as this. Little exhortation was needed, however, to convince the workers of the need for united action. It had become evident that their seething discontent could not be held in check much longer. Although he continued to counsel restraint, Wilson recognized the rising tide of dissatisfaction.

"A strike should be the very last resort under any and all circumstances," Wilson said in the spring of 1901, "but if it becomes absolutely necessary to strike—if every argument has proven unavailing and every other expedient has failed—then strike and strike hard; but before doing so, be sure you are ready. Be sure that you can win."

But even as he uttered this admonition the first rumblings of trouble came from the midwest. In April, 1901, the men on two or three sections of the Missouri Pacific Railroad near St. Louis went on strike to enforce a demand that their wages be increased from $1.10 to $1.25 a day. Fearing a general strike, the management hastened to avert further trouble by increasing the wages of track laborers on the Missouri Pacific and Iron Mountain Railroad in Missouri to $1.25 a day.

The failure of the Maine Central strike a few months later, the first stoppage of work ever officially authorized by the Brotherhood, emphasized the danger of hasty action and lack of preparation. In June, 1901, the management of the Maine Central Railroad met a demand from its track employes for increased wages and improved working conditions by offering a wage increase of 10 per cent. It refused, however, to negotiate a rules agreement with Brotherhood representatives. Although no other organization on that system had been able to obtain an agreement the Joint Protective Board was not satisfied.

Opposed to a strike, Wilson hurried to the scene. Irked, however, by the refusal of the general manager to answer his request for a conference, and swayed by the persuasive arguments of those who favored drastic action, Wilson sanctioned a strike and left to attend to urgent business elsewhere. At 5:00 p.m. on June 10, 1901, the strike of maintenance of way employes on the Maine Central officially became effective. But the imprudence of this hasty action soon became apparent. Only about half the men actually went on strike, and even before the walkout began, desertions occurred among members of the Joint Protective Board. Apparently whistling in the dark, the July, 1901, issue of the "Advocate" carried this comment on the strike: "We had earnestly hoped that a settlement would have been reached in time for its details to be published in this issue, but . . . as we go to press the situation is little changed from what it was a week ago."

On July 3 Wilson called the strike off and the men returned to work. Only the Herculean efforts of the Board chairman and the unofficial support of the members of other railroad labor organizations had prevented an irreparable disaster. The men returned to their jobs under an agreement with the company that they would not be discriminated against for their part in the strike or because of membership in the Brotherhood. The strike gained nothing for the employes beyond the wage increase previously offered by the company.

Some members were outspoken in expressing dissatisfaction with the outcome, but in commenting on the failure of the Maine Central men to support the strike fully, Wilson said: "It must be remembered that they jumped into the fray on the shortest possible notice and with the least possible preparation. They had neither the experience of strikes nor the sinews of war . . . The call to strike came to them very much as the cry of fire comes to persons who are in the midst of peaceful slumber."

But if it served no other purpose, the strike had been a salutary lesson in restraint to the officers of the Brotherhood, and it had given the railroads forceful notice that maintenance of way workers were prepared to strike if necessary. "We want the railway companies to understand that we know our rights and will have them, even if we have to strike to get them," Wilson said in further comment on the Maine Central strike.

Even before the Maine Central strike had begun, the course of events was already leading to the Brotherhood's second and much more successful strike. On April 18, 1901, a committee representing maintenance of way workers on the Canadian Pacific Railway met the general manager of that road at Montreal to request a substantial increase in rates of pay (wages of trackmen were as low as $1.15 a day) and the negotiation of an agreement containing the following rules among others: a fair trial and the right to appeal in discipline cases; pay for time lost because of unjust suspension or dismissal; the time and one-half rate for work performed after ten hours or on Sundays; promotion based on seniority and merit; leave of absence and pass privileges both for employes and committeemen; the payment of employes' expenses when they were required to work away from their regular boarding places; a rule covering certain composite service; no discrimination against, suspension, or discharge of employes for serving on grievance committees; no discrimination against employes for membership in the Brotherhood; a sixty-day notice by either party for changes in the agreement.

At the conference, the general manager insisted that the committee should have presented their grievances to local officials before coming to him. The committee replied that they were authorized to represent at least 90 per cent of the railway's maintenance of way workers, and that under the company's established rules it would be futile to handle with minor officials such matters as were contained in the employes' request. An exchange of letters between the committee and the general manager brought no tangible results. The Canadian Pacific was obviously being supported by other Canadian railways in its opposition to the committee's proposals. Its wage rates for trackmen were already as high as, or higher than, the rates paid by other Canadian roads, who had no wish to see wage rates go higher. In addition, the railway managements realized that the negotiation of an agreement between the Canadian Pacific and the Brotherhood would be tantamount to a recognition of the union as the bargaining agency for the employes. Unquestionably this was a result which they were particularly anxious to avoid. The general manager did agree, however, to make an investigation of the employes' request and to call the committee back to Montreal by the end of May.

While the conferences were in recess, the company increased the wage rates of a number of its trackmen. This move the committee construed as an attempt by the company to divide the employes. In early June, the company distributed a document containing "Rules Governing the Service of Section Foremen and Sectionmen," bearing no signature but containing some of the basic provisions of the rules requested by the committee. The committee accepted this as additional evidence of an effort by the company to discredit the Brotherhood. Moreover, reports from various points over the system indicated that false rumors were being circulated about the conduct and the activities of committee members while they were in Montreal, and that individual employes were being sounded out on their attitude in the event of a strike. Reports were also received that the company had employed twice the number of trackmen usually worked during that season of the year, and that the foremen had been instructed to rush their work and get their tracks in shape by the end of May. Obviously the company was preparing for trouble.

To assure the railway company of the organization's sincere wish to bring about a peaceful settlement of the dispute, on May 13 Wilson wrote a letter to the general manager outlining in detail the objectives and purposes of the Brotherhood and its wish to act in good faith in entering into any agreement with a railroad company. He received no reply. It was apparent, therefore, when the committee returned to Montreal at the end of May that the die had been cast and that a test of strength between the Brotherhood and the Canadian Pacific Railway Company was in the offing. Subsequent conferences accomplished little, and on June 13 Wilson approved a strike call to be effective at 6:00 a.m., June 17.

On the morning of June 17, maintenance of way men on approximately 10,000 miles of track operated by the Canadian Pacific simultaneously quit work. The company attempted to minimize the strike in statements to the newspapers, but reports to strike headquarters indicated that it was about 95 per cent effective. Wilson later estimated that about 5,000 workers went on strike but that approximately 20 per cent returned to work in a few days. In "The Calcium Light," Wilson gave a detailed outline of the progress of the strike, and quotations from letters, items, and editorials appearing in Canadian newspapers indicated that a part of the citizenry and some newspapers favored the strikers. Other newspapers viewed the strike with disfavor and attempted to ridicule Wilson and the Brotherhood. The following is quoted from "The Calcium Light":

"On July 6th [1901] the same paper [the "Montreal Herald"] contained the following:

" 'It is not easy to withhold sympathy with the cause of labor wherever it may be struggling against capital for rights that are either scantily recognized or contemptuously ignored; but in the case of the trackmen's strike on the Canadian Pacific Railway, the merits of the case weigh so heavily in favor of the company that it is the duty of the true friends of labor to dissuade workmen from prolongation of a hopeless struggle. The trackmen entered upon the conflict seriously handicapped by the fact that the Canadian Pacific Railway Company pays higher wages than are paid on the other systems with which it is a competitor. Knowing that this was the case, the trackmen threw up their employment in the hope of coercing the company into granting still higher wages. Mr. Wilson, the president of the Brotherhood, admits these facts; but he says that the employes of the Grand Trunk and Intercolonial, who are paid lower wages than those of the Canadian Pacific, are not members of the organization of which he is the head, and the Brotherhood is not called upon to fight for those who are outside its ranks. The statement may be true, but it will not satisfy the public. It is against that strong elementary principle of British fair play, which is the usual standard of justice in cases of this kind, that the company which pays the highest wages should be compelled to pay still higher, before the others are brought up to its level. That is why Mr. Wilson has failed to gain public sympathy in this strike; why he has failed to get the support of kindred organizations, and why the Canadian Pacific are bound to win in the struggle. One of the most hopeless features in this strike is that the men have not even a case that can go to arbitration. They are fighting for a minimum wage of a dollar and a half a day—small enough remuneration, it is true—but the company pays a minimum of a dollar and a quarter while others are paying only one dollar and ten cents, and surely Mr. Wilson has sufficient intelligence to realize that before he can logically ask the C. P. R. for more he must first get the railways who pay one dollar and ten cents for the same class of labor up to the dollar and a quarter standard. There is good reason for supposing that the Brotherhood in this instance chose as the target for assault the Canadian Pacific, because that system—in consequence of its length of mileage, stretching as it does from the Atlantic to the Pacific—is more vulnerable than other railways. The principle is neither fair nor just. The company, assured of public sympathy, have already practically won the fight. The men who still remain out will, if they are well advised, return to work.'

"The statement made in the foregoing article that the minimum wage was $1.25, is incorrect; the minimum wage paid is $1.15.

"In strong contrast with the foregoing is the following editorial from the Inland Sentinel:

" 'Without entering into the merits of the case against the special constables arrested near Ashcroft last week, charged with intimidating workmen, the fact that the company's officials are compelled to have recourse to such extreme measures in order to have necessary work done on the track is scarcely in accord with their oft reiterated declaration that they have no difficulty in obtaining men to fill the strikers' places. Even ten dollars a day and board failed to tempt more than a mere handful of men to go to work upon a mud slide east of this point. The truth of the matter is they find it almost impossible to get any one to accept work at any price. The reason is not hard to find and lies in the fact that the general public recognize the justice of the claims of the striking trackmen for a living wage, and are in hearty sympathy with the movement. In addition to this the men upon whose sympathies the company relied as a reserve force upon which they could fall back and use as a lever to compel the strikers to submit, know full well that they would not be advancing their own interests by taking up the work, and they object to being made the tools of the company, only to be cast aside when the struggle is over. Meanwhile the strikers stand firm and the condition of the track is daily becoming, according to our reports, more and more deplorable, and traveling more hazardous, facts that cannot but be potent factors in bringing the company to a sense of their responsibilities leading eventually to a satisfactory settlement of the dispute.' "

Opponents of the strike tried to make capital of the fact that the trackmen on the Canadian Pacific received five cents a day more than trackmen on other roads. Why, Wilson was asked repeatedly, had he not called a strike on the Grand Trunk Railway instead? Wilson replied that the men on the Grand Trunk were not union men and had not called on the Brotherhood to secure increased wages and better working conditions for them; but the men on the Canadian Pacific had contributed part of their meager earnings to support the Brotherhood and were entitled to its services.

Wilson pointed out further that the cost of living had increased (he produced a comparative list of food prices to prove his point), that the country prospered, and the railway company had increased its dividends. "The contention that maintenance of way men should continue to work for less than an equitable share of the wealth they create, because the same class of men on other roads continue to do so, is absurd," Wilson said. "If men employed by one railway company are being deprived of their rights is it fair for the public to condemn them when they band themselves together and make united efforts to bring about improved conditions for themselves and families, because the same class of men on other roads have not got brains or courage enough to do likewise?"

By July 1 the situation had become critical and the company strove desperately to break the strike by importing laborers to take the places of the strikers. Wilson appealed to the Canadian government to enforce the Canadian Alien Labour Law restricting the importation and employment of aliens. As the strike continued, train service employes became alarmed because of the unsafe condition of the tracks, and took action at several meetings deploring "the continuance of the strike" and urging conciliation to bring about a fair settlement. Wilson was undoubtedly under tremendous pressure at this time to bring the strike to an end, but he stood steadfast and determined.

On July 31, Wilson, the chairman, and the secretary of the employes' committee were arrested on a charge of criminal libel but were released on bond. The charges were purportedly brought by a former committeeman named Montgomery whom Wilson accused of deserting the employes' ranks and whom he had flayed severely in a letter to the strikers on July 4. Wilson was certain, however, that Montgomery had not instigated the suit alone. "It is clear to my mind that the Canadian Pacific Railway company is hedging behind Montgomery," Wilson said in a letter dated August 1, 1901, to the strikers. "I was told three weeks ago that the advisability of having me arrested was being considered at the general offices of the Canadian Pacific Railway company, on the charge of inciting men to destroy property. A few days later I was informed that the company had decided to place Montgomery between themselves and your organization and have me arrested. . . .

"The Brotherhood of Railway Trackmen having funds on hand, and a few fearless friends living in Montreal not wearing C. P. R. collars, who came forward and executed bonds, are the only things that prevented your president, chairman and secretary from being locked in cells prepared for criminals.

"Will you uphold the C. P. R. company and its mercenaries, in their unscrupulous actions, or will you declare your souls your own, and support those who are fighting your battles in an honorable, manly and law-abiding way?"

The suit was later dropped after the strike had been settled.

In August, a conciliation committee composed of the Genereal Chairmen of other labor organizations on the Canadian Pacific attempted to bring about a settlement of the strike, but Wilson would not accept the proposed terms of settlement, which he declared "would mean an unconditional and disgraceful surrender upon the part of the trackmen." At this point the members of the Board of Adjustment of the Brotherhood of Railroad Trainmen arrived in Montreal to assist in the conciliation proceedings, and it was chiefly through their intercession that an agreement to end the strike was reached.

The strike terminated on August 30, 1901, after a plan for settlement had been agreed to by the company and the Brotherhood. The company confirmed the concessions it had granted before the strike and promised to negotiate an agreement for permanent employes at the end of six months. In the meantime, the Brotherhood was to show it had a responsible organization to represent the employes.

At the conferences the following March, the company contended that by the terms of the settlement the organization was authorized to represent only the permanent first and second men in maintenance of way gangs, and proposed arbitration of the representation dispute. The situation was critical. The rank and file members had supported the strike intrepidly, and they were essential to the future success of the Brotherhood. The Brotherhood stood its ground and won its argument that its source of authority derived from all workers under its jurisdiction and that it must negotiate for all of them.

The conferees reached a satisfactory agreement on working rules, but the question of wage increases had to be left to an Arbitration Board composed of three members. Each party selected an arbitrator, and a court justice was chosen as the third man. Speaking for the Brotherhood, Wilson stressed the company's prosperity and the rise in the cost of living since 1897. On May 8, 1902, the Arbitration Board rendered an award granting an increase of 20% over 1897 wage rates to Canadian Pacific maintenance of way workers. By June, 1902, the committee had completed its work and a printed copy of the agreement signed with the railway company was furnished to each member on that road.

The effects of the Brotherhood's victory on the Canadian Pacific were far-reaching. The strike had been called not only to obtain higher wages and a rules agreement, but to secure recognition of the union by the railway company. Other railway companies in both Canada and the United States had followed the progress of the strike closely, and the Brotherhood's success undoubtedly forced railway managements in both countries to revise their estimates of the potential strength of this growing organization, which they had given but slight consideration in the past.

The reverberations from the strike were soon evident. On the same day the Arbitration Board released its wage award for Canadian Pacific workers, the Grand Trunk Railway in Canada issued a circular notice granting to similar classes on that road wage increases which Wilson estimated amounted to $100,000 a year. A short time before, a resolution had been introduced in the Canadian Dominion Parliament to establish a minimum wage of $1.50 a day for maintenance of way employes on government roads. Although the records of the Brotherhood do not indicate the fate of this resolution, its introduction reflected the trend of thinking and showed that the unsatisfactory conditions under which maintenance of way men worked had been forcefully brought to the forefront by the strike.

The strike, however, had not been won without considerable cost to the organization. On October 1, 1901, the Brotherhood levied a special assessment of $1.00 on all members to replace money borrowed from the Insurance Fund to conduct the strikes on the Maine Central and the Canadian Pacific.

Meantime, the Brotherhood had continued its progress on other roads. In July, 1901, the "Advocate" reported that the Seaboard Air Line Railroad had reduced its working day to eleven hours in summer and nine hours in winter, an average reduction of three hours. And as the great strike became history, the Brotherhood prepared to begin a period of unprecedented growth and expansion.

"The first year of the twentieth century, the year just closed," the "Advocate" said in January, 1902, "has marked the most important epoch in the annals of our Brotherhood. The growth of the Order during this time was greater than during any similar period in its history. . . . Much of the good that has resulted, such as higher wages, shorter work days, better houses to live in and more generous concessions in the matter of pass privileges, etc., has followed closely upon the completion of system organizations on the several railways where concessions were made."

During 1901, the Brotherhood issued charters to 96 subordinate divisions and enrolled 6,000 new members. In January and February, 1902, it enrolled approximately 1,500 new members, 1,012 in February alone. "The advance guard is now safely out of the wilderness and they have blazed the way for others to follow," Wilson said in reviewing the Order's rapid growth.

The fact that the organization suffered growing pains was evidenced by an announcement in July, 1902, that the membership had become so large that Grand headquarters could no longer maintain the membership records in book form, and that a card system had been adopted. Applications for membership continued to pour in; more than 700 were received during the month of October. "The Order was never in better shape numerically and financially than at the present time and its future was never more hopeful," the "Advocate" said in November.

The rapid and continued growth of the Order, however, simply mirrored its success on the Canadian Pacific and on roads in the United States. In March, 1902, the "Advocate" commented on an understanding reached with the Chesapeake

& Ohio Railway. Previously, foremen had been required to work the equivalent of 8 or 10 days a month in overtime hours without extra pay. They received no expenses when they were away from their headquarters in emergencies. Track laborers received $1.00 a day, except on one or two small divisions where they received $1.10, and were often required to lay off to absorb overtime.

The concessions agreed to by the company granted track foremen 20¢ an hour for all work in excess of 10 hours a day. A foreman discharged or suspended could appeal from the supervisor or division engineer to the superintendent. Most track laborers received from $1.10 to $1.20 a day, plus 15¢ an hour for extra work at night or on Sundays. Track foremen sent to work at wrecks, slides, washouts, or other emergencies were to be furnished meals and lodging by the company. This understanding had been reached after the company had denied the committee a conference and the men had voted almost unanimously to strike if their request for improved wages and working conditions could not be settled.

On April 25, 1902, representatives of the Brotherhood completed negotiations on what was probably one of the most comprehensive of the early agreements reached with a railroad company in the United States. On that date the management of the East St. Louis & Suburban Railway Company signed an agreement giving maintenance of way employes the right to a speedy, fair, and impartial trial in the event of trouble; the right to be represented at hearings by fellow employes of their own choosing; the right to appeal to the general manager; pay for time lost because of improper discharge; a nine-hour day with pro rata pay for the tenth hour of service and the time-and-one-half rate for work performed after the tenth hour or on Sundays; promotion based on seniority, merit and other qualifications being equal; the recognition of seniority in force reduction; and free transportation after six months' service. The company agreed to grant leaves of absence to committeemen and to practice no discrimination against employes for serving on grievance committees or for membership in the Brotherhood. In addition, the agreement listed rates of pay and specified that employes would be paid on the fifth and twentieth day of each month.

An agreement of this kind on every railroad in the United States and Canada had long been Wilson's goal, but most railroads continued to oppose the organization of their maintenance of way workers. Wilson outlined some of the methods being used to discourage unionization. Railway officials, he said, would first try to learn which employes were members of the union and threaten them with discharge. If this had no effect, they would talk about "promotion." As a last resort, they would grant a voluntary increase in wages. This last method often brought the desired result, and Wilson deplored the shortsightedness of many workers who felt they had no further need for the Brotherhood after their wages had been increased. He cited one instance in which the company had retracted a wage increase as soon as the Brotherhood had become dormant on the system through losses in its membership. In order to save $4.00 a year in Brotherhood dues, Wilson pointed out, the men had surrendered $47.00 a year in wage increases.

Unskilled in the fine points of collective bargaining, Joint Protective Board members, too, found themselves being exploited. In one instance, the general manager of a railroad took a quick vote of the Board members before the adjournment of the first conference on the settlement of existing grievances, and none opposed the company's unsatisfactory offer. Wilson cautioned Board chairmen against permitting a vote to be taken before the company's proposition could be discussed privately by members of the Board.

In Canada, too, railway managements were reluctant to recognize the Brotherhood as the bargaining agency for their maintenance of way employes, even after its success in the Canadian Pacific strike. F. H. Fljozdal, who later served as President of the Brotherhood from 1922 to 1940, has told of the conditions that existed on the Canadian Northern Railway, where he was employed, before the company recognized the union in 1905.

The men held union meetings at night, he recalled, because the company would not permit them to be off during the day. On one occasion, many of the men had traveled 25 or 30 miles on their handcars on a bitterly cold night to install a lodge at Belmont, Manitoba. The meeting was being held in a room behind a store. In the midst of the meeting, the general superintendent walked in and delivered an ultimatum that any man who was not at work at seven o'clock the next morning would no longer have a job with the company. All the men were back at work on time the following day, but many of them had lost a night's sleep traveling in the bitter cold and shoveling snow from cuts. Fljozdal considered the superintendent a favorable official who was simply following orders. The outcome, had he been less friendly to the union, can only be conjectured.

In 1902, Fljozdal received $45.00 a month as foreman. He ordinarily worked ten hours, although he was on call twenty-four hours a day. By threatening to strike, foremen were able to secure a wage increase of $5.00 a month, even though they had no organization to represent them at that time. Fljozdal found $50.00 a month a meager sum indeed on which to support a family of eight. Deciding that no job at all could be little worse than the one he had, Fljozdal took a course of action almost unheard of in those days: he visited the superintendent in his private car. The superintendent received him courteously but made it plain that he could not deal with individual employes.

"Then it would be necessary that we ask for a wage increase collectively before you would consider it?" Fljozdal asked.

"Oh, I'm not encouraging organization," the superintendent replied. "We don't want an organization on our system." But the superintendent's remarks convinced Fljozdal that it was only through united action that the workers could hope to obtain justice.

In 1904, Fljozdal served on a committtee seeking union recognition. The company had denied him a leave of absence to attend the conference; so he went without it. The management agreed to meet the committee formally within six weeks to negotiate an agreement, but the official conducting the conference emphasized the penalty that could be levied against an employe for being off without leave of absence. Thereupon the secretary of the committee said that unless the company permitted Fljozdal to return to work, no member of the committee would return. When Fljozdal left the conference he learned that instructions had already been issued relieving him of his job as section foreman, but these instructions were canceled almost immediately by telegram. Shortly thereafter the company recognized the union, and Fljozdal became the first General Chairman on the system.

In the late summer of 1902, the Brotherhood began encountering trouble from another source. In September of that year, Wilson warned the membership against the blandishments of a rival organization, the United Brotherhood of Railway Employes, which had been formed on the Pacific coast to enroll railroad workers of all crafts. Citing the unhappy fates of the Knights of Labor and Debs' American Railway Union, Wilson cautioned maintenance of way workers not to affiliate with the U. B. of R. E. It had been reported, he said, that in June, 1902, track and bridge and building men on the Canadian Northern Railway had suspended work in obedience to an order from the U. B. of R. E., but found themselves stranded as other crafts negotiated agreements and returned to work. Eventually they decided they had made a mistake and returned to work without gain beyond restoration to their jobs.

Maintenance of way workers could receive from their craft organization, the B. of R. T. of A., the help they so sorely needed, Wilson pointed out. That they did need its protection desperately is evidenced by a letter written to the "Advocate" in November, 1902, by a track laborer on a southern railroad who said that he received less than $18.00 a month in wages with which to support his family.

In spite of discouraging odds, the Brotherhood strove incessantly to improve the welfare of its members. By the end of 1902, it had been able to negotiate agreements with two other large railroads, the Atlantic Coast Line and the Norfolk & Western, and at the same time to obtain concessions on various roads where written agreements could not be obtained. When the fourth biennial convention convened in St. Louis, Missouri, on December 1, 1902, therefore, the problems to be handled were those of a growing organization.

The convention created two new offices: that of Grand Secretary-Treasurer, a post filled by Wilson since 1896, and that of editor of "The Advance Advocate." In an atmosphere of complete harmony, it also adopted all of Wilson's recommendations practically as he submitted them. Certain changes were made in the laws of the Insurance Department. The convention decided also that in the future, assessments levied by Joint Protective Boards must be sent direct to the Grand Secretary-Treasurer. Joint Protective Boards were prohibited from entering negotiations on proposed agreements until the Grand President's approval had been obtained and funds to defray expenses had been collected. Working cards were to be issued to members paying quarterly dues (membership certificates had formerly been issued). The Canadian Pacific strike had demonstrated the impracticability of attempting to pay strike benefits, and this feature was dropped from the laws. The convention voted to change the name of the order to the "International Brotherhood of Maintenance of Way Employes" in keeping with its expanded jurisdiction over all classes of maintenance of way workers.

Prior to the convention, several chapters of a Women's Auxiliary had been formed and Wilson invited them to send representatives to the convention. At the convention, the first Grand Lodge of the Women's Auxiliary was formed under the aegis of the Grand Division of the Brotherhood, with Mrs. Alice C. Mulkey as International Grand President.

The convention re-elected Wilson Grand President and elected C. Boyle Grand Secretary-Treasurer by acclamation.

The continued flood of new members created additional problems for the Grand Division. More than 1,500 new members enrolled during the month of March, 1903, and by the end of the year the Brotherhood had a membership of about 40,000, judging from the meager information available. In 1900, three rooms had been ample to house the offices of the Order, but in the early part of 1903 it became necessary to move the offices to larger quarters, for ten or twelve rooms were now needed.

Meanwhile, in answer to persistent demands from shippers, farmers, and the public, Congress had passed the Elkins Act (February, 1903) in an attempt to prevent rebates to favored shippers and general fare- and rate-cutting by the railroads, which it had vainly tried to do in passing the Interstate Commerce Act in 1887. The latter act had established a commission of five members to guard against violations of the law, which was intended to regulate abuses within the railroad industry. The commission, however, could not fix rates or enforce its own decisions. The Elkins Act, which marked an important step in the regulation of interstate commerce by the Federal government, forbade variations by the railroad companies from their published rates, but left the general power of rate fixing in their hands.

On July 10, 1903, the Canadian Parliament passed a significant piece of labor legislation in enacting the Railway Labour Disputes Act of 1903 to "aid in the settlement of railway labour disputes." Although the act provided machinery for investigation, mediation, conciliation, and arbitration, it imposed no penalty for the failure of either party to abide by the findings of boards of arbitration. Its chief virtue was its purpose to inform the public of the facts concerning labor-management disputes on Canadian railways. It was the forerunner of later governmental laws seeking to settle labor disputes.

The success of the Brotherhood in obtaining higher wages and better working conditions for its members continued through 1903. On April 6, 1903, maintenance of way men on the Canada Atlantic Railway went on strike to obtain concessions which the management had refused to grant. On June 26, Wilson negotiated a satisfactory settlement with the management and called the strike off.

In the June, 1903, issue, the "Advocate" summarized the concessions gained on railroads in the United States and Canada since the Protective Department was formed in 1898. During this five-year period, the "Advocate" said, the Brotherhood had secured agreements for maintenance of way employes on about 40,000 miles of railroad, and the wage increases obtained, directly or indirectly, amounted to more than $10 million a year. Other benefits included free house rent, transportation privileges, a shorter work day, seniority, and impartial investigation in discharge.

But as the Brotherhood grew, other persons, noting the vast number of unorganized maintenance of way workers, began to form rival organizations. In the spring of 1903, J. I. Sheppard, a lawyer in Fort Scott, Kansas, formed the "National Union of Railway Trackmen." Sheppard ridiculed the fact that the Wilson union had been able to organize but a comparatively small percentage of maintenance of way men during the sixteen years of its existence, and boasted that the new union would take care of this shortcoming quickly.

Almost six years later, when the N. U. of R. T. amalgamated with the I. B. of M. W. E. (February, 1909), Sheppard had not obtained one tangible concession for his members on any railroad, although he had been able to maintain a membership of some 5,000.

As the year 1903 closed, the Brotherhood was able to point to some important achievements. In December, 1903, a new schedule had been obtained on all government roads in Canada raising the minimum wages of section men above the minimums paid on privately-owned roads. At that time, the "Advocate" reported, agreements were in effect with the following railroads: the Canadian Pacific, the Canada Atlantic, and government roads in Canada, and the Atlantic Coast Line, the East St. Louis & Suburban, the Chesapeake & Ohio, the Norfolk & Western, the Seaboard Air Line, the Central of Georgia, and the Florida East Coast in the United States. On other roads where the employes were only partially organized, valuable concessions had been obtained even though formal agreements had not been signed with the management.

During 1903, the Brotherhood had established 200 lodges and enrolled 15,000 new members. The bank reserve and working capital had increased 300 per cent during the year, and the "Advocate" stated that thousands of members of the Brotherhood would work full time during the winter for the first time at wages higher than they had ever received before for similar work.

Early in 1904, Wilson warned his membership against four rival organizations among those then in the field soliciting membership among maintenance of way workers. The first of these was the Sheppard organization at Fort Scott, Kansas. The second had been formed on the one-big-union principle by an ex-telegrapher who had been unable to secure office in his own union. The third was under the control and direction of a Chicago detective, and the fourth had been organized in Pennsylvania by a former member of the Brotherhood who had been a delegate to the 1902 convention. Aside from their considerable nuisance value, there is nothing to indicate that these or any other rival organizations ever seriously retarded the growth of the Brotherhood.

But Wilson soon found his attention diverted from the minor irritations of rival organizations to the more ominous battles looming with railroad managements. An agreement had been signed with the Atlantic Coast Line Railroad in December, 1902, but the company refused to agree to improvements requested by the Joint Protective Board in January, 1904, and ordered its roadmasters to discharge all employes who would not agree to stand by the company and withdraw their support from the committee. Wilson thereupon called a strike effective at noon on February 11, 1904.

Three weeks later, on March 3, 1904, Wilson revoked the strike call. Although the men had voted almost unanimously for a strike, it was soon apparent that they did not know what a strike actually entailed. Frightened by the tactics of the company in discharging several foremen and ordering others out of company houses, the men began returning to work within a few days. On a second ballot, taken while the strike was on, two-thirds of the men refused either to vote or to vote for the continuance of the strike.

Chastened by his experience on the Atlantic Coast Line, Wilson cautiously took a strike vote on the Southern Railway before entering negotiations with the management of that road in the spring of 1904. Only one-third of the men voted to strike if a satisfactory settlement could not be reached. Although discouraged by this lack of support from the men, Wilson nevertheless entered the conferences and secured concessions on working rules.

In spite of the upsurge in its fortunes, the Brotherhood was making progress only through the slow and painful process of attrition. It had been able to negotiate satisfactory schedules during 1904 on the Boston & Maine and the Bangor & Aroostook, but most railroad managements continued their opposition to unionism; and they were being unwittingly aided and abetted, Wilson found, by the very men the union was trying to protect. In one instance, the foremen on a particular railroad had withdrawn their membership from the Brotherhood because it also represented the laborers. As a result, the wages of laborers were reduced so low that the foremen had difficulty securing men. One foreman was discharged for incompetency because he could not keep his gang filled with laborers at 85¢ a day.

The record membership of the Brotherhood and the success it had attained in improving the conditions of maintenance of way workers made Wilson's return to office a foregone conclusion when the fifth biennial convention of the Brotherhood convened in St. Louis, Missouri, on November 14, 1904. Both Wilson and Grand Secretary-Treasurer Boyle were re-elected by acclamation. In view of the Brotherhood's constant expansion, the convention authorized the Grand President to appoint a committee to select and buy a suitable office building for the Brotherhood, either in St. Louis or in some other city of central location, but this plan was not carried out until 1913, when the Grand headquarters were moved to Detroit, Michigan. It also instructed the Grand President not to carry on negotiations to bring about an amalgamation between the Brotherhood and Sheppard's N. U. of R. T. unless the latter organization appointed a committee for that purpose. A change in the laws made Grand and protective dues of $4.00 a year payable semi-annually in advance. Initiation fees remained as formerly: $3.00 for each foreman or other official and $2.00 for each laborer or apprentice.

The two-year period following the 1904 convention was a period of victory mixed with defeat. Although Wilson was able to report wage increases obtained on various roads—some on roads where the Brotherhood already held contracts and others as a result of the Brotherhood's organizing activities—in this same period occurred the Brotherhood's longest and most disastrous strike.

Somewhat concerned with the failure of the men to enforce the rights the organization had obtained for them, in the spring of 1905 Wilson urged the membership to read their contracts in order to understand their rights and how to secure them, and outlined the wage losses that could be sustained through failure to do this. For the benefit of maintenance of way workers on western roads, who were not well organized, Wilson pointed out that they were receiving from 25¢ to 50¢ a day less than the section men on some New England roads, who were well organized.

As the summer of 1905 wore on, trouble began to take definite shape in the west. Not only had the management of the Denver & Rio Grande Railroad refused the demands of the Brotherhood and offers of arbitration, but it had, in effect, insulted the organization by granting wage increases to other organized groups on the road. Wilson ordered a suspension of work effective at 6 p.m., August 2, 1905, because of "unjust discrimination, intolerable conditions of employment, broken faith and assaults on character." The company employed every means possible to break the strike and recruited strike-breakers of every type and description from all parts of the country. As the strike dragged on through the fall and winter, Wilson repeatedly reiterated the intention of the Brotherhood to continue the strike until a victory had been won. In February, 1906, the Grand Executive Committee levied a special assessment on all members to aid in prosecuting the strike "for an indefinite period or until an honorable settlement is effected."

On May 7, 1906, Wilson called the strike off after nine months and five days. There was little cause for jubilation in the ranks of the Brotherhood. Nothing of a tangible nature had been gained. The strike had been costly to the company, however, and it served as prima facie evidence that the Brotherhood was prepared to carry on protracted strikes, if necessary, to gain improved conditions for maintenance of way workers. Organization on the Denver & Rio Grande, however, had been broken by the strike and for the time being at least was dead.

At the sixth biennial convention held in Toronto, Ontario, Canada, beginning December 3, 1906, Wilson and Boyle were again re-elected Grand President and Grand Secretary-Treasurer by acclamation.

The year 1907 opened auspiciously. The "Advocate" was able to report continued progress not only in obtaining agreements on several roads for the first time, but also in renewing old agreements on more favorable terms. In the April, 1907, issue the "Advocate" printed in full a schedule effective February 1, 1907, on the Bangor & Aroostook Railroad as a type of agreement to be commended to maintenance of way workers on all roads.

General financial and economic conditions throughout the country in the fall of 1907, however, gave an ominous outlook for 1908. The railroads reduced their expenditures for maintenance work considerably. In some instances they cut expenses by reducing hours worked; in others by reducing both pay and hours worked. Layoffs were heavy and unemployment became widespread. The December, 1907, issue of the "Advocate" contained a warning to maintenance of way workers to organize for a defense of concessions already gained. This same issue, however, was able to report substantial gains made by the Brotherhood. At that time, the "Advocate" said, negotiations for schedules were pending on the Baltimore & Ohio, the Baltimore & Ohio Southwestern, and the Mobile & Ohio Systems. Excellent progress had been made in the work of organizing the Missouri, Kansas & Texas, the St. Louis & San Francisco, and numerous branches of the New York Central.

Since 1901, when it obtained its first agreement (on the Canadian Pacific), the "Advocate" continued, the Brotherhood had signed agreements on twenty-odd railroads operating some 70,000 miles of track, and the aggregate increase in wages obtained through the efforts of the Brotherhood amounted to more than $12 million a year. A list of important roads with whom it had negotiated agreements included the following not previously mentioned: the Canadian Northern and the Intercolonial & Prince Edward Island in Canada, and the Illinois Central, the Soo Line, and the Southern in the United States.

During 1907, 20,000 new members had been enrolled in the Brotherhood. In implementing the Brotherhood's organizing activities, Wilson made every effort to illustrate concretely the advantages of membership. In one instance he made a comparison to show that on the Baltimore & Ohio Railroad, where the Brotherhood was not recognized, foremen received $45 and $50 a month. On the Norfolk & Western Railroad, however, where an agreement was in force, foremen received $58 a month, with overtime for Sundays, fifteen days' vacation with pay, annual card passes, and enjoyed rules governing promotion, seniority, and the investigation of grievances.

In wage negotiations, railroad managements frequently cited lower wage rates being paid on competing roads. This brought into focus the thought of joint demands and an attempt to standardize wages, but the business depression of 1907-08 brought such plans to an end for the time being.

The year 1907 witnessed, too, a growing restiveness on the part of system Joint Protective Boards. System officers had at times been lax in the handling of system funds, and the method of having all finances sent to Grand headquarters at

St. Louis and thence disbursed to the various General Chairmen and their committees, had not only been necessary but had proved to be safe and economical. System divisions, however, were now demanding a greater responsibility in the conducting of the affairs of the Brotherhood. This was a sign of healthy growth.

On December 16, 1907, C. Boyle resigned as Grand Secretary-Treasurer, and the Grand Executive Committee appointed S. J. Pegg to succeed him.

The year 1908 had hardly begun before tragedy struck. On February 7, John T. Wilson died, the victim of an unfortunate occurrence at his home two days earlier. At age 47, Wilson was in the very midst of life, and his death came as a stunning shock to the men he had served so faithfully for 21 years. With an abruptness almost startling, that portion of the Brotherhood's history which can be termed the Wilson era had come to an end.

Wilson was buried at St. Louis on February 11 amidst expressions of sympathy from all parts of the continent. "A great tragedy has been enacted and a great man has lost his life," the "Advocate" said. "It is beyond the power of tongue or pen to describe the sadness which fills the hearts of those who have been most intimately associated with our fallen leader during the years of his championship of the cause of down-trodden humanity. . . . His trials, perplexities and disappointments were manifold and great, but his purpose was as fixed and unyielding as adamant. Nothing daunted him; nothing checked his desire to relieve distress among his craftsmen—his people. . . . They thought the fates had decreed their lives should be spent in . . . a state of abject slavery, but John T. Wilson showed them that it was man's greed and not God's laws that was responsible for their condition. . . . All honor and glory to his name and his deeds. . . . In his death labor and oppressed humanity have indeed lost an ardent and resourceful champion whose motto in life was to 'do right all the time, everywhere and by all people.' "

A more personal insight into the character of Wilson is given in a letter written in May, 1931, by S. J. Pegg, former Grand Lodge Secretary-Treasurer, concerning the annual Memorial Day ceremony in St. Louis in Wilson's memory.

"To many of our members the name John T. Wilson is just another name," Pegg wrote. "The man, and what he accomplished for our organization, are matters of history. . . .

"When the Order of Railway Trackmen of America was organized in 1887 . . . only section foremen were accepted to membership. In those days, especially in the South, sections were much longer than they are today and, as only one man on each section was eligible to membership, you can readily understand the tremendous mileage an organizer had to cover to reach but a comparatively few men. Had John T. Wilson remained on his section there is not the least doubt but that he would have been advanced to supervisor or roadmaster and perhaps to a much higher office. Instead, he chose to serve the men in the maintenance of way department as an organizer traveling on foot or legging it with a section crew on the old rubble car over the right of way. . . . When night came he went to rest in the same quarters as those occupied by the section crew, very often an old hovel or a discarded box car through which the sun and rain came without interference. His food was very plain fare and very often he went without food, unless he happened to come to a village where there was a store and there get his biscuits and cheese, washing them down with water from the railway ditches. . . .

"To give you a better idea of the sterling qualities and indomitable courage with which he carried on his undertakings, I might refer you to the Canadian Pacific strike which lasted for some eleven weeks. The organization had very little money with which to finance a strike against a railway which at that time was one of the largest and strongest financially on the continent. . . . In order to carry on the strike after the Brotherhood money was exhausted, John T. Wilson was forced to secure loans from his friends and mortgaged his own home and everything that he possessed to furnish the wherewithal to pay the expenses of the strike which finally resulted in the greatest victory our Brotherhood has ever known. . . .

"John T. Wilson and his men represented only a bare majority of the employes in the maintenance of way department on this railway. Indeed, I have heard since that he represented not more than one-third of the employes in paid-up membership, but he so imbued his followers with the spirit of resistance that they took courage and stood by him shoulder to shoulder until victory was acclaimed."

In accordance with the laws of the Brotherhood, A. B. Lowe, First Vice President, automatically succeeded Wilson as Grand President. Born in Scotland on November 11, 1845, Lowe emigrated to Ireland with his parents eighteen months later. At age 13 he came to America, and since that time he had lived in Canada with the exception of a few years spent in track work in the United States. Entering railroad service in a section gang at age 17, Lowe had followed no other vocation except for his Brotherhood activities. He did his first organizing work for the Canadian Brotherhood in 1893, and not only helped organize maintenance of way workers throughout the Dominion, but played a vital part in the amalgamation of the Canadian order and the Wilson organization.

When he stepped into the breach created by Wilson's death, Lowe was much in the position of a man who is forced to change horses in the middle of a stream. Wilson's driving personality had so long dominated the affairs of the Brotherhood that it seemed almost impossible that another could fill his place without advance warning or preparation. Moreover, the affairs of the organization had been moving at a rapid pace, and a critical point had been reached in the evolution of the Brotherhood from an amoeba-like order struggling for survival to an organization that had become truly international in scope. As Lowe picked up the reins of the fallen leader, he had little time to get his bearings. But his long years of experience in Brotherhood work stood him in good stead, and as the country recovered from the short-lived panic, Lowe was able not only to continue effectively the program of organization already so well developed by Wilson, but to lay plans for future expansion. In June, 1908, the "Advocate" set as a goal by 1912, the 25th anniversary of the founding of the Brotherhood, a membership of 100,000 and a $1 million treasury surplus. At that time, according to an estimate appearing in the "Advocate," the Brotherhood had approximately 50,000 members. Whether this figure represented an actual paid-up membership, however, is not certain.

When the seventh biennial convention was called to order in New Orleans, Louisiana, on December 7, 1908, Lowe urged cooperation and affiliation with the central labor bodies or federations of the American Federation of Labor and the Dominion Trades and Labour Congress of Canada, inasmuch as the Brotherhood was affiliated with both these national organizations.

The convention adopted certain changes in the laws of the Insurance Department, including a provision for a policy of $250.00 at rates ranging from 25¢ to 60¢ a month, depending on age (18 to 55), and concurred in a recommendation that after 75 per cent of the maintenance of way employes on a whole system or on a large branch of any system, who were eligible to membership, had organized, they be allowed to establish a system organization and be assisted in securing a contract. Lowe and S. J. Pegg were elected to succeed themselves as Grand President and Grand Secretary-Treasurer, respectively.

In the two years that followed, the organization continued its success in obtaining improved schedules and in signing agreements on additional roads. Early in 1909, the Brotherhood moved its offices to a new location in St. Louis, continuing its process of expansion. Later that year, system federations of various railroad labor organizations affiliated with the American Federation of Labor were formed on several railroad systems in a move to develop greater cooperative action on individual railroad systems. In February, 1910, S. J. Pegg became editor of the "Advance Advocate" in a rearrangement of duties at headquarters.

On December 15, 1909, the General Chairmen of the Brotherhood from various systems met in St. Louis to attend what was probably the first regional association meeting of system officers. Their primary purpose was to discuss questions of mutual interest, but the meeting was so successful that they decided to form a permanent organization to be known as the "System Division Association" to meet annually. General Chairmen, Vice Chairmen, and Secretaries of system divisions organized in the I. B. of M. W. E. were eligible to membership in the association.

In the spring of 1910, officials of the Southern Pacific Railroad refused to meet the Brotherhood committee to discuss a request for improved conditions, and issued instructions to the men either to give up membership in the Brotherhood or leave the service of the company. Lowe called an apparently unsuccessful strike on the Texas lines of that system effective June 1, 1910. A month later, he called a strike on the Delaware & Hudson Railroad, effective July 2, because of the refusal of the company to agree to a rules schedule or to grant wage increases. The D. & H. strike was successfully terminated on August 13, when the company agreed to increase wages, grant improved working conditions, and recognize the right of their employes to bargain collectively through the Brotherhood.

Few questions of major importance confronted the eighth biennial convention held in Boston, Massachusetts, beginning September 5, 1910. The delegates to the convention were cordially welcomed to Boston and given a place of honor at the head of a mammoth Labor Day parade which lasted two hours. At a meeting of the General Chairmen's Association on September 2, one of the highlights of the convention, F. H. Fljozdal discussed the Canadian Lemieux Act, called "The Industrial Disputes and Investigation Act of 1907," intended to foster voluntary arbitration of labor disputes and to minimize strikes. Under this act the government could conciliate and investigate labor disputes, the status quo remaining until a report was rendered. The Lemieux Act and the Railway Labour Disputes Act of 1903 indicated a growing concern of the government in the settlement of labor-management problems.

The convention re-elected A. B. Lowe Grand President and S. J. Pegg Grand Secretary-Treasurer by acclamation.

The process of winning recognition and negotiating agreements road by road had now necessarily become the chief objective of the Brotherhood. This procedure, to be effective, required the strengthening of system divisions. Following the convention, therefore, Lowe urged each system to create a fund for defraying the expenses of its Joint Protective Board members in conferences with management. He suggested that regular system division dues be substituted for the system assessments usually levied. This was one of the most important steps ever taken toward strengthening the system organizations. It is obvious that system division dues established as an integral part of a member's total dues payment would provide a much more stable and effective means of income to the system than the levying of irregular assessments.

The Brotherhood continued its steady progress during 1911. In June, Lowe reported that each of the first five months of the year had gone far beyond the corresponding month of 1910 in membership. Negotiations were successfully concluded on various roads in the eastern and southern regions of the United States for increased wages and improved working conditions. In the early part of the year, conciliation awards under the Lemieux Act in Canada recommended substantially increased wages on the Canadian Pacific, the Grand Trunk Pacific, and the Canadian Northern west of Port Arthur. "The total increases granted on Canadian roads this spring," the "Advocate" said in May, "approximate $200,000 a year."

"An era of prosperity is sweeping over the country," said the "Advocate," "and those alive to the changed financial conditions are pressing to the front with claims for a fair share of the increase and meeting with much success in their mission." But many railroads, continuing their open opposition to the efforts of the Brotherhood to organize their systems, apparently did not feel that their maintenance of way employes should share in the nation's prosperity.

"The supervisor has been around and has requested all the foremen to lay down their membership or they would be discharged," said a letter to the "Advocate" signed only by certificate number. The "Advocate" commented: "We note that on one or two roads in the south the minor officials who have noted the progress being made toward organizing their road have succeeded to a certain extent in intimidating their foremen in an endeavor to make them withdraw out of the organization under pain of dismissal." And the officials of a far-western road were reported as "discharging all their employes in the maintenance of way department who refuse to withdraw from their trade organization and sign a statement that they are satisfied with their present wages and conditions."

The first strike of the year occurred in the early spring. The chairman of the General Managers' Association at Chicago, Illinois, had refused to reply to a request from the employes that a committee of management be formed to meet with them to discuss a proposed contract. Effective at 6:00 p.m., May 1, 1911, Lowe sanctioned a strike of maintenance of way employes on six railroads in the Chicago terminals. Defeat was soon evident, however, when many of the men who had pledged themselves to respond to the strike call failed to do so.

On September 16, 1911, Lowe called another strike, this time on the Delaware, Lackawanna and Western Railroad, because of the refusal of the company "to grant any concessions whatever on a schedule of working rules and rates of pay submitted to them by a committee representing the trackmen of the system." The president of the road had not only refused to meet Lowe and the committee, but had declined Lowe's offer to arbitrate the issue and had sanctioned the discharge of some members of the employes' committee. Although the attitude of the press and the public was encouraging to the strikers, Lowe called the strike off within a few weeks after a number of the men had returned to work and a majority of those still on strike voted to do likewise.

In spite of these scattered defeats, the Brotherhood continued to make progress on many roads. Lowe leaned toward conciliation and arbitration in the settlement of disputes with the railroads. On December 20, 1911, an Arbitration Board rendered its award in a dispute with the Cincinnati, Hamilton and Dayton Railroad. Although dissatisfied with the small wage increases granted, Lowe said the Brotherhood would abide by the award as it had agreed to do.

The January, 1912, issue of the "Advocate" contained a notice that in the future, Grand Lodge would not advance funds to cover the expenses of a Joint Protective Board or a grievance committee of any system, but that it would be necessary for each system to raise money to cover its own expenses as a good many systems were already doing.

In the same issue, Lowe reported that the committee he had appointed, in accordance with instructions of the 1910 convention, to investigate the cities of Chicago, Detroit, St. Louis, and Washington as a site for the permanent headquarters of the Brotherhood, had collected a vast amount of data which would be submitted to the delegates at the coming convention.

A summary of the organization's activities during 1911 indicated that wage increases obtained for maintenance of way workers during that year approximated considerably more than $2¼ million. Lowe urged increased organization and pointed out the immense possibilities of the Brotherhood if all the more than 526,000 maintenance of way workers in the United States and Canada were members.

Following a change in the Canadian government in September, 1911, Lowe had received reports of wholesale dismissals and suspensions of members of the Brotherhood on government roads for alleged political partisanship. In March, 1912, he met with government railway officials and obtained an understanding that investigation must precede dismissal or suspension, as required by the agreement; that charges would not be brought unless the employe's conduct was clearly wrong; and that accused employes laid off before the conference who were found innocent would be paid for time lost.

The conciliation award rendered in 1911 under the Lemieux Act had been accepted by the Canadian Pacific and the Canadian Northern. Despite repeated conferences, however, the Grand Trunk Pacific had not agreed to abide by the recommendations of the Conciliation Board. In August, 1912, Lowe announced that the Grand Trunk Pacific had finally accepted the award. While the conciliation proceedings were in progress, Grand Lodge had urged railroad workers in the United States to try to obtain the passage of a Federal law similar to the Lemieux Act.[1] Criticism had apparently been leveled at Grand Lodge officers for their reliance on conciliation and arbitration rather than more drastic action when the railroads refused to meet the requests of their employes for improved conditions. Lowe accepted the settlement on the Grand Trunk Pacific as a vindication of his policies.

"The strike is a relic of a bygone age and should never be used only as a last resort . . .," the "Advocate" said. "There are occasions when a strike may accomplish results and win out for the men, but it should never be used until every honorable effort has failed."

In order to save time at future conventions, the 1910 convention had decided it would be wise to have committees

---

[1] p. 68

appointed prior to the convention who could investigate the various matters to be handled and be prepared to report to the convention. This new plan had been placed in operation before the biennial convention met in St. Louis, Missouri, beginning November 11, 1912.

"The years 1911 and 1912 have been the best years of our organization's history," Lowe told the convention. ". . . the best in new schedules received, new contracts made, in revisions and extensions of the contracts . . . in the improvements that have come to the homes of our people through these revisions and new contracts."

The selection of a city in which the permanent headquarters of the Brotherhood would be located was one of the important questions before the convention. Grand Lodge employed a staff of 27 persons in St. Louis and its offices occupied more than 5,000 square feet of floor space. With from 25 to 100 organizers in the field, General Chairmen and Joint Protective Boards on more than 50 roads, and with a host of subordinate lodges under its jurisdiction, the establishment of a permanent headquarters for Grand Lodge had become essential to the development of plans for future expansion. The cities of St. Louis, Washington, Chicago, and Detroit were voted upon by the delegates, and Detroit received a majority of the votes cast.

The convention decided that each member would be required to pay 50 cents semi-annually to create an emergency fund; and that thereafter the minimum dues to be charged by subordinate lodges semi-annually would be 25 cents.

Grand President Lowe and Grand Secretary-Treasurer Pegg reported that the insurance fund was in bad condition, and that the insurance rates had not been sufficient to put the Insurance Department on a self-sustaining basis. The convention adopted a motion leaving in the hands of an insurance committee the task of revising the laws and rates of the Insurance Department to place it on a sounder financial basis.

The convention re-elected Lowe Grand President and Pegg Grand Secretary, and elected Alex Gibb to fill a newly-created office: Treasurer and Editor and Manager of the "Advocate."

The attempt of the 1912 convention to bring about a revision of the laws and rates of the Insurance Department soon ran aground on the shoals of legal technicality. A legal opinion obtained by the insurance committee held that although the convention had full authority to make the changes itself, it could not delegate this authority to a committee. As a result, the laws and rates of the Insurance Department remained as they were prior to the convention.

Early in 1913, the Grand President and Grand Executive Committee purchased a large building, formerly used as a residence, at 27 Putnam Avenue (later changed to 61 Putnam Avenue), Detroit, Michigan, and the permanent headquarters of Grand Lodge were moved to this location in March, 1913.

The year 1913 passed apparently without any occurrences of momentous importance. But appearances were deceptive: both within the Brotherhood and in Europe, explosive forces were being generated that were soon to be detonated with destructive suddenness. During 1913, the "Advocate" reported, increased wages and improved conditions of employment had been secured on 23 different railroad systems. Twenty revisions had been secured through conferences and 3 through arbitration. "The above results were obtained without interruption of work, and the best of feeling prevails between the officials and employes," the "Advocate" said.

By early 1914 it had become apparent that the heavy burden of looking after the far-flung activities and interests of the Brotherhood was beginning to exact its toll of Grand President Lowe. "This has been one of the most arduous seasons that I have experienced since I joined the organization, and the strain of all these negotiations is beginning to tell upon me," he said in his monthly letter to the membership in March. A few weeks later he reached the definite decision to give up active duty in the organization he had served so faithfully for twenty-two years. Failing health and the strenuous schedule of work to be done, he said in his farewell letter to the membership, had convinced him that "the right thing to do was to transfer to other and younger shoulders the burden which was liable to break me down."

In commenting on Lowe's resignation, the "Advocate" said: "In looking back over the long trail which he has traveled we find it beautifully straight and clean. . . . We salute him and wish for him many years of peace, happiness and contentment in the thought of duty well and faithfully done."

On April 11, 1914, the Grand Lodge officers met and elected T. H. Gerrey to succeed Lowe as Grand President. Gerrey had begun his railroad career as a track laborer, and had worked in that job for eighteen months at 45 cents a day—hours from sunrise to sunset. Later, he had worked seven years as foreman of construction, ten years as work train foreman and conductor combined, and ten years as track foreman. He had been a member of the Brotherhood for fourteen years, serving eight years as local chairman and four years as General Chairman on the Norfolk and Western Railway before his election as Grand Vice President in 1912.

It is apparent that during this period of time the Brotherhood was in a state of transition. With the death of Wilson and the resignation of Lowe, control had passed entirely from the hands of the "old guard," and sentiment toward a new leadership had not as yet crystallized sufficiently to be effective. When Gerrey took office, less than five months remained until the next convention. Like a ship becalmed, the Brotherhood rode out the intervening time.

Meanwhile, in Europe only a spark had been needed to ignite the highly-inflammable nationalisms, the fears, and the distrusts that had been building up on the European continent. The assassination of the heir-apparent to the Austro-Hungarian throne on June 28, 1914, proved to be the spark that set the conflagration. On July 28, Austria declared war on Serbia. A few days later, Germany invaded France and Belgium, and the holocaust called World War I was under way. For more than four years the world was ravaged by a war that brought death, destruction, and devastation to many European countries. Not only did it greatly alter the course of history, but indirectly it had a tremendous effect on the future of the Brotherhood.

And as the war raged in Europe, storm clouds gathered on the horizon as the Brotherhood prepared for its tenth biennial convention. Ironically enough, the damaging blow that so seriously threatened the future of the organization was struck not from without but from within. In one afternoon the delegates to the convention were able to accomplish what rival organizations and antagonistic railroad managements had been unable to do in twenty-seven years: split the union asunder and send its strength recoiling upon itself.

CHAPTER IV

WORLD WAR I AND AFTER

THE tenth biennial convention of Grand Lodge convened in Winnipeg, Manitoba, Canada, beginning September 7, 1914. The early sessions gave little indication of the underlying tension between certain groups of delegates. But outside the convention hall, in hotel lobbies and hotel rooms, events were progressing toward their seemingly inevitable climax.

Following the usual preliminaries, the convention began consideration of several important questions. The Grand Executive Committee reported that the Insurance Department had ceased to exist in August, 1913. When the program adopted by the 1912 convention to place the insurance fund on a sounder financial basis could not be placed in operation because of an adverse legal opinion, the committee reported, the special assessments necessary to keep the department in operation had become so heavy that members carrying insurance refused to pay them and withdrew from the Insurance Department. As a result, the insurance fund was exhausted, and outstanding claims had been paid from the general fund.

The routine business of the convention continued until September 11. Soon after the afternoon session that day had been called to order, a group of delegates withdrew from the convention. The minutes of the convention give only the barest outline of the conflict which had so quickly developed into a crisis.

A delegate from New Orleans, Louisiana, first rose to a question of privilege. He said that a committee representing lodges from the United States had approached the delegates from Canadian lodges concerning a slate said to have been framed by the Canadian delegates from which members of lodges in the United States had been excluded, and that they had been informed that the slate would go through.

A delegate from Massachusetts also rose to a question of privilege and asked the leaders of the Canadians if they had refused to grant any concession on the division of officers of the Brotherhood. Receiving no reply, he moved that a committee of dissolution be appointed. The motion was lost.

He then moved an indefinite adjournment of the Grand Lodge convention. When this motion was defeated, approximately twenty delegates left the convention hall (a standing count the following morning showed that twenty delegates from the United States still remained in the convention).

Grand Vice President Irwin assumed the chair after Grand President Gerrey had requested permission to retire. After Gerrey had left the hall, the delegates adopted a motion requesting Grand Secretary Pegg to interview him to ascertain whether he intended to return. At 4:00 p.m. Pegg returned and reported that a committee representing the seceding delegates was prepared to meet a committee from the delegates still in session to try to compose the differences between the two groups. Shortly before the convention adjourned for the day, A. E. Barker told the delegates that the conference between the two committees had accomplished nothing.

When the convention opened on the morning of September 12, Grand President Gerrey addressed the convention briefly and tendered his resignation, effective at once. The Grand Lodge officers elected A. E. Barker to act as President until the election of officers could be held in the regular order of business.

In later years, hardly two delegates who attended the 1914 convention gave the same reason for the split in its ranks, although the convention minutes indicated that the dissension arose over the election of officers. A circular letter issued by Gerrey and S. J. Pegg on September 25, 1914, gave these possible reasons for the secession movement: resentment over the feeling that the headquarters building at Detroit had been bought with money supplied in part from system division and emergency funds; inability of the two factions to reach an agreement on a slate of officers; the feeling that systems in certain sections of the country had been neglected; and the refusal of the convention to permit the General Chairmen to vote the strength of their systems.

This division in the Brotherhood ranks probably arose from a combination of reasons. Perhaps the most realistic appraisal that can be made is that it stemmed primarily from the efforts of rival factions to secure control. Whatever the immediate cause or causes may have been, however, the organization had been seriously weakened by a secession movement which many delegates later felt could have been avoided had diplomacy and tact been used at the proper time.

The convention continued in session through September 16. Any hopes that the recalcitrant delegates would return to the folds of the Brotherhood, however, were soon dashed. On September 14, the seceders met in Detroit and elected T. H. Gerrey President and S. J. Pegg Secretary-Treasurer of a rival organization, the "Brotherhood of Maintenance of Way Employes", with headquarters at Greensboro, North Carolina.

In the meantime, the convention obtained an opinion from counsel that the delegates in session constituted the legal body of the Brotherhood, and that insofar as the organization was concerned, the seceding delegates had no rights except as individuals.

The convention abolished the office of Treasurer and Editor of the "Advocate" and restored the combined position of Grand Secretary-Treasurer. It also voted to hold conventions triennially in the future and elected Barker Grand President and George Seal Grand Secretary-Treasurer.

Allan E. Barker, the newly-elected Grand President, had been serving as General Chairman on the Grand Trunk Pacific System in Canada at the time of his election and had many years of experience in Brotherhood work. Many of the delegates who had withdrawn from the convention and allied themselves with the Gerrey group represented systems on which the Brotherhood held agreements, and the new President found his ability as a speaker and an organizer taxed to the limit as he set about salvaging the fortunes of the divided organization.

The Brotherhood began the year 1915 with high hopes of repairing much of the damage that had been done at the 1914 convention. In February, 700 new members enrolled, and President Barker announced the establishment of a new department at headquarters for the purpose of tracing delinquent members and promoting the enrollment of new members. Nevertheless, the split in its ranks continued to be a menacing obstacle to the organization's future progress.

Meanwhile, a rising wave of protests against low wages and poor working conditions had been sweeping through the ranks of workers in all parts of the nation. Early in the year, Frank P. Walsh, Chairman of the United States Commission on Industrial Relations, which later rendered a report on the causes for the industrial unrest and dissatisfaction in America, made a speech in which he proposed that the wages of section men be increased to $2.00 for an eight-hour day. In contrast, the "Advocate" pointed out, section foremen on unorganized roads were receiving from $50.00 to $60.00 a month, and section men from $1.35 to $1.50 a day.

At that time, more than 2,600,000 workers in the United States held membership in labor unions. The biggest American unions were those connected with transportation. They had a combined membership of some 667,000.

In 1913, A. B. Lowe, then President of the Brotherhood, had lauded the Canadian Lemieux Act, intended to aid in the settlement of industrial disputes, as a good law for maintenance of way workers. But experience had begun to prove otherwise. Conciliation methods under the act were cumbersome and caused long procedural delays during which the men could neither strike nor the company declare a lockout.

"The Canadian Lemieux Act is a stumbling block to the workers of Canada, and the framers of the Act meant it to be such," the "Advocate" said. "The sooner this Act is amended, or repealed, the better it will be for organized labor."

Barker called the first strike of his administration at 6:00 p.m., on May 7, 1915, against the Soo Line Railway. At that time, track foremen on the Soo Line received from $52.00 to $62.50 a month, except in a few large yards where the rates were slightly higher. Track laborers received $1.50 a day for a ten-hour day, or $39.00 a month. During the winter months, their hours were reduced to eight, and they received $1.20

a day, or $31.20 a month. The Brotherhood had asked for a wage increase of 10 per cent, but the negotiations came to an abrupt halt in early May. The company had discharged the members of the employes' committee and threatened the dismissal of every man who held membership in the Brotherhood.

The strike resulted in an inglorious defeat for the Brotherhood. Although 90 per cent of the men had voted to stand by the committee and suspend work if necessary, the strike was called off after four or five days because only a comparatively few men responded to the strike call.

It may appear paradoxical to say that the Brotherhood could sustain these defeats and still make substantial progress. But even lost strikes had their effect; for strikes were costly to the railroads. It is unfortunate that the money spent by the railroads to oppose the organization of their maintenance of way workers was not used to improve the indefensibly poor wages and conditions of these men. It appears, however, that some railroad officials had a morbid dread of labor unions. In a speech said to have been delivered at a roadmasters' convention and later carried in a circular distributed on a western railroad, a special roadmaster was quoted as saying about Brotherhood organizers:

"For your information I am advised from a very reliable source that your system is being covered by these agitators. . . . If you allow these fellows to get a hold and disorganize your forces you will never see the end of it until such time as you exterminate it. . . . There will be no more section foremen's union or International Brotherhood of Maintenance of Way Employes on the .... Line. We have exterminated it forever and any foreman who mentions it in the future will be discharged (applause)."

Some railroad managements, however, who were favorable to the principle of collective bargaining, felt that the maintaining of harmonious relations with their employes was much to be preferred to costly strikes. In early July, Barker announced that the first maintenance of way rules agreement on the Northern Pacific Railway had been signed effective June 24, 1915.

In the spring of 1915, an organization called the "Canadian Brotherhood of Railway Employes" began soliciting membership among maintenance of way employes in Canada in an attempt, no doubt, to capitalize on the split in the ranks of the Brotherhood. It met with little success, however.

The Gerrey organization, too, was beginning to reap the harvest of disunity. In a circular addressed to all lodge secretaries on July 16, 1915, Gerrey said that an organization known as the "Order of Railway Workers" was trying to organize maintenance of way men on the New York, New Haven & Hartford Railroad. Gerrey stressed the urgent need for funds and asked that lodges and individual members lend money to the Gerrey order, such loans to be payable one year from date with interest at 6 per cent per annum. Assets of the organizations, the circular said, were valued at $1,000.00.

The growing concern of the government with labor-management problems and a recognition of the right of workers to organize were revealed in a report issued by the United States Commission on Industrial Relations containing a majority recommendation that workers be given the right to form and maintain labor organizations without penalty.

By the end of 1915, a heavy foreign and domestic demand for all types of commodities and products (the foreign market was chiefly for materials of war) had brought about an improvement in business conditions. The affairs of the Brotherhood, too, were on the upgrade.

"As far as our own organization is concerned," the "Advocate" said with respect to 1915, "it has been a year of reconstruction and organizing. With our organization in a run-down and chaotic condition at our last convention, we are pleased to state that splendid progress has been achieved in the year past, our financial and numerical gain being very gratifying."

But as business conditions improved, the workers found the purchasing power of their already low earnings reduced by the relentless increase in the cost of living. In the spring of 1916, a number of unorganized maintenance of way workers on the Central of New Jersey Railway went on strike spontaneously in protest against low pay and long hours. They sought an increase in pay from $1.75 to $2.00 a day and a reduction in hours from ten to eight.

In Canada, meantime, Barker and the committee obtained an agreement from the general manager, effective March 1, 1916, readjusting and leveling up rates of pay on government-owned railways. Later, a new schedule negotiated for government roads, effective June 1, 1916, contained important rules changes and established higher wage rates.

Signs of trouble made their appearance at this time on the Boston & Maine Railroad. The section men on that road had requested certain working rules and an increase of 10 per cent in their wages of $1.80 a day. When a settlement could not be reached, Barker called a strike effective at 6:00 p.m., May 16, 1916. Approximately 2,000 foremen and trackmen left their jobs. Many of the strikers were able to obtain other employment at wages much higher than they had received on the railroad. By the end of two months, numerous strikers had returned to work after the company granted a wage increase of 10c a day, and the strike could not be considered an unalloyed victory for the Brotherhood.

The plight of wage earners had continued to grow more desperate because of the increase in the price of commodities due to the war, and the Brotherhood succeeded in securing favorable settlements of wage increase requests on various systems.

In June, the organization won an important court case, an outgrowth of the 1914 split in its ranks. Following the convention, a former General Chairman of the I.B.M.W.E. who had joined the Gerrey-Pegg movement, began court proceedings to obtain for the seceding systems the system division funds held by Grand Lodge. On June 19, 1916, the court refused to recognize the rights claimed by the seceders and not only dismissed the complaint but ordered the complainants to pay the court costs.

After two years, the Brotherhood had made a considerable recovery from the trend toward deterioration that had been apparent at the 1914 convention. "Our membership has increased by thousands, our organizing activities have extended to many new railroad systems and generally a strong, vigorous growth has been experienced," the "Advocate" said in January, 1917. "Many new contracts for wage increases and working agreements have been entered into and our members have been benefited by wage increases approximating $2½ million annually."

At this time, both the nation and the Brotherhood were on the threshold of an era that was to witness developments of tremendous importance. The protest throughout the nation because of the rapid rise in the cost of living had now reached a strident crescendo. It was estimated that during the month ending February 15, 1917, the combined price of 27 principal foods increased 4 per cent. And to this acute economic problem had been added the imminent threat of active participation in the war by the United States.

Although during the early months of the war the majority of the people in the United States favored the allies, a strong undercurrent of neutrality prevailed, and it was not until Germany began her ruthless submarine warfare, culminating in the sinking of the Lusitania in 1915, that popular resentment flared against Germany and her allies. On April 6, 1917, after almost three years of an unparalleled attempt to maintain neutrality, the United States declared war on Germany.

The plans and activities of the Brotherhood were for the time being at least dwarfed by the repercussions that followed the declaration of war. In April, Barker had announced plans to revise during 1917 every agreement held by the Brotherhood, but the swift flood of events stifled this ambitious project.

The war, too, had brought into focus the need for a revamping of the Canadian railway system. In May, 1917, the majority report of the Dominion Royal Commission, appointed to investigate railway conditions in Canada, recommended a plan increasing government ownership of railroads.

The entry of the United States into the war, however, had not lessened the determination of maintenance of way workers to secure improved wages and working conditions through strikes if necessary. For more than a year, maintenance of way men on the Missouri Pacific, Iron Mountain & Southern Railway had been trying to secure a conference with the management to discuss the need for a wage increase. At that time, section foremen received $60.00 a month and the men under them as little as $1.50 a day.

Not only had the company repudiated its promise to give the men a conference on their request, but had discharged their spokesman, an employe with twenty years' service. On June 23, 1917, the men went on strike for a wage increase of 25 per cent and improved working conditions. Estimates placed the first wave of strikers at 4,000, a number later increased to 6,000. Approximately 1,000 members enrolled in the Brotherhood on the Missouri Pacific after the strike began. The strike faded into oblivion as the rapid-fire developments of the next few months gave entirely new direction to the Brotherhood's activities.

On September 3, 1917, the Brotherhood held its first triennial convention in Detroit, Michigan, and made several important changes in its laws. The first of these was the adoption of the quarterly method of paying dues. The convention changed the laws to provide that dues must be paid quarterly thereafter on or before the first day of April, July, October, and January of each year.

Like its membership, the Brotherhood found itself caught in the spiral of rising prices, necessitating a greater income to meet increased expenses. Initiation fees for new members were established at $1.00, $2.00, and $3.00, depending on the monthly income of the applicant, and Grand Lodge dues were increased to $8.00 a year. System dues were to be set by each system and each lodge could establish local dues of not less than 50¢ a year.

Because of the war, the convention decided that efforts to maintain the Ladies' Auxiliary should be discontinued until conditions were more favorable.

The question of allowing colored maintenance of way workers to join the Brotherhood had become pressing. After much discussion, the convention voted to permit colored workers to affiliate with the Brotherhood in allied lodges.

The convention also voted to reaffiliate with the Dominion Trades and Labour Congress of Canada (affiliation with that body had been previously ended), adopted a resolution calling for an eight-hour day for all workers, and re-elected Barker Grand President and Seal Grand Secretary-Treasurer by acclamation.

Had the delegates been able to peer even briefly into the future, it is certain that many other far-reaching changes would have been adopted, for the next few years were to witness not only a spectacular rise in the fortunes of the Brotherhood and a healing of the wounds of dissension that had been inflicted at the 1914 convention, but a succeeding period of internal strife and disintegration. For the time being, however, the immediate problem before maintenance of way workers was to bridge the gap between inadequate wages and rapidly mounting prices. From December, 1915, to December, 1917, food prices alone increased almost 50 per cent.

The problems of the railroads, too, had become acute with the entry of the United States in the war. The need to haul more troops, supplies, and ammunition quickly became paramount. By the end of 1917, the rail transportation system had become hopelessly bogged down. Operating individually under their time-honored system of competition, the railroads could no longer meet the country's emergency needs. A centralized system of control to provide swift and dependable transportation had become vital to the prosecution of the war. In a proclamation dated December 26, 1917, President Woodrow Wilson placed the railroads under government control. This action established the United States Railroad Administration with William G. McAdoo, Secretary of the Treasury, as Director General of Railroads.

The rising tide of complaints from railroad workers because of low wage rates and poor working conditions was one of the critical problems before the Director General as he assumed control of the railroads. On January 18, 1918, he created a Railroad Wage Commission under the chairmanship of Franklin K. Lane, Secretary of the Interior, to investigate and report on the wage situation among railroad employes. In appointing the commission, McAdoo said:

"The creation of this Commission is the culmination of a large number of complaints and demands of employes which have been pending before the railroad managers for some time past. . . . They came in all forms, from various classes of railroad labor organizations and from various groups of unorganized employes of the railroads."

The Lane Commission began hearings late in January. A delegation of Brotherhood representatives headed by Barker went to Washington to prepare arguments to be laid before the Commission. Barker appeared before the Commission on February 13, 1918, and presented the Brotherhood's case in behalf of maintenance of way workers. Barker told the Commission that the low wages being paid by the railroads were not attracting workers to the maintenance of way department; that there was no uniformity in wage rates between different roads; that the wages of skilled men were too low; that the cost of living made existing wage rates wholly inadequate; that the practice on many roads of paying the time and one-half rate for work outside of regular work hours or on Sundays and holidays should be extended to all roads; that an eight-hour day should be put into effect; and that wage rates should be standardized on all roads.

Barker asserted that quick relief from existing conditions was urgently needed to overcome the critical situation confronting the railroads. "The men ask only a living wage, which the railroads are not paying," he told the Commission. The report of the Lane Commission, submitted to Director General McAdoo on April 30, 1918, showed that section men received an average wage of only $50.31 a month in 1917, with correspondingly low earnings for other maintenance of way classes.

On May 25, 1918, the Director General issued General Order No. 27 granting wage increases to railroad workers, effective January 1, 1918, based on the Lane report, to be added to wage rates in effect in December, 1915. All wage rates under $46.00 a month were increased by $20.00. From a percentage standpoint, the complicated formula increased wages above $46.00 a month from 43 per cent for those receiving $46.01 to 0 per cent for those in higher wage brackets. No increase at all was granted to employes receiving more than $250.00 a month.

General Order No. 27 also established an eight-hour day with overtime pay at the pro rata rate for service beyond eight hours. In addition, it created a Board of Railroad Wages and Working Conditions to hear and investigate disputes pertaining to these subjects referred to it by the Director General.

A myriad of protests followed the issuance of General Order No. 27 because of the inequalities and differences in the wage increases granted. Representatives of the Brotherhood submitted to the Director General a proposal to establish certain uniform wages and standard rules in the maintenance of way department. Scores of General Chairmen were summoned to Washington to appear before the Board of Railroad Wages and Working Conditions. Effective September 1, 1918, the Director General issued Supplement No. 8 to General Order

No. 27 ordering wage increases for maintenance of way employes estimated to amount to $75 million a year and establishing rules governing working conditions.

Supplement No. 8 granted wage increases ranging from 12¢ an hour for track laborers to $25.00 a month for foremen and certain other classes, and established the following minimum rates: Bridge and building foremen, $115.00 a month; assistant bridge and building foremen, $105.00 a month; track foremen, $100.00 a month; bridge and building mechanics, 53¢ an hour; bridge and building helpers, 43¢ an hour; track laborers, 28¢ an hour.

The rules to be incorporated in existing agreements covered such matters as promotion and seniority rights, discipline and grievances, hours of service, overtime, and calls. Eight hours, exclusive of the meal period, were to constitute a day's work, with pro rata pay for the ninth and tenth hours of service and the time and one-half rate thereafter. A minimum allowance of three hours was provided for calls.

Although Supplement No. 8 did not by any means meet the request of the employes, it marked a definite milestone toward the attainment of fairer wages and better working conditions.

Another important declaration of the Railroad Administration was also having a tremendous effect on the fortunes of the Brotherhood. In General Order No. 8, issued February 21, 1918, the Director General of Railroads said:

"No discrimination will be made in the employment, retention, or conditions of employment of employes because of membership or non-membership in labor organizations."

This clause became railroad labor's Magna Charta. By prohibiting railroad managements from continuing their campaign of coercion and intimidation to discourage organization by railroad workers, it opened the way for the Brotherhood to widen immensely its organizing activities on railroads throughout the United States.

By the latter part of the year, the membership had increased fourfold. To take care of the rapidly-increasing membership, a new printing plant had been installed and a new two-story building erected adjacent to the Grand Lodge headquarters to house the printing plant and the growing staff of the Grand Secretary-Treasurer's Department.

In the meantime, conferences had been under way toward an amalgamation of the Brotherhood and the Gerrey-Pegg organization. The Director General had made it plain that maintenance of way workers must form one organization before they could expect to have their wage cases and grievances handled effectively by the government. As a result, committees representing the two organizations began negotiations. After conferences extending over several months, the two committees agreed that each organization would hold a special convention to discuss the question of consolidation.

A special convention of the I.B.M.W.E. met in Detroit, Michigan, on August 12, 1918. President Barker announced that since July 1, the Brotherhood had enrolled 9,000 new members, 3,274 in the first eight days of August alone. The Brotherhood, he said, then had approximately 32,000 members, the rival organization 6,000 or 7,000 (the 1919 convention report placed the figure at 8,000).

Barker also told the convention that on July 23, the Executive Committee of the American Federation of Labor had voted to turn over to the Brotherhood, after the amalgamation had taken place, the railway shop and roundhouse laborers, who had no organization to represent them but were organized on a number of roads under A.F. of L. federal charters.

The convention selected a committee of ten to meet with a like committee from the Gerrey organization in Cincinnati, Ohio, on August 15, to complete the amalgamation. At the Cincinnati meeting, the two committees reached an agreement reuniting the two factions of the Brotherhood. The committees changed the name of the organization to the "United Brotherhood of Maintenance of Way Employes and Railway Shop Laborers," and the name of the "Advance Advocate" to the "Advance Guide."

The committees decided that the next Grand Lodge convention would be held in September, 1919, established initiation fees for new members at $3.00, Grand Lodge dues at $8.00 a year, and subordinate lodge dues at a minimum of 60¢ a year, and re-elected Barker Grand President and George Seal Grand Secretary-Treasurer.

Progress, meanwhile, was being made on Canadian roads also. In the early part of 1918, a conciliation award established increased rates of pay on the Canadian Northern Railway. In later negotiations, wage rates were leveled up to the Canadian Pacific wage scale, effective June 1, 1918.

On July 26, 1918, the Canadian Railway War Board, consisting of officials from the various railways in Canada, called representatives of railway labor to Montreal to discuss the application to Canadian railways of General Order No. 27, issued in the United States by the Director General of Railroads. A movement by the Brotherhoods toward this end had been under way for several months. The conference completed plans for the creation of Canadian Board of Adjustment No. 1 to handle disputes between Canadian railways and their employes. This board was to be composed of twelve men, six selected by the railways and six by the employes. An implementing agreement was signed on August 7, 1918. This board is still in existence.

On November 8, 1918, the Canadian Railway War Board entered into an agreement with the Brotherhood putting into effect for Canadian maintenance of way workers the terms of Supplement No. 8 to General Order No. 27, issued by the Railroad Administration in the United States. A national agreement signed on March 7, 1919, covered practically every railway in Canada and established more uniform wage rates, standardized working conditions, the eight-hour day, overtime rules, and other favorable conditions of employment. This was the first national agreement negotiated by the Brotherhood.

The beginning of government control of railroads in the United States had placed before the Railroad Administration a tremendous backlog of unsettled grievances. To meet this exigency, the Railroad Administration inaugurated an important method of settling disputes between the railroads and their employes: the use of "Adjustment Boards" to decide controversies growing out of the interpretation and application of agreements established by orders of the Railroad Administration.

On November 13, 1918, the Brotherhood joined with the Order of Railway Telegraphers, the Brotherhood of Railway Clerks, and the Switchmen's Union of North America in an agreement with the regional directors for the railroads under government control, establishing Adjustment Board No. 3 to dispose of controversies arising for this group of organizations. This board was to consist of eight members, four selected by the railroads and four by the employes.

The orders of the Director General of Railroads, however, had not eliminated the opposition of some railroad managements to the organization of their maintenance of way employes. The Pennsylvania Railroad and certain other carriers had refused to enter into a written wage agreement or contract with the Brotherhood. On January 8, 1919, Barker issued a strike vote to members of the Brotherhood on the Pennsylvania System. Shortly thereafter he received a telegram from the Director of Division of Labor, United States Railroad Administration, urging him to suspend negotiations with the officials of the Pennsylvania Railroad and assuring him that conferences would be authorized to pave the way for a national agreement for maintenance of way workers on all railroads in the United States. Emphasis on negotiations, therefore, changed quickly from a system to a national level.

The almost incredible growth of the Brotherhood during this period of time is revealed by the fact that members paying dues to July 1, 1918, totaled only 17,000. New members enrolled at a fantastic rate during the ensuing twelve months, however, and at one time Grand Lodge was at least twelve weeks behind in the crediting of dues payments and the handling of correspondence. For some time, the working of a night shift of clerks became necessary to take care of the huge backlog of work. By the end of June, 1919, the membership approached the 200,000 mark.

The rapid growth of union membership on the railroads in the United States under government control had tempted other persons to form rival organizations. Such an organization, "The American Brotherhood of Railway Trackmen," under Robert H. Eaves as president and with headquarters at Bonne Terre, Missouri, had been active in Missouri and adjacent states for several years. For a time the Eaves' organization prospered, but as the Brotherhood expanded its coverage, the membership of the Eaves' order dwindled. In July, 1919, the two organizations signed an amalgamation agreement.

Some 1,800 delegates attended the regular convention of Grand Lodge, which remained in session in Detroit, Michigan, for two weeks beginning September 8, 1919. A parade through the streets of Detroit by 3,000 delegates and visitors was one of the highlights of the convention. Motion pictures of the convention and the parade were taken and shown in Detroit.

The convention adopted a proposal by President Barker and the Executive Board to acquire a site on which a modern building to house the offices of Grand Lodge could be erected. And it approved a plan to inaugurate a mail-order department through which members could buy goods at reduced prices.

The convention also voted to establish a Provident Department to replace the defunct Insurance Department. The sum of $200,000.00 was to be transferred from the general fund to establish the new department, and 25 per cent of Grand Lodge dues were to be transferred to this department monthly for the payment of claims. In the event of total disability or death of a member in good standing, benefits ranging from $50.00 after six months' continuous membership to $300.00 after 66 months' continuous membership were to be paid. A member's standing in the Provident Department began anew each time he failed to pay his dues as required by the laws.

Minimum quarterly dues to be charged by system divisions and subordinate lodges were set at $1.00 and 25¢, respectively.

The convention voted to re-establish the Ladies' Auxiliary, gave colored members more direct representation at Grand Lodge conventions by allowing them to be represented by white delegates, changed the name of "The Advance Guide" to "The Railway Maintenance of Way Employes' Journal," and unanimously re-elected Barker Grand President and Seal Grand Secretary-Treasurer.

But all was not harmony at the convention. The handwriting on the wall had become more legible. Dissident voices were louder in opposition to the grandiose plans of the Barker administration. Fred H. Fljozdal, who later became President of the Brotherhood, accepted defeat as Vice President rather than approve of policies which he felt were not in the best interest of the organization.

Estimates place the membership of the Brotherhood at this time at well in excess of 200,000. But as the organizing problem eased, the order encountered trouble from a new source. Several other labor organizations, including some of the building and construction trades unions, and the firemen and oilers, claimed jurisdiction over work being performed by railroad workers enrolled in the Brotherhood. Thus began a series of jurisdictional disputes with other unions which have never been entirely settled.

During the early summer of 1919, the International Brotherhood of Stationary Firemen and Oilers protested the seating of the United Brotherhood at the 1919 convention of the American Federation of Labor because of the jurisdictional dispute between the two organizations. On June 10, 1919, President Barker wrote a letter to the president of the firemen and oilers promising that the Brotherhood would turn over all shop and roundhouse employes then holding membership in the Brotherhood to the firemen and oilers and would discontinue its organizing campaign among these employes. On the strength of this letter, the latter organization withdrew its protest, and the convention seated the Brotherhood's delegates.

Barker did not tell his 1919 convention that he had written this letter. He said instead that he had told the firemen and oilers that his organization would not relinquish its jurisdiction over railway shop laborers. The convention adopted a resolution saying in effect that the maintenance of way organization had lawfully taken jurisdiction over railway shop laborers and protesting any action of the American Federation of Labor or any other organization to take over the men it represented. Thus the convention unknowingly repudiated the very action that had brought about the seating of its delegates at the A. F. of L. convention.

Effective January 1, 1920, the American Federation of Labor suspended the Brotherhood because of its refusal to comply with an order of the Executive Council ordering it to relinquish control over certain classes of employes claimed by the carpenters and joiners, the painters and decorators, and the firemen and oilers. Its charter was not reinstated until June 12, 1922.

As the year 1919 closed, the Brotherhood reached another important objective. Early in the year, following the promise of the administration to negotiate an agreement covering all railroads, a proposed national agreement had been prepared by some thirty-five Brotherhood representatives and submitted to the Railroad Administration. Conferences with the administration on this agreement began in March, 1919, but because of the heavy backlog of work before government officials, the work could not be completed until late in the year. At that time, a committee of sixteen officers of the Brotherhood signed a national agreement with Walker D. Hines, then Director General of Railroads, effective December 16, 1919, covering the hours of service and working conditions of maintenance of way employes throughout the United States. Although the Brotherhood did not receive all the concessions it had requested the national agreement marked another important step forward, and it established agreements on roads where they had not previously existed.

The greatest disappointment among the membership arose from the failure of the national agreement to provide a wage increase. Some members criticized the Grand Lodge officers soundly for not calling a strike to enforce their wage demands. The "Journal" urged the men to support the organization to protect themselves when the railroads were returned to private ownership, which seemed imminent.

The situation reached a crisis early in 1920 when Barker notified all members to begin a strike at 7:00 a.m., February 17, 1920, because of the failure of the administration to heed the employes' demands for a living wage. He canceled the strike call on February 14 when the government promised relief and President Woodrow Wilson agreed to set up machinery to act on the employes' request for higher wages.

By this time, the so-called Plumb Plan had become a hotly-debated issue. When the war ended with the signing of the armistice on November 11, 1918, the question of the return of the railroads to private ownership became a potent subject of controversy. Glenn E. Plumb, a Chicago lawyer, formulated a plan for continued operation and control of the railroads by the government, and a bill had been introduced in Congress to make the Plumb Plan effective. The railroad labor organizations favored government operation of the railroads, and fifteen of them joined in establishing the newspaper "Labor" for the express purpose of promoting the Plumb Plan. The Brotherhood was one of the original founders of "Labor" and made the second largest contribution ($12,000.00). The Plumb Plan died when Congress passed the Transportation Act of 1920 returning the railroads to private ownership on

March 1, 1920; but "Labor" continued on as the official voice of the standard railroad labor organizations.

In the intervening years, railroad labor has completely reversed its stand on government ownership of railroads in the United States. In 1920, the ruthless hostility of the railroads toward labor unions under private ownership was still fresh in the minds of railroad workers. Low wages, poor working conditions, and the penalty of dismissal for union membership had been their lot on many railroads. Under government control, their wages had been increased, national agreements providing improved working conditions had been signed with the Railroad Administration, discrimination or penalty for union membership had been ended, and for the first time, workers on many railroad systems had been able to join their craft union without fear of retaliation by railroad managements. It is not strange in these circumstances, therefore, that railroad employes looked with apprehension on the return of the railroads to private ownership.

Although many railroads did seek, after the end of government control in 1920, to smash the railroad Brotherhoods and to bring about a return to the labor-management conditions that existed prior to 1918, they were for the most part only temporarily successful. As time passed, collective bargaining on the railroads became an accepted fact. The passage of the Railway Labor Act of 1926 and the amended Act of 1934 created a stable method of collective bargaining procedure between railroad management and the unions. Today, the railroad Brotherhoods are diametrically opposed to government ownership of railroads in the United States. They fear the regimentation of workers that might result and they feel that the welfare of both their members and the railroads can better be protected and advanced under a system of private ownership and free enterprise.

Early in 1920 Grand Lodge completed plans to make effective the action taken at the 1919 convention. The "Journal" announced that lodge secretaries would soon receive full descriptive price lists and illustrated catalogs of mittens, gloves, overalls, shoes, and other articles to be sold under the Brotherhood's Cooperative Direct Selling Plan.

The cover of the February issue of the "Journal" depicted the proposed new home of the Brotherhood, a twelve-story office building to be erected in Detroit on a site purchased at Columbia and Clifford Streets. But these plans never reached fruition; the venture resulted in a heavy financial loss, and a new headquarters building was not constructed until thirty years later.

Jurisdictional disputes, too, were becoming more serious. Early in the year, the officers of Grand Lodge adopted a resolution protesting any attempt on the part of the American Federation of Labor, or any organization affiliated with that body, to take jurisdiction over any members of the Brotherhood. The resolution had particular reference to workers represented by the Brotherhood at shops, roundhouses, stores, yards, offices, power plants, pumping stations, fuel departments, and so on.

As spring approached, the top-heavy ramifications of Barker's policies toppled his administration. Effective March 18, 1920, Barker resigned as Grand President. "For several weeks," the "Journal" said, "the Grand Executive Board has been in session inquiring into certain conditions over which controversies have arisen from time to time. Acts and policies of the Grand President did not meet with the approval of this supreme body under the laws of the Brotherhood. . . .

"In its investigation of conditions the Grand Executive Board found matters unsatisfactory. Each and every step taken was most carefully considered. The interests of the United Brotherhood and its members were the thought constantly kept uppermost in the minds of those who were participating in the inquiry.

"In the end it became apparent that differences of serious import could not be harmonized and action was taken requesting that the Grand President place his resignation in their hands."

The resignation of Barker ended the most fabulous era in the history of the Brotherhood. During government control, the membership of the Brotherhood had increased stupendously. No one can give the peak figure exactly because quarterly membership figures do not reflect the overlapping of new members who join in the last month of a quarter and are placed in good standing for the following quarter. Estimates have run as high as 300,000, but this could well be an exaggeration. Ill-equipped to handle the tremendous expansion, Grand Lodge floundered in the tide of new members and money which poured into headquarters.

A conspicuous characteristic of the Barker administration had been its lack of ordinary business acumen. The affairs of Grand Lodge were in a sadly muddled state. The Brotherhood had entered into certain contracts and commitments in connection with the erection of the new building and the operation of the mail-order department and had made various unsound investments of Brotherhood funds, all of which had placed the organization in a serious financial predicament.

E. F. Grable, then a Vice President and formerly General Chairman on the Illinois Central System, was elected to succeed Barker. In his youth, President Grable had served an apprenticeship in the carpenter's trade and at age 23 became a member of the carpenters' union. He entered the service of the Illinois Central Railroad at Chicago as a carpenter in 1895. From 1901 to 1908 he acted as superintendent of bridges and buildings on the Memphis Division. He next worked as building inspector on the Missouri Pacific Railroad. He left this position to return to the Illinois Central, where he worked for six years until his discharge for refusal to relinquish his membership in the Brotherhood.

Buffeted by financial troubles, torn from within by dissension, and harassed by persistent rumors of every variety that alarmed the membership and caused agitation for a special convention of Grand Lodge, the organization set about to calm the chaotic sea of doubt and suspicion. The job before Grable was an unenviable one.

On March 31, 1920, George Seal resigned as Grand Secretary-Treasurer, and Samuel J. Pegg was elected to succeed him.

Along with the passing of the Barker regime went the long-established custom of presenting the retiring Grand Lodge President with a high silk hat and a cane.

To the woes Grable had inherited were soon to be added the troubles that came with the end of government control of the railroads. The Transportation Act of 1920 had fixed the terms under which the railroads were to be returned to private ownership and had established machinery for dealing with labor-management difficulties on the railroads. Title III of the act created a United States Railroad Labor Board of nine members to be appointed by the President of the United States, three members representing the railroads, three representing labor, and three the public. The Board had power to hear and decide disputes over grievances, rules, or working conditions, and to investigate conditions relating to wages, hours of labor, and other working conditions.

The Act prescribed that in determining wages the Board should take into consideration the following factors as well as "other relevant circumstances":

1. The scale of wages paid for similar kinds of work in other industries;
2. The relation between wages and the cost of living;
3. The hazards of the employment;
4. The training and skill required;
5. The degree of responsibility;
6. The character and regularity of employment; and
7. Inequalities of increase in wages or of treatment, the result of previous wage orders or adjustments.

Title III also provided for the establishment of adjustment boards by voluntary agreement between the carriers and employe organizations. The Labor Board could decide questions which adjustment boards could not settle. If there was no adjustment board to which the dispute could be submitted, it could be referred directly to the Labor Board. The law provided no means, however, except the pressure of public opinion, for enforcing decisions of either an adjustment board or the Labor Board.

With the return of the railroads to private ownership, the railroad labor organizations set about promptly to obtain increased wages and improved working conditions. On April 28, 1920, a proposed agreement adopted at a meeting of General Chairmen of the Brotherhood in Chicago was sent to the officials of all railroads in the United States, along with a demand for a wage increase. The wage dispute eventually reached the Labor Board, and on July 20, 1920, the Board issued Decision No. 2 granting increases in wages to railroad workers effective May 1, 1920. The decision increased the wage rates of maintenance of way men from 8½¢ to 15¢ an hour.

Following the issuance of Decision No. 2 in the United States, Wage Agreement No. 3, dated March 7, 1919, between the Railway Association of Canada (Canadian Railway War Board) and the Brotherhood, was amended to put increased wage rates in effect as of May 1, 1920.

With the return of the railroads to private ownership, the railroads began anew an attempt to divide and disrupt the Brotherhood. They carried on a vigorous campaign to induce foremen and minor supervisory officials to withdraw from the Brotherhood and establish a separate organization apart from the skilled and semi-skilled laborers; but they met with little success.

In November, 1920, the Brotherhood's Cooperative Department announced that it was ready to take orders for shoes, gloves, overalls, hose, blankets, and shirts, and that samples of goods to be sold were being sent to General Chairmen for distribution to lodge secretaries. Within a few months, however, it was evident that this rash venture into the mail-order business was a dismal failure. Not only did the membership decline to buy these goods in the anticipated quantities, but protests were received that the shoes being sold did not bear the union label. In addition, many of the "samples" were being put to direct use by lodge secretaries to whom they had been sent.

Barker had made contracts to purchase several factories to manufacture the merchandise to be sold by the Brotherhood, and had also made a contract for the purchase of goods from a Toledo, Ohio, firm. The Grable administration prepared to dispose of the factories purchased, and the Toledo firm agreed to furnish merchandise direct to the members from the factory at wholesale prices.

When the members found that the shoes did not bear the union label and that the prices being charged approximately equaled ordinary retail prices, they refused to buy the goods. Thereupon, the Toledo firm entered suit against the Brotherhood for damages of $750,000.00 This litigation resulted in the impounding by the court of Brotherhood funds on deposit in a Cleveland, Ohio, bank, and caused both the Brotherhood and its Grand Lodge officers considerable embarrassment until the matter had been disposed of by the court.

This unfortunate experience convinced the officers and members of the Brotherhood that it should stay out of the mail-order business or similar cooperative ventures and devote its entire time and energy to the welfare of its membership in the way of improving their wages and working conditions. It has consistently followed this policy since that time.

But even more serious problems were beginning to plague the Grable administration. The issuance of Decision No. 2 of the Labor Board had been followed almost immediately by a severe business depression. During the latter part of 1920 some 3½ million persons were thrown out of work, and it was estimated that by the spring of 1921 300,000 railroad workers had lost their jobs.

As early as 1919, the United States Chamber of Commerce had declared open war on labor unions and championed the open shop, and as economic conditions grew more depressed, business girded its loins to smash the unions and slash the wages of workers. Led by Vice President W. W. Atterbury of the Pennsylvania Railroad, the railroad group began a movement to abrogate the national agreements and reduce wages. Atterbury launched a particularly vitriolic attack against the railroad labor organizations.

On December 29, 1920, the Atlanta, Birmingham & Atlantic Railway served notice on its employes that wages would be reduced effective February 1, 1921. The railroad labor organizations expressed the opinion at the time that this small road had been selected by the General Managers' Executive Association as a test case to determine the extent to which the railroads could go in reducing wages. In Decision No. 89, dated February 21, 1921, the United States Railroad Labor Board directed the carrier, in effect, to cancel its wage reduction order.

The A. B. & A. refused to comply with the Board's decision, and on March 5, 1921, the employes of that road, including maintenance of way workers, went on strike. On February 26, 1921, the employes of the Missouri & North Arkansas Railroad had gone on strike under similar conditions. In January, 1921, the Erie Railroad had arbitrarily placed a wage reduction in effect, and the Labor Board found that it, too, had violated Decision No. 2 of the Board through its action.

In the meantime, the carriers continued to seek wage reductions and an abrogation of the national agreements. One phase of their program met with success on April 14, 1921, when the Labor Board issued Decision No. 119. In this decision the Board terminated the national agreements effective July 1, 1921, and directed that the representatives of the carrier and the employes on each railroad system negotiate a new agreement. If the parties could not agree by July 1, the Board would promulgate the rules. By Addendum No. 2 to Decision No. 119, the Board directed that in the event of a deadlock on rules, the rules promulgated by the Railroad Administration, except those fixing punitive pay for overtime, would remain in effect until the Board could reach a decision.

Decision No. 119 was the first of several stunning blows suffered by railroad employes. On June 1, the Labor Board rendered Decision No. 147 reducing the wages of all railroad workers by approximately $378 million a year, effective July 1, 1921. The reductions for classes in the maintenance of way department ranged from 7½¢ to 10¢ an hour.

The railroad labor organizations bitterly denounced Decision No. 147 and threatened to strike, but those affiliated with the American Federation of Labor later decided to withhold any strike action until the Labor Board had passed on the general issues then before it.

As an aftermath of Decision No. 147, Canadian lines brought pressure to bear to impose a similar reduction in wages, which Canadian railway workers found they were compelled to accept in the circumstances.

But the ebbing fortunes of the Brotherhood were to encounter still other adversities before the year ended. Earlier in the year, a committee representing the Pennsylvania System Joint Protective Board had called at Grand Lodge to settle various disputes between the system and Grand Lodge, particularly an accounting by Grand Lodge for system division funds. A Wayne County, Michigan, judge acting as arbitrator by court decree had brought about a settlement of the matters in controversy, and apparently the situation had been disposed of amicably and to the complete satisfaction of the committee.

In November, 1921, however, the Pennsylvania System withdrew from the jurisdiction of the Brotherhood and formed a system organization called the "Pennsylvania System Fraternity" to represent maintenance of way workers on that road. The name of this organization was later changed to the "Maintenance of Way Employes' Union," but the maintenance of way men on the Pennsylvania System remained outside the jurisdiction of the Brotherhood for sixteen years.

Meanwhile, the strikes on the A. B. & A. and the M. & N. A. had continued, and an assessment of 50¢ was levied on each member to aid in the continuance of the strikes.

As the year closed, the Labor Board issued Decision No. 501 in settlement of the dispute between the Brotherhood and the railroads on rules and working conditions arising out of the abolishment of the national agreement. The decision came as a distinct disappointment to the employes, for it required the payment of the time and one-half rate only after the tenth hour of service and thus had the effect of establishing the ten-hour day.

Another important issue now began to take shape. Because of the continuance of depressed business conditions, the railroads had served notice on their employes on October 14, 1921, of a proposed further reduction in wages. The employes countered with a request for a wage increase. They had long insisted that the plight of the carriers was due to the financial manipulations of interests that controlled the railroads and to lack of economy and efficiency in operation, and not because of the substandard wages being paid to railroad workers.

The dispute eventually reached the Labor Board in March, 1922. At the Board hearings (April, 1922) the employes insisted that they could not live on the wages being paid, and many section men and their wives were brought from various parts of the country to testify before the Board. The Labor Board, however, gave little heed to the testimony presented by these witnesses as to their substandard living conditions because of low wages. Decision No. 1028 reduced the wages of some 400,000 maintenance of way workers from 1¢ to 5¢ per hour, effective July 1, 1922. Ironically, the lowest-paid classes were among those receiving the 5¢-an-hour wage cut. A dissenting opinion by the labor members of the Board said:

"According to data contained in the majority report, the minimum hourly rate of pay for section men on the railroads

A. B. Lowe
Second Grand Lodge President
1908-1914

T. H. Gerrey
Third Grand Lodge President
1914

A. E. Barker
Fourth Grand Lodge President
1914-1920

E. F. Grable
Fifth Grand Lodge President
1920-1922

F. H. Fljozdal
Sixth Grand Lodge President
1922-1940

E. E. Milliman
Seventh Grand Lodge President
1940-1946

Maurice J. Tobin, U. S. Secretary of Labor, breaking ground for the new headquarters building—April 27, 1950. Left to right: Wm. Jewkes, Ottawa, Ontario, Brotherhood's oldest member; A. Shoemake, Secretary-Treasurer; T. C. Carroll, President; Maurice J. Tobin; Frank X. Martel, President, Detroit and Wayne County Federation of Labor; Harold D. Truax, Commissioner of Finance, Highland Park, Michigan.

→

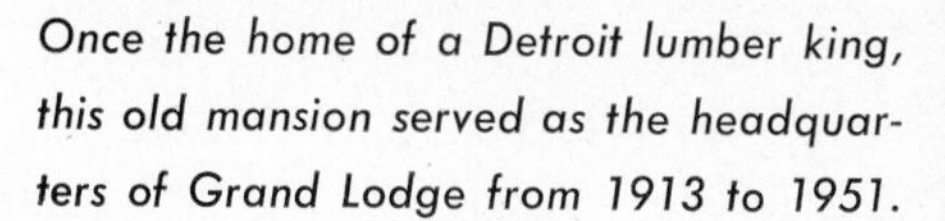

Once the home of a Detroit lumber king, this old mansion served as the headquarters of Grand Lodge from 1913 to 1951.

New international headquarters of the Brotherhood at Highland Park, Detroit, Michigan, dedicated October 30, 1951. ←

Members of Central Committee of Canada who negotiated the Brotherhood's first national agreement in 1919. Front row, left to right: W. Jewkes; G. W. Murray; A. McAndrew, Vice-Chairman; W. Dorey, Chairman; W. Aspinall, Secretary; J. J. O'Grady. Back row: G. H. Cummings; J. G. Geraldi; P. Woods; W. Crampton; G. J. Maggs; F. Foster; W. Cullen.

Grand Lodge officers, 1952-1955. *Seated—Secretary-Treasurer A. Shoemake (left) and President T. C. Carroll. First row, standing—Vice President T. F. Holleran, Vice President T. L. Jones, Vice President George Hudson, Vice President W. Aspinall, Vice President J. H. Hadley, Vice President Louis Vogland and Vice President W. K. McKee. Second row—Statistician and Research Director Frank L. Noakes, Executive Board Members J. A. Huneault, C. L. Lambert, Ralph Freccia, and J. P. Wilson and Executive Board Chairman M. C. Plunk.*

President Carroll and Secretary-Treasurer Shoemake *clasp hands after the laying of the cornerstone completes the new headquarters building.*

of the United States will, under this decision, be 23 cents. This means earnings for a full-time 48-hour week of $11.04."

Other decisions rendered by the Labor Board at that time ordered reductions in the wages of shop craft employes, clerks, and signal department employes. No reductions were made during 1922 in the wages of engine and train service employes, nor in those of all classes of non-operating employes.

As July 1, the effective date of the wage cuts, drew nearer, demands that a strike be called in protest against Decision No. 1028 became tumultuous. Grable vacillated between action and inaction; he wavered between decision and indecision. Arrangements to call maintenance of way workers out on strike were made, and then canceled at the eleventh hour.

"In the present situation I know it is difficult for the membership in general to understand all the angles to the controversy," Grable said in a letter to the membership outlining his reasons for not calling the strike. "I realize that our members are righteously indignant at having been forced to accept another reduction in wage rates which were far too low even before the cut was put into effect. But I also know that nothing is ever accomplished by blindly rushing headlong into a situation without counting the cost. Our members want relief. They want a living wage. They want bearable conditions. They are willing to make any necessary sacrifices to secure them. However, they do not want to make needless sacrifices and they do not want to be led into traps which may have been laid for them and from which there is no way out except defeat and the loss of much more than has yet ever been suggested.

"I realize there is but little use in my letter to our members this month to deal with anything other than the strike situation. The shop crafts struck on July 1. Coming into contact with our members the question has been asked times without number why the executives of the maintenance of way did not put into effect the strike vote which was taken some time ago.

"There is but one answer to that question. It has seemed best to your chief executive and other Grand Lodge officers that the strike order should not be put into effect so long as there is a chance of securing justice for our members in a better way. Had our organization agreed with the shop crafts that we should go out in concert with them on July 1 and remain out until the grievances of all classes who struck were satisfied we should certainly have kept our part of the agreement. However, no such agreement has been entered into. . . .

"In conforming to the policy outlined early in July numerous conferences have been held with the managements of different roads in an attempt to have them return to the rates in effect before the last decrease or even above that figure. Where our representatives have been unsuccessful in inducing their management to do this the controversy has been immediately carried to the Railroad Labor Board. . . . We are firm in the belief that we shall be able to have re-established rates of pay not less than, and most likely in excess of, the rates established under Decision 147."

But Grable's explanation failed to calm the wave of angry resentment and criticism from maintenance of way workers over his failure to call them out on strike with the 400,000 shopmen who left their jobs on July 1, 1922, in protest against the wage cut. In fact, large numbers of maintenance of way employes and clerks had walked out with the shopmen in unauthorized strikes.

After the shopmen's strike had been in progress for two months, Harry M. Daugherty, Attorney General of the United States, requested an injunction from a Federal court against the strikers. The granting of the injunction, which the shop crafts declared was the hardest blow ever dealt labor by the Federal courts, broke the strike. With the defeat of the shopmen, company unions were established among shop employes on a number of roads, and the standard organizations of the shop crafts did not regain representation rights on many systems for years.

The failure of the shopmen's strike increased the bitterness that threatened to demoralize the membership of the Brotherhood in the United States and the steady drop in membership reached an alarming degree. As the Grable administration reeled from the destructive blows being rained upon it, difficulties had arisen from another source.

On April 23, 1922, J. O. Raley, former Vice President of the Brotherhood, had called a meeting of the General Chairmen on the Central of Georgia, Georgia, Atlanta & West Point and Western Railway of Alabama, New Orleans & Northeastern, and Alabama Great Southern Systems. Raley fostered the idea that skilled and so-called unskilled workers should not be in the same organization. This group of General Chairmen formed an organization called "The Order of Skilled Railway Maintenance of Way Employes" with headquarters at Macon, Georgia, and elected Raley president. Later, the Alabama Great Southern and the New Orleans & Northeastern Systems withdrew from this rival organization; but the agreements held by the Brotherhood with the three remaining railroads, covering foremen and mechanics, were taken over by the Raley organization.

When, therefore, 700 delegates convened in triennial convention of Grand Lodge in Detroit, Michigan, beginning October 2, 1922, the troubles of the Grable administration had been augmented and compounded. Feelings ran high, and it was quite obvious that the delegates were determined to make drastic changes in the official family of the Brotherhood.

In his report to the convention, President Grable attempted to allay the rising tide of dissatisfaction. "I am sure most of you will appreciate that the period through which we have passed since our last convention has been a most trying one," he said. "Every organization upon the American continent has been beset by trials greater than those of any previous period. It is a matter of gratification that our organization has been able in a measure to meet the problems which have arisen from time to time and at this time with the opportunity before us in this convention to unify the support of our loyal membership, our Brotherhood can emerge from the chaotic conditions of the past to a brighter and better day. . . .

"I am not unmindful that all has not been accomplished that we have hoped for. Some may contend that your officials should have followed different policies from those which have been followed. These are criticisms that can be made by those so inclined no matter what had been done . . . I ask that the delegates reserve judgment until such time as they have information upon which to base intelligent opinions. I am sure you will best serve the interests of our Brotherhood if you will do this."

It might be said in all fairness to Grable that he had assumed the Presidency at one of the most critical times in the history of the Brotherhood. Not only was the organization torn from within by internal strife, but the buffeting pressure from external sources, particularly in the form of drastic wage cuts, had become almost overwhelming. Whether anyone else could have done a better job than Grable in meeting the recurring crises that beset the Brotherhood is a question that can never be satisfactorily answered.

The convention took a decided stand in condemning company unions, some of which were being formed by former officers and members of the Brotherhood.

With respect to jurisdictional disputes, it adopted a policy of not transferring any disputed class of workers to other organizations until a referendum vote of the particular craft had been taken to ascertain whether that class wished to make the transfer. This action caused Grand Lodge some embarrassment in its subsequent negotiations on jurisdictional disputes with other unions, particularly the firemen and oilers and the clerks (concerning representation of stores department employes).

The convention also adopted a system of issuing dues stamps instead of working cards to cover dues payments, and approved a plan to strengthen system divisions under which two or more systems could join to form one system federation. This made it possible for smaller systems to affiliate with larger systems, or for two or more small systems to form a federation.

Favorable consideration was given to a proposal to move Grand Lodge headquarters to St. Louis, Missouri, but this plan never materialized because of the heavy expense involved in moving and in acquiring a new headquarters building.

The convention revised the laws of the Provident Department, established at the 1919 convention, and placed it under the jurisdiction of the Grand Secretary-Treasurer.

The election of Grand Lodge officers clearly reflected the dissatisfaction of the delegates with the past administration. They took action to reduce the number of Vice Presidents from fourteen to five, and elected a completely new Executive Board.

Grand Lodge dues were reduced from $2.00 to $1.50 a quarter. The minimum dues to be charged by system divisions were increased to $1.50 a quarter.

Regardless of whether the Grable administration did or did not deserve the abundant criticism being heaped upon it, the delegates were in no mood for compromise. The guillotine was poised, and the convention, completing its attempt to eradicate all traces of the Grable regime, elected F. H. Fljozdal to succeed Grable as Grand President and Elmer E. Milliman to succeed Samuel J. Pegg as Grand Secretary-Treasurer.

From the vantage point of some thirty years later, it is not difficult to isolate the two prime reasons for the downfall of the Grable administration. In the first place, Grable had been selected as President to straighten out the badly-tangled internal and financial affairs of the Brotherhood. There were those who thought he had not undertaken the job with sufficient forcefulness and determination. It is evident from the records, however, that he did make the attempt. It is also evident that in the process he was overwhelmed by external forces, particularly the decisions of the United States Railroad Labor Board ordering severe reductions in wages.

It was the reaction of the Grable administration to these wage cuts that formed the second indictment of those who were dissatisfied with the trend of events. Many delegates felt that the Grand Lodge officers had not met the challenge of these Labor Board decisions with sufficient vigor and forthrightness. The bitterness of railroad workers toward the Board's wage decisions is readily understandable. The extent to which the Board slashed wages is apparent from the following figures for track laborers, one of the lower-paid classes of workers:

Date Effective	*Established by*	*Minimum Hourly Wage*
Sept. 1, 1918	Supplement No. 8 to General Order No. 27	$ .28
May 1, 1920	Decision No. 2 (U.S.R.R. Labor Board)	.36½
July 1, 1921	Decision No. 147 (U.S.R.R. Labor Board)	.28
July 1, 1922	Decision No. 1028 (U.S.R.R. Labor Board)	.23

In commenting on the wage rates established under Decision No. 1028 for lower-paid men in the maintenance of way department, the labor members of the Board said in a dissenting opinion:

"The rates of pay established under this decision will mean annual earnings far below any minimum standard of subsistence which has been formulated, even below those of most conservative employer groups. . . . We believe that in this decision the Labor Board is affecting hundreds of thousands of families; it is touching the proper nurture of hosts of children."

These were the unpromising circumstances in which Grable surrendered the reins of leadership to the new President.

CHAPTER V

THE CRITICAL YEARS

THE years immediately following the 1922 convention were indeed a period of crisis. Could the Brotherhood survive the vicissitudes of the post-war era? Could it extricate itself from its financial difficulties? Could it restore the shattered hope and faith that threatened to prostrate its membership? Could it wrest from hostile railroad managements the higher wages and improved working conditions so sorely needed by the men it represented? Could it settle its jurisdictional problems successfully? Could it overcome the threat of rival organizations and company unions?

On the surface, perhaps, an affirmative answer to all these questions would have seemed rash at that time. But superficial evaluation could take little account of the hard core of determination and courage, formed in the hearts and minds of maintenance of way workers through years of deprivation and struggle, that gave the Brotherhood a hidden and incalculable source of strength. Gathering up the scattered fragments of its shattered fortunes, the organization began the tedious ascent to the heights from which it had fallen. And in this difficult enterprise it needed the highest type of leadership.

No better man than Fred H. Fljozdal could have been selected to untangle the snarled threads of the Brotherhood's affairs. Of even temperament, sober habits, and unquestioned integrity, Fljozdal soon had the complete confidence of his membership with few exceptions.

Born in Kxarxirdi, Iceland, on December 19, 1868, Fljozdal emigrated to America with his parents at age eight. His father took up homesteading in southern Minnesota and became one of the pioneer settlers of Yellow Medicine County. When he was fifteen years old, Fljozdal worked as a water boy on a construction gang for the Great Northern Railroad in slack seasons on the farm. In 1888, he went to work at Duluth, Minnesota, laying track for a street car company converting from horse to electrical power.

In 1900, he accepted a job as section foreman at Sprague, Manitoba, with the Canadian Northern Railway, later to become a part of the Canadian National System. He joined the Brotherhood in 1902 and was elected lodge secretary. He became the first General Chairman of the Canadian Northern System in 1905 and held that position until his election as Vice President of the Brotherhood in 1918. He served as a member of the Grand Lodge Executive Committee from 1914 to 1918. His refusal to approve some of the policies of President Barker brought about his defeat as Vice President at the 1919 convention.

"Organized labor generally has, for the last three years particularly, had to face a concerted movement against bettering the wages and working conditions of the millions who toil," President Fljozdal said in his first message to his membership.

"On the railways, the relinquishment [of control] by the United States Government marked the beginning of concerted action by the Railway Executives to reduce wages and working rules and, as by common consent, our organization was singled out as a convenient target for such purposes. . . .

"However, a turn in the road has been reached. Those who were of the opinion that railway workers were paid princely salaries have since discovered that such was not the case. There are no more harbored illusions as to why such insidious propaganda was spread throughout the country.

"With the cooperation of every man in our composite organization, we shall be able to forge ahead and take our place as a progressive, determined and stronger factor in the labor movement."

The growing dissatisfaction of the membership was reflected in a decline of more than 50% in the number of members in good standing to April 1, 1923, compared with the same period in 1920. The immediate job before the new President, therefore, was to resell the Brotherhood to maintenance of way workers. During the first few years of his administration, he traveled thousands of miles, attending mass meetings wherever they could be arranged, to carry the message of the Brotherhood directly to maintenance of way men. Whenever he received letters of complaint from points of trouble, Fljozdal made it a policy to visit those points so that he could talk to the men personally.

Fljozdal knew, too, that in the difficult fight ahead to raise the living standards of his members, a program of coordination and preparation was essential. He selected Leo E. Keller, then Secretary-Treasurer of the Louisville & Nashville System Division, to become the first director of the newly-created Department of Statistics and Research. It is the function of this department to gather and compile statistics to be used in wage negotiations, at conferences with railroad managements, at hearings before governmental boards, and for informational purposes. During the thirty-two years of its existence, this department has become a valuable adjunct to the Brotherhood's collective-bargaining activities.

After the failure of the shopmen's strike of 1922, company unions became an epidemic in the railroad industry, not only among the shopmen but in other departments as well. In a short time, the Brotherhood found itself confronted with company unions (or "system associations" as they were euphemistically called) on a number of roads. On some railroads the company unions represented only foremen, on others the foremen and employes in the class of mechanic, and on some railroads the entire maintenance of way craft. Reasserting its representation rights over company unions was a task which occupied the Brotherhood for many years.

An improvement in the low wage rates of maintenance of way workers, which had been slashed unmercifully by the United States Railroad Labor Board in 1921 and 1922, was another serious problem before the Brotherhood as Fljozdal began his administration. The optimistic promise of President Grable in July, 1922, that wage rates would be restored to a level at least equal to those established by Decision No. 147 of the Labor Board had not materialized. Decision No. 1267, rendered by the Board on October 21, 1922 (effective October 16), had granted a wage increase of 2¢ an hour to track foremen, assistant track foremen, machine operators, laborers, and other low-paid employes, but had not increased the wages of the remaining maintenance of way classes.

Some progress in improving wage rates was being made on individual roads, however, and in Canada a new schedule granted wage increases to maintenance of way classes effective November 1, 1922. By May, 1921, the Canadian government had taken over the Canadian Northern, the Grand Trunk, and the Grand Trunk Pacific Railways, in addition to the other lines it owned. In October, 1922, the government amalgamated all its lines into the Canadian National Railways, the largest single system in North America with some 22,682 miles of line.

The new year brought with it a gradual recovery from the business depression, and in January, 1923, the Brotherhood began a general movement to obtain higher wages and improved working conditions. By early June, settlements granting wage increases had been negotiated on a number of roads, and by the time the dispute reached the Labor Board, only about thirty railroads were involved. Settlements on individual roads continued, and when Fljozdal and other witnesses appeared to argue the case before the Board, only three major railroads and a few smaller systems remained as parties to the dispute.

In stressing the inadequate wages received by maintenance of way workers, Fljozdal pointed out that trackmen were receiving as little as 25¢ an hour, and that outside employers paid from 100 to 200 per cent more. Because wage settlements had already been negotiated on many roads, the Board in Decision No. 1861 remanded the dispute to the parties concerned for further negotiations, with the stipulation that final agreements would be effective June 1, 1923.

Jurisdictional disputes, rival organizations, and company unions had now become a serious threat to the Brotherhood.

Ever since the amalgamation in 1899, the Brotherhood (and the Canadian organization before that time) had represented signalmen on Canadian railways. In the late spring of 1923, it relinquished any further claim to represent this class of Canadian railway workers.

A rival organization, the "Canadian Brotherhood of Railway Employes," had made its appearance on the Intercolonial Railway in 1910 on the principle of one big union for all railway workers. It made no particular effort to organize maintenance of way men, however, until 1923. On May 17, 1923, a vice president of this Canadian organization sent a circular letter to the secretaries of all lodges of the Brotherhood in Canada denouncing the Brotherhood and inviting Canadian maintenance of way workers to join this rival organization.

In reply to a letter from President Fljozdal remonstrating against this action, the president of the C. B. of R. E. said that a few years earlier he and A. E. Barker, then President of the Brotherhood, had reached an understanding that if the Brotherhood would relinquish any claim to represent shop laborers in Canada, this rival organization would not seek to organize maintenance of way workers. He contended that the Brotherhood had broken the agreement made by Barker. It was not until 1925 that the two organizations reached an agreement under which the Brotherhood gave up any claim to the right to represent shop laborers in Canada. Although this rival organization has continued to be active, it has never been able to make any appreciable inroads on the membership of the Brotherhood in Canada.

The decline in membership had now indeed become of serious concern to the Fljozdal administration. From October 1, 1922, to October 1, 1923, the Brotherhood suffered a loss in membership of more than 44,000. Effective September 1, 1923, Grand Lodge began the first of a series of intensive membership drives carried on intermittently during the 1920's.

Adequate rules covering punitive pay were high on the Brotherhood's agenda at this time, and at its regular annual meeting on August 16, 1923, the Policy Committee of the Brotherhood inaugurated a movement to obtain the time and one-half rate on all railroads for work performed in excess of eight hours and on Sundays and holidays.

By the fall of 1923, the wage disputes remanded to the parties concerned by the Labor Board in Decision No. 1861 were still unsettled on seven systems and had again been submitted to the Board for decision. In Decision No. 2049, the Board granted wage increases of 1¢ and 2¢ an hour, effective June 1, 1923, to employes represented by the Brotherhood on the roads concerned. Laborers and other low-paid workers were among those receiving the meager increase of 1¢ an hour.

"The past year has proven a very eventful one for organized labor in general and our organization in particular," Fljozdal said in his message to the membership in December, 1923. "The year 1922 was a year of reaction and depression and reflected itself in wage decreases and the slackening of industry generally....

"With renewed vigor organized labor has rallied its forces in working order and has been steadily pressing onward with an occasional check but no backward movement.

"The year 1923 then has been a great year for education and organization of the worker. . . . As we then confidently and with hope and belief in the future leave the old year behind, we cannot help thinking and believing that the year 1923 has been a year of preparation and tilling wherein the seeds of progress and enlightenment will take root."

As the year closed, the strike which began in February, 1921, on the Missouri & Northern Arkansas Railroad was officially declared at an end (December 22, 1923). During the strike, the carrier had obtained many indictments against railroad workers and citizens friendly to the strikers. With the calling off of the strike, the courts dismissed pending indictments. President Fljozdal expressed the opinion that the great majority of employes who wanted to return to the service of the company would eventually be restored to their jobs.

The strike on the Atlanta, Birmingham & Atlantic Railway was also eventually called off. Although the strikes on both these roads were ostensibly lost, the employes had still achieved a victory in a very material sense. Their bitter resistance to the wage cuts was undoubtedly a strong deterrent to other railroad managements who had contemplated the slashing of wages and an abrogation of agreement rules.

On December 20, 1923, the Chairman of the Grand Executive Board announced that 95 per cent of the membership had voted in a special election to change the laws of the Provident Department in accordance with a referendum petition inaugurated by a subordinate lodge. The new laws provided for the payment of benefits, on death or permanent total disability, ranging from $50.00 after six months of continuous membership to $300.00 after sixty-six months. New or reinstated members who had reached age 55 at the last joining or rejoining date could not participate in the benefits of this department. Members who became delinquent through failure to pay dues as required by the laws forfeited previously accumulated rights in the Provident Department and began a new period of standing upon reinstatement of membership.

The dissatisfaction of railroad workers with decisions of the United States Railroad Labor Board on wages, rules governing working conditions, and grievances had now reached a high pitch. On January 31, 1924, the chief executives of sixteen standard railroad labor organizations met in Washington, D. C., to draft an amendment to the Transportation Act of 1920 to abolish the Board and to establish in its stead new machinery for settling collective bargaining controversies between the railroads and their employes. A bill containing the proposals of the unions was later introduced in Congress as the Railway Labor Act.

At the outset, opposition to the bill by railroad officials was intense. To bolster the railroads' arguments, more than fifty representatives of company unions appeared at hearings before a Senate sub-committee and repeated testimony advanced against the bill by railroad executives. Congress did not pass the Railway Labor Act until two years later.

Meanwhile, a wage controversy in Canada had reached the critical stage. In the fall of 1923, a request of Canadian maintenance of way employes for a wage increase of 5¢ an hour had been referred to a Board of Conciliation under the Lemieux Act. The railway managements refused to accept the Board's award granting wage increases. The Brotherhood had agreed to accept the award, although it fell short of their demands, but rescinded this action following the management's refusal and issued a strike ballot.

Effective April 1, 1924, Supplement "A" to Wage Agreement No. 7, negotiated with the Railway Association of Canada, settled the dispute and established the eight-hour day with time and one-half for time worked in excess of eight hours. This agreement became universal for all railways in Canada.

Improved wage schedules were also being negotiated on roads in the United States. A new agreement granted wage increases to the 17,000 maintenance of way employes of the Southern Railway which in some instances brought wage rates to a figure considerably higher than those established by Decision No. 2 of the Labor Board.

Effective May 1, 1924, the Brotherhood began a new membership drive. "The results of the drive last fall were highly pleasing, and resulted in a substantial increase in membership," Fljozdal said. "In fact, the increase in the membership has continued and is now growing daily." Many systems inaugurated supplementary membership campaigns, and although the membership figures were still far from satisfactory, the continued drop in membership had been checked and a degree of stability attained.

The July, 1924, issue of the "Journal" announced that company unions on six roads had been a complete failure, and that the Brotherhood had won representation ballots over company-sponsored organizations. In defending the pending Howell-Barkley Bill (Railway Labor Act), a Congressman pointed out that not one railroad company union had appealed a dispute to the Railroad Labor Board, nor to any tribunal created by or connected with the railroads, and that these unions were manifestly maintained by the railroads.

"Surely," he said, "no member of Congress would contend that any bona fide labor union exists where the management absolutely controls the actions of the representatives of these so-called unions and pays all expense incurred for time lost and hotel expenses, and so forth, of the representatives."

Victories by the Brotherhood over company unions continued as the workers awoke to a realization of the true situation.

As the depression of 1921-22 declined and business conditions improved, the nation began a period of expansion and prosperity. But the worker and the farmer found their incomes lagging behind the crest of living costs. Dissatisfied with the attitude of the Harding and Coolidge administrations toward the welfare of the nation's workers, labor supported almost unanimously the candidacy of Senator Robert M. LaFollette, running for the presidency of the United States on the Progressive ticket in 1924. Although Senator LaFollette received almost 5 million votes, the greatest ballot ever polled by a third-party candidate, President Coolidge was re-elected by a substantial plurality over LaFollette and the Democratic candidate.

On November 26, 1924, the Labor Board issued Decision No. 2687 disposing of a long-standing dispute between maintenance of way workers and twenty-four railroad systems on certain rules governing working conditions. The Board granted the time and one-half rate to laborers around shops and yards for work in excess of eight hours, but decided that maintenance of way classes should receive the penalty rate only after the tenth hour of continuous service. The Board also held that employes called to perform work not continuous with their regular work period would be allowed the time and one-half rate with a minimum of two hours' pay, and that the time and one-half rate would apply to work performed on Sundays and holidays.

In a letter dated December 20, 1924, to the Chairman of the Labor Board, Fljozdal protested the Board's failure to grant the penalty rate to maintenance of way men after eight hours' work. "The reasons set forth in Decision No. 2687 for denying Maintenance of Way employes this basic rule," he said, "appear to be based wholly upon the financial effects upon the carriers, and completely ignore the human rights and welfare of the employes. In fact, I am surprised indeed at the reasons advanced by the Board for denying us the punitive rates, and I emphatically hold that the Board must have been in error when influenced by such reasons."

Through subsequent negotiations on various roads not covered by the decision, the Brotherhood was able to secure a part or all of the improved rules established by Decision No. 2687. Although the decision was unsatisfactory, it did provide some relief from onerous conditions. But progress toward higher earnings had been slow indeed. The average straight-time hourly earnings of 39.5¢ received by maintenance of way workers in the United States in 1922 had increased to only 40.7¢ in 1924.

The wide disparity in wage rates for the same class of work, not only from system to system but at various locations on the same railroad, had long been criticized as inequitable by the Brotherhood. Established on the basis of supply and demand rather than a similarity of work performed, rates of pay for identical occupations might vary considerably from one part of the system to the other. In an effort to correct such conditions, the representatives of the Brotherhood on the Louisville & Nashville System filed a request with the management of that road for an adjustment of unfair differentials and inequalities in rates of pay existing in all classifications in the maintenance of way department.

The dispute eventually reached the Labor Board. In Decision No. 2752, the Board granted a sum of approximately $78,000.00 a year to be used in standardizing the rates of pay of track and bridge and building foremen and assistant bridge and building foremen. The Board refused, however, to give consideration to the leveling up of the wage rates of other classes of employes. Inasmuch as the employes in these three classes comprised only a comparatively small percentage of the total employes in the maintenance of way department, the Board's decision touched only the surface and left many of the most glaring inequalities in wage rates unchanged.

Maintenance of way workers had now become vociferous in their demands for higher earnings, and early in February, 1925, plans were completed for the launching of another general wage increase movement. During the spring and summer, wage agreements providing higher rates of pay were negotiated on numerous roads. In the late summer, a dispute covering twenty-seven railroads on which settlements could not be reached was docketed with the Board.

"Behind us are two more years of hardship, undernourishment and general wage injustice," said President Fljozdal in submitting the wage increase petition to the Board, "before us is such relief as this Board, in its wisdom, deems just.

"The railroad managements are here to protest the relief we are asking for. They will show you the financial results of an increase and will probably ask you to look upon our request in the light of so many dollars and cents. . . .

"We ask you to look upon our requests in the light of happier and healthier children, more education for the future people of our prosperous country who will come, in part, from our families."

Fljozdal pointed out that according to figures compiled by the Interstate Commerce Commission, 74.8 per cent of 388,238 employes in the maintenance of way department earned $75.00 a month or less during 1924, and that only 3.5 per cent earned $125.00 or more. "Can this be just and reasonable," he asked, "when those below that figure include not only laborers, but carpenters, painters, section foremen, mechanics' helpers, etc.?"

By this time, however, railroad workers had learned to expect little relief from the Board. (Parenthetically, E. F. Grable, former President of the Brotherhood, had been appointed as a labor member of the Labor Board by President Harding following Grable's defeat at the 1922 convention.) Moreover, the future status of the Board had become decidedly uncertain. The unions were reluctant to take cases to the Board, in which they had little confidence. The cases docketed with the Board up to December 31, 1923, had averaged 3,120 a year, but during 1924 the number had decreased by nearly 75 per cent from this yearly average to only 841; and these disputes were largely of minor importance. Paradoxically, the railroads now joined with their employes in condemning the Board, although for different reasons, and the Brotherhoods actively sought the abolishment of the Board through the passage by Congress of the Railway Labor Act.

One of the severest indictments against the Labor Board was its failure to establish a living wage for low-paid railroad workers. In a debate in the United States Senate on the Howell-Barkley Bill (February 13 and 14, 1925), Senator C. C. Dill from the State of Washington said:

"The Railroad Labor Board has held down the wages of the men who have in charge the duty of taking care of the roadbeds of the railroads of this country. I believe it is a matter of public interest—I feel it is a matter of public safety—that these men who look after the railroad roadbeds, over which trains run, should be paid such salaries that they will not be continually worried about whether or not they are going to have enough at the end of the month to feed and clothes their families. . . .

"When we stop to think that these men are receiving an average of $880.00 per year, for 12 months, $73.33 a month, no argument whatever on the part of anybody is needed to convince one that that is not enough to take care of a family decently. . . .

"In January, 1923, 171,363 Maintenance of Way men received an average of $72.00 a month. In February, 1923, 171,977 received an average of $63.00 a month. Think of it, the winter month of February, and an average wage of $63.00 a month! . . .

"These men who are today so poorly paid that they can not decently provide for their families are held down by the Labor Board and prevented from being given the extra pay for overtime that is given other classes of railroad employes who are better paid."

In a letter to President Coolidge, dated December 23, 1924, President Fljozdal said: "The discontent with the Board is widespread and deeply felt by the railway employes in general and particularly as to the Railway Maintenance of Way Employes, who are very poorly paid by the railways and have received very little consideration by the Railroad Labor Board, regardless of the fact that the work of this class of employes is of an arduous nature and requires competent men."

Thus the indictment against the Labor Board grew. Certain of the transportation organizations by-passed the Board in pending disputes concerning wages and working conditions which the carriers insisted should be referred to the Board. Through negotiations the Brotherhoods were able to obtain a more favorable settlement on individual properties than the Board had granted in similar cases by decision. The inability of the carriers to force the Board to assume jurisdiction in unsettled disputes which the employes refused to submit, created a definite dissatisfaction with the Board on the part of the carriers.

The outcome of a representation dispute on the Atchison, Topeka & Santa Fe System, meanwhile, had been unfavorable. The Brotherhood lost representation rights over certain classes of workers on that road when, at the instigation of the company, the employes formed a company union called the "Association of Maintenance of Way and Miscellaneous Foremen, Mechanics and Helpers" to supplant the Brotherhood.

Their inability to make any appreciable progress toward improving their low wages had created a feeling of discontent and frustration among maintenance of way workers. In the summer of 1925, President Fljozdal attempted to bolster their flagging spirits with a message of optimism and confidence.

"The general tendency is for a great number of people to look at matters in a somewhat pessimistic manner, focusing their vision on the dark side of things only," he said. "As the result of the general election of 1924 it was predicted by many that we would have unheard of prosperity, while others asserted things would go to 'pot.' Neither of these predictions have come quite true. The prosperity rays are of a rather pale hue—but, neither are the clouds as dark as some would have us believe. However, the general tendency among the majority of people seems to be reflected in a note of hope and expectancy for the future. Slowly but surely the pendulum is swinging back again from the extreme reaction which set in shortly following the war.

"The financial interests of the country seemingly concentrated at that time upon the demolition and destruction of unionism in our land. But in spite of their powerful attacks and regardless of the persistency of their efforts, labor is weathering the storm and is emerging out of the arena with their ideals more firmly imbedded and their principles more thoroughly accepted. But it has cost sacrifices, heartaches and hard work. . . .

"Our own Brotherhood as an important link in the labor movement shows great signs of progress.

"May each man of our craft recognize this fact and add their individual influence towards the establishment of a greater organization, which means greater benefits to the men and their families."

When the regular triennial convention met in Detroit, Michigan, beginning September 14, 1925, President Fljozdal was able to report considerable progress in eliminating company unions. Twenty-five roads had been infested with rival organizations or company unions sponsored by railroad managements. On thirteen of these roads, the Brotherhood had won a complete victory. On six roads it had won a partial victory, losing representation rights for some classes of employes but retaining them for other classes. On only six roads had the Brotherhood lost representation rights entirely. At least nine rival organizations, he reported, were active in soliciting membership among maintenance of way workers.

With respect to wages, Fljozdal said: "Insufficiency of our wages and the need of improvements therein was the fundamental cause in the establishment of our great Brotherhood and has been the reason for the many sacrifices made to maintain our Brotherhood. In the face of most bitter opposition . . . we have made progress.

"There remains much to be done toward bringing our wages to a just and reasonable level. Present rates do not permit us to maintain a proper standard of living and save something for sickness, unemployment, or old age.

"It must ever be the aim of our Brotherhood to strive cautiously, continuously, and energetically for a rate of pay that will place our craft and those dependent upon us in a position to enjoy more fully the better things of life.

"A wage that merely permits us to meet the day-to-day cost of necessities is not a living wage, not a just wage, not a reasonable wage—but is clearly an obsolete wage."

The financing of the Provident Department established at the 1919 convention had also become a matter of serious concern. It was evident that the department could no longer be continued on the current basis. The delegates voted to discontinue the payment of total disability claims and decided that a referendum vote of the membership should be taken to determine whether the Provident Department would be continued.

The action taken at the 1922 convention permitting the establishment of system federations through the combining of two or more individual systems, had brought about a strengthening of system organizations. Twenty-one system federations had been formed in the three-year period, Fljozdal reported.

In an effort to settle two of the Brotherhood's major jurisdictional disputes, the convention adopted a resolution providing that the Brotherhood would transfer to the standard organizations of the firemen and oilers and the clerks, respectively, shop laborers and stores department employes then represented by the Brotherhood, when these organizations were in a position to receive them by proper transfer. In conformity with this action, the convention shortened the name of the Brotherhood to the "Brotherhood of Maintenance of Way Employes."

The convention adopted a resolution approving greater cooperation with railway managements where it was possible; approved a concerted campaign by the standard railroad Brotherhoods to destroy company unions; endorsed the proposed Railway Labor Act; and condemned the Communist movement in the United States.

In three years, under the able administration of President Fljozdal, the Brotherhood had made a gradual recovery from the low point of the early 1920's. Although the problems of finances and reduced membership were still serious, the policies adopted to overcome these difficulties were beginning to bring favorable results. The re-election of Fljozdal as Grand President and of Milliman as Grand Secretary-Treasurer reflected the confidence of the delegates in the Brotherhood's new leaders.

It might be noted that the Brotherhood was fortunate in having the services of a competent attorney, George Brand, Sr., in its efforts to extricate itself from its difficulties. It was with his expert counsel and invaluable help that the organization had been able to pass successfully through this critical three-year period.

By referendum ballot following the convention, the membership voted to establish a new department to replace the Provident Department. This new department was to be known as the Death Benefit Department. Benefits payable at the death of a member in good standing ranged from $50.00 after 12 months' continuous membership to $500.00 after 72 months; except that members who had reached age 55 at date of joining or reinstatement could accumulate maximum benefits of only $150.00 after 36 months' continuous membership. Members granted withdrawal cards or unemployment cards could continue to maintain their standing in the Death Benefit Department by paying Grand Lodge dues. To finance the new department, Grand Lodge dues were increased from $6.00 to $10.00 a year, the additional $4.00 to be used to maintain the department.

One of the primary purposes, in the establishment of the Provident Department, in providing benefits on the basis of length of continuous membership, had been to encourage members to keep themselves in good standing. Undoubtedly this feature became an important factor in the maintenance of a stable membership. At the same time, this department was able to provide benefits which many of the lower-paid members could not or would not have obtained in any other way.

Late in 1925, the Brotherhood won another important battle in its fight against rival unions. When the management of the Chesapeake & Ohio Railway refused to recognize the purported right of the Order of Skilled Maintenance of Way Employes (formed by J. O. Raley in 1922) to represent certain classes of maintenance of way workers on that road, that organization submitted a representation dispute to the Labor Board. In its Decision No. 3977, rendered on December 2, 1925, the Board denied the claim of this rival organization.

Raley had resigned as president of this organization in 1923 and returned to his job on the railroad, and J. M. Hancock had been elected to succeed him. In 1925, Raley rejoined the Brotherhood and used his influence to bring the activities of this rival organization to an end. It was not until 1927, however, that the Raley organization finally disbanded.

As the year 1926 began, one of the prime objectives of the railroad labor organizations was to obtain the passage of the Railway Labor Act, introduced in Congress in 1924 as the Howell-Barkley Bill. Both labor and management were dissatisfied with the results achieved under Title III of the Transportation Act of 1920, and mutual agreement had crystallized on the need for a revision of the law.

Months had passed since the Labor Board had held hearings on the Brotherhood's request for wage increases, and still the Board had rendered no decision. "To now seven precious months have passed and still silence and more silence prevails," commented an editorial in the "Journal." "Ominous rumblings are heard—the discontent is getting more pronounced. The more radical elements within our Organization are finding food for propaganda and dissension. The faith in fair play and just consideration of those entrusted with the well-being of these Maintenance of Way men is severely shaken and well may they doubt that any relief will ever be forthcoming from the Labor Board . . . Its usefulness is near the zero mark with the thermometer still dropping, indicating, if possible, less consideration than ever . . . The only bright light on the horizon is the possibility of the enactment of the new Railroad Labor Act."

Opposition to the Howell-Barkley Bill had, however, arisen in Congress. President Coolidge suggested that the representatives of the railroads and the labor organizations try to reach an agreement on the principles involved. Subsequent negotiations between representatives of the railroads and the Brotherhoods resulted in a redrafted bill introduced in Congress in January, 1926, and finally enacted into law as the Railway Labor Act of 1926 in May.

The new law repealed Title III of the Transportation Act of 1920 and abolished the United States Railroad Labor Board. It established instead a Board of Mediation consisting of five members to mediate unsettled disputes at the request of either party or on the Board's own initiative, and provided for the arbitration of disputes by voluntary agreement. In the event any dispute threatened substantially to interrupt interstate commerce, the act authorized the appointment of an Emergency Board by the President of the United States to make an investigation and render its report to the President within 30 days after its creation.

The act emphasized the principle that it would be the duty of the carriers and their employes to make and maintain agreements covering wages and working conditions, and declared the right of the employes to organize and select their representatives "without interference, influence, or coercion exercised by either party over the self-organization or designation of representatives by the other."

"This law is the result of an agreement between the Standard Railroad Labor Organizations and a great majority of the Railway Managements," President Fljozdal said. "It is the first time in history that both sides appeared before Congress and agreed upon labor legislation. It can be made to serve the mutual interests of both sides if honestly and fairly applied, and that is the intention of the Brotherhood of Maintenance of Way Employes."

The railroad labor organizations placed great faith in the new act to bring relief from the oppressive conditions that had grown up under the administration of the Railroad Labor Board; and over a period of twenty-eight years the Act, as subsequently amended, has provided an important and effective means of settling collective-bargaining disputes on the railroads. But the Brotherhoods soon found that the Act of

The first of these was the failure of the language of the Act to place a complete ban on company unions, as the
1926 contained two major defects.
Brotherhoods had anticipated. The Act also provided for the establishment by agreement of Boards of Adjustment on a national, regional, or system basis to settle disputes arising out of existing agreements; but it contained no provision to enforce the obligation to create these boards. This proved to be another serious defect in the law.

The carriers had refused to agree to national adjustment boards and the employes objected to system boards. Where system boards were subsequently established, they proved to be ineffective. The Brotherhood adopted the policy of attempting to form regional boards of adjustment, which seemed to be the only compromise. The carriers, however, adhered to their policy of insisting on the establishment of a system board for each individual railroad, and eventually the situation became almost completely stalemated. Inasmuch as system boards were invariably made up of representatives of the railroad and the employes on a particular system, they could be little more effective than system conference committees. Thus the employes found that they were without an impartial tribunal to which unsettled grievances could be appealed for decision. Unsatisfactory compromises on grievances were the only solution in many instances.

The immediate problem before the Brotherhood following the passage of the Railway Labor Act was the long-overdue improvement of wage rates in the maintenance of way department. Before it ceased to exist, the Labor Board in Decision No. 4197, had remanded to the interested parties the wage disputes that had been pending before the Board for months. It became necessary, therefore, that these disputes be progressed under the new law, and General Chairmen on properties where disputes had been remanded by the Board's decision immediately reopened negotiations with their managements. On roads not covered by Decision No. 4197, requests were filed with the management for wage increases of approximately 5¢ an hour.

Maintenance of way workers held high hopes of obtaining fair play under the new law. Certain it is that they had displayed the utmost patience during the long unfruitful years of trying to obtain relief from the Labor Board. But the railroads continued to resist any movements to increase wages, and many railroad workers had not yet realized that a strong organization is the only sure method of obtaining improved conditions under any law or in any given set of circumstances.

The success of the railroad Brotherhoods in securing the passage of the Railway Labor Act emphasized the advantages of unified action, and in May, 1926, the chief executives of the railway labor organizations formed the Railway Labor Executives' Association "for the purpose of cooperative action to obtain and develop consistent interpretations and utilization of the Railway Labor Act, and for other purposes affecting the labor activities of the associated organizations." The chief executives of the Brotherhood have maintained continuous association with this organization since that time.

The heads of four of the five engine and train service organizations (the engineers, the firemen and enginemen, the conductors, the trainmen, and the switchmen), often called the "operating employes," later withdrew from the association: the Brotherhood of Railroad Trainmen in 1937, the Brotherhood of Locomotive Engineers in 1942, and both the Brotherhood of Locomotive Firemen and Enginemen and the Order of Railway Conductors in 1950. The Firemen and Enginemen re-affiliated with the R.L.E.A. effective January 1, 1955. With the exception of the Firemen and Enginemen and the Switchmen's Union of North America from the operating group of railroad Brotherhoods, the association is now composed of the chief executives of organizations in the "non-operating" [1] group.

Meanwhile, the Brotherhood had closed out another of the ventures of the Barker regime. The 1925 convention had instructed that a survey be made to determine the advisability of developing the site purchased at Columbia and Clifford Streets in Detroit for the erection of an office building. An investigation revealed that the erection of the proposed building would not be feasible, and the property was sold. The Brotherhood suffered a net loss in this transaction of more than $153,000.00.

By this time, another serious problem which has since become of deep concern to both the railroads and their employes had arisen. The post-war years witnessed a substantial increase in the number of highway buses and trucks in use, and on July 27, 1926, the Interstate Commerce Commission began an investigation "into and concerning the opera-

---

[1] Non-operating employes may be defined as those not engaged in the actual operation of trains: maintenance of way employes, clerks, shop employes, signalmen, telegraphers, etc.

In 1955 the following organizations were affiliated with the Railway Labor Executives' Association:

- Brotherhood of Locomotive Firemen and Enginemen
- Switchmen's Union of North America
- Order of Railroad Telegraphers
- American Train Dispatchers' Association
- Railway Employes' Department, A. F. of L.
- International Association of Machinists
- International Brotherhood of Boilermakers, Iron Ship Builders, Blacksmiths, Forgers and Helpers
- Sheet Metal Workers' International Association
- International Brotherhood of Electrical Workers
- Brotherhood Railway Carmen of America
- International Brotherhood of Firemen & Oilers
- Brotherhood of Railroad Signalmen of America
- Brotherhood of Railway and Steamship Clerks, Freight Handlers, Express and Station Employes
- Brotherhood of Maintenance of Way Employes
- National Organization Masters, Mates & Pilots of America
- International Longshoremen's Association
- National Marine Engineers' Beneficial Association
- Hotel & Restaurant Employes and Bartenders International Union
- Railroad Yardmasters of America
- Brotherhood of Sleeping Car Porters

tion of motor buses and motor trucks by or in connection or competition with common carriers subject to the Interstate Commerce Act." Thus began the history of one of the various forms of competing transportation, subsidized either directly or indirectly from public funds, that have gradually whittled away much of the railroads' most lucrative passenger and freight business and have caused the abolishment of the jobs of many railroad workers.

The advantageous position reached by highway truck lines in the transportation field has been due to their being permitted to use roads and highways built and maintained at public expense. The railroads, on the other hand, built their own right of ways and maintain them without public subsidy. Much has been said about the land grants to the railroads by the Federal government in the early days of railroad construction; but statistics show that the free transportation they were required to furnish to the government as a result of these land grants far exceeded the original value of the grants. Another competitive advantage enjoyed by highway truckers is their ability to pick and choose the cream of freight traffic. Thus the railroads, transporting all types of freight as a true common carrier, receive on the average far less revenue than do truck lines for each ton of freight hauled.

The extent to which competing forms of transportation have encroached on the business of the railroads since 1930 is shown by the following table from the "Yearbook of Railroad Information—1954 Edition":

DISTRIBUTION OF COMMERCIAL TRAFFIC IN THE UNITED STATES*

	1953d	% of Total 1953d	1944	% of Total 1944	1940	% of Total 1940	1930	% of Total 1930
MILLIONS OF FREIGHT TON-MILES								
Steam Railroads a	614,000	52.5	745,573	69.4	378,352	62.0	388,500	75.0
Great Lakes b	115,000	9.8	105,620	9.8	87,593	14.3	71,000	13.7
Rivers and Canals	70,000	6.0	31,385	2.9	22,412	3.7	9,087	1.8
Motor Trucks	200,000	17.1	58,047	5.4	62,007	10.2	20,345	3.9
Oil Pipe Lines	170,000	14.5	132,864	12.4	59,277	9.7	27,900	5.4
Electric Railroads	1,000	0.1	1,339	0.1	849	0.1	1,148	0.2
Airlines	450	—	71	—	14	—	4	—
Total	1,170,450	100.0	1,074,899	100.0	610,504	100.0	517,984	100.0
MILLIONS OF PASSENGER MILES								
Steam Railroads	31,800	45.9	95,663	74.2	23,816	64.5	26,876	68.5
Electric Interurban	650	0.9	2,042	1.6	950	2.6	2,400	6.1
Inland Waterways c	1,500	2.2	2,187	1.7	1,317	3.6	2,800	7.2
Buses	20,500	29.6	26,920	20.8	9,800	26.5	7,080	18.0
Airlines	14,800	21.4	2,178	1.7	1,052	2.8	73	0.2
Total	69,250	100.0	128,990	100.0	36,935	100.0	39,229	100.0

* Includes intercity freight traffic by private as well as contract and common carriers, except coastwise and intercoastal traffic. a—Includes Mail and Express. b—U.S. domestic traffic only. c—Includes Great Lakes. d—Estimated by Association of American Railroads.

Source: Interstate Commerce Commission; Public Roads Administration; Office of Chief of Engineers, U.S. Army; Civil Aeronautics Board; and others.

By the latter part of 1926, the movement to obtain higher wage rates had been successful on various roads in the United States. In Canada, a new schedule effective January 16, 1927, granted wage increases approximating 2¢ and 3¢ an hour to all classes of maintenance of way workers.

The movement to obtain higher wages continued into 1927, and early in the year the Brotherhood won a gratifying vote of confidence from maintenance of way workers on the Boston & Maine Railroad. At a wage conference, the management had questioned the authority of the committee to represent the men. A secret ballot issued by the carrier was tabulated by representatives of the company and the Brotherhood on March 1, 1927. Ninety-eight per cent of the men voted for the Brotherhood over a company union.

Wage negotiations begun in 1926 under the Railway Labor Act had now reached the final stage on several roads. On May 16, 1927, the Brotherhood's first arbitration proceedings under the new law began at Louisville, Kentucky, on the request of maintenance of way employes of the Louisville & Nashville Railroad for a wage increase. The hourly rates of track laborers on that road ranged from 26¢ to 38¢ an hour and averaged 30.52¢.

Vice President T. C. Carroll, later to become President of the Brotherhood, served as the employes' representative on the Arbitration Board. A number of maintenance of way workers and the wives of some workers testified before the Board as to the substandard conditions under which they lived because of the low wages paid by the company.

The majority report of the Board, rendered after several weeks of testimony, granted an increase of $6.00 a month to foremen and from 1¢ to 3¢ an hour to other classes. In an opinion accompanying the award, Carroll said that he had concurred with the public member of the Board in this wholly inadequate award with great reluctance as the only means of securing some measure of relief for the workers.

Similar arbitration proceedings on the Chicago & Northwestern System began on July 8, 1927, before a six-man board which rendered a wage-increase award on August 15.

The struggle of the railroad Brotherhoods against company unions received substantial legal support when a Federal judge in Texas ordered the Texas & New Orleans Railroad Company to refrain from having "their officers, servants and agents" attempt to dictate to their clerical forces the form of organization they should have.

The adverse effects of the activities of company unions and rival organizations, and the demoralization that had infected the membership in 1921 and 1922, had not yet been fully overcome. Nevertheless, the membership had become impregnated with a stability that reflected the patient optimism and soundness of Fljozdal's policies. He well knew that the maintaining of a sound organization on each system was a prime requisite in building for the future. In the face of opposition from some quarters, he insisted that Grand Lodge lend financial assistance to system divisions that had become moribund until they could be rehabilitated. The wisdom of this policy during these critical years became more and more apparent as time passed.

The dangers of disorganization were being forcibly impressed on maintenance of way workers by the reaction of the management on roads where the membership had fallen to a dangerously low point. Representatives of the Brotherhood had been withdrawn from one southeastern road because of lack of membership. In the early part of 1927, a roadmaster on that system issued instructions ordering a 5¢-an-hour wage cut for track laborers. The men had said they could not afford to pay dues; but the wage cut amounted to approximately seven times the quarterly dues they would have paid to the Brotherhood for protection against just such a contingency.

The November, 1927, issue of the "Journal" editorially flayed the continued efforts of some railroad managements to establish company unions under the Railway Labor Act of 1926. "That the employes have consistently lived up to the letter and spirit of the Act cannot be denied," the "Journal" said. "That some railroads have flagrantly violated both is also a fact.

"The principal underlying cause for the existence of a 'Company Union' on any railroad, where the employes already have a voluntary organization of their own, is the desire of the management to prevent wage increases and check any expression of independence in the breasts of the men concerned. Such actions, which includes coercion and intimidation will never result in harmonious relations between employes and employers."

To settle a representation dispute in Canada with the Order of Railroad Telegraphers, the Brotherhood relinquished the right, effective December 1, 1927, to represent towermen or levermen operating switches or signals at railroad intersections.

Although nothing of a spectacular nature had been achieved by the Brotherhood during 1927, the year had been a period of steady accomplishment. "In looking back over the twelve months ending November 1," President Fljozdal said in December, 1927, "we can truly say that it has been a year of progress and advancement for our organization. . . . This period has seen more money added to the wages of our men than in any other year since the issuance of Decision No. 2 by the United States Railroad Labor Board in 1921."

When the twenty-third regular convention met in Detroit, Michigan, beginning September 10, 1928, it was apparent that the Brotherhood had reached a comparative state of maturity and had established a plateau of stability from which to carry on its future activities. The total paid-up membership had changed little since the 1925 convention. During the three-year period, almost 100,000 new or delinquent members had been enrolled, but this potential gain had been canceled by an approximately equal number of members who became delinquent.

"I have repeatedly pointed out," Secretary-Treasurer Milliman said in his report to the convention, "that we cannot expect to make very material net gains in our membership strength until we can devise ways and means of reducing our membership turnover. . . . We experienced a turnover of over 150 per cent during the last three year period."

He emphasized, however, that during the last fiscal year the number of new and reinstated members had substantially exceeded the number who had become delinquent, a trend that if continued would aid materially in increasing the strength of the Brotherhood. One of the more serious factors contributing to the heavy turnover in membership was the instability of employment in the maintenance of way department. The Brotherhood's membership records reflected the heavy turnover in the railroads' labor force resulting from their general policy of reducing forces during the winter and increasing them during the summer. Many workers went from job to job as forces were reduced or increased.

In a detailed report to the convention, President Fljozdal outlined many of the problems and the accomplishments of the Brotherhood. Of fifteen rival organizations in the field since 1921, six were still active: The Canadian Brotherhood of Railway Employes, the Brotherhood of Railroad Bridge and Building Mechanics and Helpers, the United Railway Track Laborers' Association, the American Federation of Railway Workers, the Pennsylvania System Fraternity, and the Track Foremen's Association of America (established on the New York, New Haven & Hartford Railroad before the Brotherhood started organizing the men on that system).

Of twenty-nine company unions formed since 1921, nineteen still remained in existence. Where the records were complete, they indicated, Fljozdal pointed out, that railroad managements had taken an active part in promoting and establishing company unions. In one instance, a carrier failed to act in good faith under the Railway Labor Act and delayed a wage increase request for two years. When the employes became thoroughly disheartened, the carrier sent its officials over the road to enroll the men in a company union. It was found, too, that former representatives of the Brotherhood had been actively engaged in supporting three of the twenty-nine company unions and eight of the fifteen rival organizations.

In trying to regain representation rights on systems where company unions had been established, Fljozdal found himself in much the same predicament that confronted John T. Wilson in his attempts to gain recognition for the Brotherhood some thirty or forty years before, with this difference: In the early days, railroad managements had been openly hostile to the organization; now they tried to hide their opposition behind the pseudo-respectability of company unions. Moreover, fear on the part of the men of reprisals by the company and their general inertia toward change were difficult obstacles to overcome.

Numerous jurisdictional disputes had been handled by the Brotherhood, the report outlined, many of them involving controversies with the firemen and oilers over the representation of shop laborers. Other disputes had been handled with certain shop craft organizations, the telegraphers, the signalmen, and the carpenters and joiners.

One of the major objectives of the Fljozdal administration had been to secure the time and one-half rate for work performed on Sundays and holidays and after the eighth hour of service. Fljozdal reported that 162 railroad units grouped under 69 major systems in the United States were then paying the penalty rate for Sunday and holiday work. In refusing to pay the penalty rate after eight hours' work, the railroads were discriminating against maintenance of way workers, he asserted. Practically all other groups of railroad workers in the United States then enjoyed this condition of employment. Canadian maintenance of way workers, however, were more fortunate. They received the time and one-half rate both for work performed on Sundays and holidays and after eight hours.

Since the 1925 convention, Fljozdal reported, the Brotherhood had secured wage increases on practically the entire railroad mileage in Canada and on 104 railroads in the United States. The following selected figures from a detailed wage analysis showed the modest but continued upward trend in earnings in the United States:

	Average Earnings	
	October, 1922	*October, 1927*
Bridge and building foremen	$163.00 per mo.	$174.00 per mo.
Section foremen	118.00 per mo.	129.00 per mo.
Bridge and building carpenters	.568 per hr.	.621 per hr.
Section men	.329 per hr.	.359 per hr.

The convention voted to return to the practice of issuing serially-numbered dues receipts in place of the dues stamps used since the 1922 convention. It adopted resolutions approving the principle of the five-day week with no reduction in pay, requesting that a movement be started to obtain time and one-half pay after eight hours' work, and condemning company unions and the use of court injunctions in labor disputes.

Reductions in force and the lengthening of sections had become perennial problems. The convention directed the Grand President to take the necessary steps to try to secure legislation regulating the length of sections and the number of men to be employed in a gang. (Later attempts at various times to secure this legislation both nationally and on a state level proved unsuccessful).

The delegates unanimously re-elected President Fljozdal and Secretary-Treasurer Milliman.

The convention had decided that future movements for wage increases and rules revisions should be handled on a regional basis in an effort to establish more uniform wages and working conditions. At a meeting in Chicago, Illinois, in November, 1928, an International Association of Grand Lodge and System Officers and Regional Associations of System Officers were formed. Although associations of this kind had functioned in the past, the constitution now officially sanctioned their creation.

The Regional Associations elected a National Committee of twelve members, three from each of four regions in the United States (northwestern, northeastern, southwestern, and southeastern), and instructed the committee to meet to consider future policies toward the unification of rules and to make recommendations to the Regional Associations on various issues as they developed.

The fifth region comprised all the railways in Canada, the Central Committee in Canada corresponding to the Regional Associations in the United States. Members of the Central Committee are system officers from railways in Canada. The President of the Brotherhood assigns a Vice President to assist the Committee. The Central Committee negotiates with the railways in Canada on a national level agreements covering wages and working conditions (a national agreement has been in effect on Canadian railways since 1919), and renders official interpretations on the rules of such agreements.

Meantime, a record number of voters had cast their ballots in the 1928 election, and the Republican nominee, Herbert

Hoover, had been elected President of the United States over his Democratic opponent, Governor Alfred E. Smith of New York. The Republicans had been continued in power principally on the strength of an unprecedented business prosperity that had followed the recession of the early 1920's. The net railway operating income of Class I railroads in the United States, for example, climbed from $600 million in 1921 to $1.2 billion (approximately double) in 1929.

Wage earners, however, did not share fully in this prosperity. Millions of workers were earning far less than the minimum standard set up by the Federal Bureau of Labor Statistics as necessary to maintain the average family in health and comfort. In this period of phenomenal business success, the average straight-time hourly earnings of maintenance of way workers on Class I railroads in the United States increased from 39.5¢ in 1922 to only 41.9¢ in 1929. They earned an average of $996.39 in 1922 and $1,062.73 in 1929. The earnings of maintenance of way workers in the lower-paid groups were well below this average figure. A decrease in the cost of living from the high point reached in 1920 had, however, furnished some relief from the standpoint of real wages.

As the year 1928 closed, business counted its swollen profits. The sobering voices of the few who counseled restraint and a curtailment of the unprecedented stock market speculation, were lost in the din of prophecies that reflected glowing optimism, and there was little indication of the financial catastrophe to follow. It was clear to many then as it is now, however, that a prosperity founded on the false principle of large profits and financial inflation, which ignores the inadequacy of the purchasing power of the worker and the consumer, cannot last.

Eleven months later and during the years of the severe depression of the 1930's, this economic truth was impressed upon the nation with a forcefulness that should not soon be forgotten. For the time being, however, the nation's economic ship continued to sail the treacherous seas of high business profits, over-expanded credit, a seriously high rate of unemployment, inadequate income for wage earners and farmers, and wild financial speculation.

After more than two years of operation under the Railway Labor Act, the National Railroad Mediation Board frankly admitted that the refusal of the carriers to agree to the establishment of national or regional boards of adjustment to decide unsettled grievances had practically nullified an important feature of the act. The need for adequate boards of adjustment was one of the important issues discussed at a meeting of the Railway Labor Executives' Association in early February, 1929.

A plan to foster greater cooperation between railway managements and the Brotherhood had long been on the organization's agenda. The first step toward this goal took place in Canada when the Canadian National Railways accepted President Fljozdal's offer of a cooperative agreement. This agreement was patterned after a similar understanding, in effect since 1925, between the railway and its shopmen. In recognition of the mutuality of interests between employer and employe, representatives of the Brotherhood and the railway agreed to accept each other's help in the solution of the problems of each and the furtherance of their legitimate aims and tasks.

This arrangement implied full cooperation by the Brotherhood with the management in maintaining the safety of its right of way and structures and the improvement of its transportation service to the public. At the conferences, such important subjects as stabilization of employment, first aid, safety first, fire protection, and education were discussed.

To conform with the policy adopted by the 1928 convention and the action taken by the International Association and the Regional Associations, on March 25, 1929, the General Chairmen in each region in the United States made request on their respective managements for a general and uniform revision of rules, including time and one-half after eight hours of service.

In early April, the Railway Labor Executives' Association decided on a program to amend the Railway Labor Act to provide means for definitely enforcing the right of employes to bargain collectively with the railroads through representatives of their own choice, to require the creation of adjustment boards to decide grievances, and to strengthen other weaknesses in the act of a less major nature that had become apparent since its passage. The Association also took action toward protecting the interests of employes in the consolidation of railroads (which was being advocated in some quarters), and to bring about the stabilization of the employment of railroad workers.

By early summer, movements in the United States to obtain improved rules governing working conditions and an increase in pay were well under way. In Canada, direct negotiations between the Central Committee and the Railway Association of Canada resulted in a general wage increase for all classes of maintenance of way workers. The increases, ranging from 1¢ to 5¢ an hour, and probably averaging about 3¢ an hour for all employes, became effective June 1, 1929. Rules changes agreed upon earlier in the year granted section and bridge and building foremen in Canada full pay for holidays and gave monthly-rated employes two weeks' leave of absence annually with pay after four years' service.

And at last the railway labor organizations were beginning to win out in their long fight against company unions. In unmistakable language, a United States Circuit Court of Appeals sustained the injunction granted by a Federal judge in Texas outlawing the company union of railway clerks on the Texas & New Orleans Railroad.

As the fall of 1929 approached, agreements had been reached on various roads in the United States granting increases in wages and the time and one-half rate after eight hours' work. But progress had not been favorable on all roads. Effective at 8:00 p.m., November 13, 1929, the Brotherhood joined with other railroad labor organizations in calling a strike on the Toledo, Peoria & Western Railway because of the failure of the carrier to meet with the representatives of the employes on requested wage increases, revisions of rules agreements, and pending grievances. The adamant attitude of the management in refusing to negotiate with the committees representing the employes had existed since 1925.

By this time, the highly-inflated bubble of the nation's economy had burst. On October 24, 1929, and again on October 29, the stock market crashed with staggering losses to speculators and investors. By November 13, the debacle was complete, and in the wake of this colossal financial liquidation the nation began the descent into the abyss of the great business depression of the 1930's.

CHAPTER VI

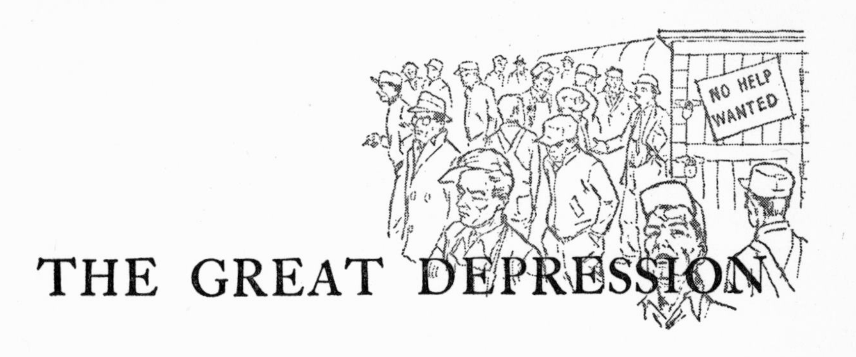

THE GREAT DEPRESSION

ONE of the most serious of the nation's mistakes during the early months of the depression was the failure to recognize that the stock market crash was a symptom of economic disease and not an isolated incident. On all sides, optimistic and complacent prophecies promised an early financial recovery and a return of continuing prosperity. Few persons saw the dismal years ahead.

By the end of 1930, however, the seriousness of the economic situation, both in the United States and in Canada, had become acutely apparent. The net railway operating income of Class I railroads in the United States had dropped from an all-time high of $1.2 billion in 1929 to $868 million in 1930, the smallest since 1922. Freight business was at the lowest point in eight years, and passenger business was less than at any time since 1906.

This sharp drop in railroad income reflected itself in drastic force reductions by the carriers. The average number of maintenance of way employes in railroad service dropped more than 60,000 from 1929 to 1930 (and more than 200,000, approximately one-half, from 1929 to 1933, when the low point of the depression was reached). The Brotherhood had enrolled 23,000 new members in 1929 and had the largest membership in years. Its goal of a further substantial increase in membership, however, became a lost hope as the railroads slashed their forces.

Railroad workers viewed, too, with some apprehension the agitation that had arisen to effect economies in the railroad industry by consolidating systems and facilities, particularly the disastrous effect this would have on an already heavy loss of jobs through force reductions.

The American Federation of Labor estimated that the income of workers in the United States had declined by more than $6 billion during 1930, that in excess of 5 million wage earners were without employment at the end of the year, and that millions of other workers had only part-time employment.

The unemployment situation had become a grave problem in Canada also, in spite of the fact that relief work totaling more than $50 million had been approved by the Minister of Labour acting in accordance with the program adopted by a special session of Parliament.

Faced with this critical business decline, any plans of the railroad labor organizations for improving the conditions of their members had of necessity to be postponed. As the economic structure of the nation crumbled, the program of labor unions became one of preserving jobs and rates of pay rather than improving job conditions.

Early in 1930, President Hoover conferred a distinct honor on President Fljozdal in appointing him as one of a five-member Good Will Commission to represent the United States at the celebration of the 1000th anniversary of the Althing (or parliament) of Iceland, the oldest democratic institution of its kind on record, which was held in the summer.

The strike on the Toledo, Peoria & Western Railroad was terminated by an agreement signed with the carrier by the cooperating Brotherhoods on July 25, 1930. Every effort of the unions, including the services of a government mediator, had failed to bring about an acceptable settlement. It had become apparent that a continuation of the strike would not influence or compel a settlement. Little of a tangible nature was obtained in the agreement settling the strike beyond provisions governing the re-employment of strikers by the company, although the company did agree that "the principle of making contracts with the representatives of the majority of the employes in service in a given class shall be regarded as the sound basis for collective bargaining."

The annual meeting of Grand Lodge and system officers, held in November, 1930, gave serious consideration to the problems confronting railroad workers because of heavy force reductions. And for three days during December, members of the Railway Labor Executives' Association met to discuss every phase of the unemployment situation. The Association unanimously adopted a joint program calling for a shorter work-day, a shorter work-week, both without reduction in pay, and relief from instability of employment on the railroads.

The Association also recognized the inroads being made on railroad employment by competing forms of transportation, and approved a program to bring about greater regulation of highway buses and trucks, pipe lines, and waterways to eliminate unfair competition with the railroad industry.

The business recession continued on into 1931, and by the end of the year almost 8 million persons were unemployed in the United States. The net railway operating income of Class I railroads in the United States shrank still further from $868 million in 1930 to $525 million in 1931. The number of railroad workers who had thus far lost their jobs exceeded 400,000.

Old-age benefits, unemployment insurance, and a reduction in the work week without a reduction in pay were being strongly advocated as a necessary means of checking the debilitating effects of the depression. President Green of the American Federation of Labor urged the inauguration of a shorter work week and requested that President Hoover call a national industrial conference to seek a remedy for the unemployment crisis. Labor insisted that only an increase in purchasing power could check the economic chaos, and pledged itself to resist all attempts to reduce wages.

When, therefore, the 24th regular convention of Grand Lodge met in Toronto, Ontario, Canada, beginning September 14, 1931, a broad outline of the problems facing the Brotherhood and its membership had already been etched on the agenda of the convention by the necessities of the economic reverses in both the United States and Canada.

"It is only stating a well-known fact when we say that the United States and Canada are now facing a severe business depression," President Fljozdal told the delegates. "In the latter months of 1929, following the historical stock market crash, the economic conditions of our two countries became upset and we are now in the throes of a world-wide depression.

"More than six million workers were idle in the United States during the past summer and millions more were working only part time. Similar unemployment conditions prevail in Canada. Banks have closed at an alarming rate, factories have closed or reduced operations, charitable resources have been overtaxed, employers, workers and farmers have suffered serious setbacks, and our captains of industry have appeared unable to meet and adjust conditions.

". . . We still have our farm lands, our factories, our railroads, our natural wealth, our working population, our same needs and desires—and yet unemployment and suffering is general. Wise men discuss existing problems, scholarly orations are made, the wage-earner is overwhelmed with sympathy for today and with promises for tomorrow, but conditions remain bad.

"Regardless of all the mass of reasons, excuses and pretended solutions presented during the past two years, our Brotherhood takes the stand that . . . a more equal division and distribution of the products of industry must be conceded before permanent economic security can be enjoyed."

The convention adopted a resolution denouncing the tendency of employers in the United States and Canada to cut wages and urging vigorous resistance to any attempt of railway managements to reduce the already inadequate wages of maintenance of way workers.

It also adopted a resolution favoring a five-day week with no reduction in pay from the six-day basis, took action favoring a Federal old-age pension law, pledged itself to renewed activity in placing men in state and national legislative bodies who are friendly to labor, declared itself in favor of greater stability of employment and union-management cooperation, and condemned company unions. It also went on record as favoring a more reasonable regulation and taxation of motor buses and trucks to place them on a fairer competitive basis with the railroad industry.

Before the severity of the depression halted the movement, Fljozdal reported, the Brotherhood had been able to obtain the time and one-half rate after eight hours' work on 28 Class I roads in the United States, with a mileage of 48,557 (20 per cent of the total Class I mileage in the United States), and on two Class II roads and one switching and terminal company. Practically all roads in Canada then paid the penalty rate after eight hours of service; thus the Brotherhood had obtained this concession on a total of 85,858 miles of line in the two countries.

In spite of the depression, the Brotherhood had been able to secure wage increases on 55 roads since the 1928 convention for a part or all of the classes represented, he said. It is obvious, however, that these increases were obtained before the carriers had felt the full force of the depression.

Strangely enough, the membership of the Brotherhood had increased by approximately 2,800 since the 1928 convention in spite of the heavy force reductions made by the railroads. This was a strong indication that maintenance of way workers felt the need for the protection of the organization during the critical years of the depression.

The convention re-elected President Fljozdal and Secretary-Treasurer Milliman unanimously.

In view of the declining revenues of the carriers, it was inevitable that sooner or later they would seek a further reduction in expenses in addition to the retrenchment that had already been made through force reductions. Late in 1931, the railroads in the United States opened informal negotiations with the chief executives of the railroad Brotherhoods on the carriers' proposal for a 15 per cent wage cut.

The Grand Lodge officers and General Chairmen of the Brotherhood met in Chicago on December 9, 1931, to discuss the situation. It is estimated that 2,000 men attended, the largest gathering of the representatives of railroad workers that had ever been held in this country. It was clearly evident that a crisis in the affairs of the railroads and their employes had been reached, and the Brotherhoods authorized their chief executives to negotiate to a conclusion with a committee representing the railroads the issues of unemployment and wages.

Formal conferences between nine railroad presidents and the chiefs of the railroad Brotherhoods began on January 14, 1932. The carriers' request for a 15 per cent reduction in wages was withdrawn when the committees reached an agreement that effective February 1, 1932, and continuing until January 31, 1933, 10 per cent would be deducted from the pay check of each employe. Basic wage rates were not to be affected, and the railroads agreed to make an earnest and sympathetic effort to maintain and increase railroad employment.

The unions agreed to this wage deduction because of the seriousness of economic conditions in the nation and with the hope that their action would help to relieve the critical distress of unemployment on the railroads. As the nation continued to slide deeper into the depression, however, little was done by the railroads toward increasing employment.

A rather dramatic sidelight to these negotiations occurred several weeks before the formal conferences began. Earlier in the year, the Chicago & Northwestern Railroad had notified its assistant foremen and trackmen that their wages would be reduced 10 per cent. The Brotherhood protested this action. When mediation failed, the organization agreed to arbitrate but the railroad company refused and put the reduction in effect December 7, 1931.

On the day before Christmas, President Fljozdal and President Fred W. Sargent of the C. & N. W. met across the conference table, and Fljozdal pleaded with the latter to rescind this action. As a result of this personal plea, President Sargent recalled the wage reduction order that had gone into effect on December 7.

One very important outgrowth of the 1932 wage-deduction negotiations was the establishment of a pattern of national handling which has been followed since that time in general movements concerning wages and working conditions affecting all carriers.

The depression continued unabated through 1932. The decline in living costs as business stagnated was more than offset by wage cuts and part-time employment. The number of unemployed persons in the United States had increased to more than 12 million by the end of 1932, and approximately 188,000 maintenance of way workers had lost their jobs. But mere statistics do not reveal the whole picture. The short work-week had become prevalent and thousands of maintenance of way workers had only two, three, or four days of work each week. Their earnings were hardly above the level of destitution.

Thus far little of a direct nature had been done by the Federal government to relieve the dire situation among unemployed and partially-employed workers.

Conditions had become critical in Canada, too, and on March 5, 1932, the Railway Association of Canada served notice on the Central Committee of the Brotherhood of the wish of the railways to reduce wages by 10 per cent. On April 8, 1932, an agreement was reached that beginning May 1, 1932, a 10 per cent deduction would be made from the wages of Canadian maintenance of way workers. The agreement was to remain in effect until April 30, 1933, and continue thereafter subject to change on thirty days' notice. The other railway labor organizations in Canada had previously agreed to a similar deduction from wages.

Old-age benefits had been advocated as one of the means of easing the effects of the depression, and early in 1932 a bill to provide a retirement system for railroad workers, sponsored by the twenty-one standard railroad labor organizations, was introduced in Congress. Sentiment in favor of social insurance plans had not as yet crystallized sufficiently, however, and the necessary support for the bill could not be mustered.

The railroad labor organizations were also vitally interested in a bill pending in Congress to regulate bus and truck traffic. "The 21 Standard Railroad Labor Organizations are pledged, by convention action, to support legislation for the regulation of bus and truck transportation in all forms," said a joint statement issued by the Brotherhoods.

"As railroad employes, having had years of experience, we are convinced that the railroads of the country can give service equal to that furnished by any other form of transportation . . . if the other forms of transportation are regulated to the same degree as are the railroads. . . . We know of no reason why forms of transportation competing with the railroad should not be regulated in the same manner."

On June 22, 1932, the Railway Labor Executives' Association issued an appeal to Congress not to adjourn in July, as was contemplated. "Adequate measures to relieve destitution, to increase employment and to safeguard the future have not been enacted and cannot be developed to meet the grave emergencies of the next few months unless Congress stays on the job," the Association said. But the important November elections were in the offing, and in spite of the unprecedented economic crisis in which the nation was then enveloped, Congress adjourned on July 16 until December 5, 1932.

Meanwhile, the financial condition of the railroads grew steadily worse. The net railway operating income of Class I carriers in the United States declined from $525 million in 1931 to $326 million in 1932. (The term "net railway operating income" refers only to income from operations. Many carriers suffered deficits during the depression years after deductions for fixed charges and other non-operating expenses were made.) As the carriers sought to retrench, they continued their heavy force reductions. More than 600,000 railroad workers had now lost their jobs.

In addition, as the year waned the carriers sought conferences with the chief executives of the railroad Brotherhoods on a 20 per cent reduction in basic wage rates which the railroads proposed to put into effect. On December 21, 1932, conference committees representing the railroads and the Brotherhoods agreed that the 10 per cent deduction from pay checks scheduled to expire January 31, 1933, would be extended until October 31, 1933, and that neither party could serve notice of a desire to change this agreement until June 15, 1933. Basic wage rates were to remain unchanged, and the carriers withdrew their demand for a wage reduction.

By this time, the 1932 election had become history and the Democratic nominee, Franklin D. Roosevelt, had been elected President of the United States by a plurality of more than 7 million votes.

The high point in unemployment was eventually reached in the spring of 1933, when about 13 million persons were without jobs. The average number of maintenance of way workers in railroad service on Class I railroads in the United States during 1933 was only 199,000 compared to 405,000 in 1929. For the first time since 1929, however, the net railway operating revenue of Class I railroads showed an upward trend, increasing to $474 million during 1933, due to the heavy reductions in expenses made by the carriers.

Meantime, railroad managements were casting about for still other ways to reduce expenses. On at least three railroads in the early part of the year, officials asked their employes to donate ten days' pay, five days in each of two successive months. This attempt, however, was soon abandoned.

On June 15, 1933, the carriers in the United States served notice on their employes for a 22½ per cent reduction in wages to become effective November 1, 1933, when the 10 per cent deduction from pay checks expired. In conferences on June 21, 1933, an agreement was reached to extend the 10 per cent deduction for another eight months until June 30, 1934.

Conditions had also grown worse in Canada, and on June 13, 1933, the Railway Association of Canada served notice of their wish to make a further reduction in the compensation of maintenance of way workers. Certain railway crafts in Canada had already been forced to accept a 20 per cent deduction, and a Conciliation Board hearing a similar case had unanimously recommended a 15 per cent deduction for still other classes. For five months, representatives of the Brotherhood in Canada opposed this further reduction in pay, but on November 17, 1933, a tentative agreement, later ratified by the membership, was entered into providing for a 15 per cent deduction from wages effective December 1, 1933, and continuing until November 30, 1934; this deduction to be reduced to 10 per cent on December 1, 1934.

The voters in the United States had rejected the Republican administration in November, 1932, chiefly because of its failure to do more to relieve the depressed economic conditions. Between that time and March, 1933, when President Roosevelt assumed office, the nation's banking system collapsed. An epidemic of bank closings impounded funds of the Brotherhood throughout the country. Banks in Detroit, Michigan, were among the first to close their doors, and Grand Lodge faced a difficult problem in trying to meet its running expenses. Promptly upon assuming office, President Roosevelt declared a bank holiday and set in motion sweeping financial and economic reforms designed to bring the nation out of the doldrums of the depression.

Motor, water, and air lines had become serious competitors of the railroads even before the stock market crash of 1929. From 1929 to 1933 the freight business of motor carriers doubled. At the same time, the revenue of the railroads in the United States from freight and passenger traffic was cut in half. The loss of business because of the depression combined with the inroads of its competitors was more than the railroad industry could stand. Many lines were thrown into bankruptcy.

On June 16, 1933, President Roosevelt signed the Emergency Railroad Transportation Act, establishing a Federal Coordinator of Transportation to guide the carriers through the difficult process of reorganization and rehabilitation. The Railway Labor Executives' Association succeeded in having provisions included in the law protecting the interests of workers in the consolidation of railroad systems or facilities.

The Act also gave substantial help to the Brotherhoods in their fight against company unions. On September 7, 1933, Joseph B. Eastman, Federal Coordinator of Transportation, notified railroad managements that certain acts of the railroads pertaining to labor organizations representing their employes were illegal under the Act. With his notice he enclosed a questionnaire concerning company unions to be filled out and returned. As a result, several railroads soon abandoned company unions on their lines.

Meanwhile, the National Industrial Recovery Act (popularly called the NRA) had been passed by Congress in June, 1933, to stimulate recovery from the depression. Coordinator Eastman suggested that the railroads, who were not covered by the Act, voluntarily raise the wages of their lower-paid employes at least to the standards set by NRA.

"To my way of thinking, Mr. Eastman's [suggestion] is very timely," President Fljozdal commented. "It is to be hoped the railroads will give it the consideration it merits.

"Surely railroads are not doing their part in the recovery program when they work employes seven days a week while literally hundreds of men in the same departments are laid off and begging for work. Or when they pay as low as 10 and 12½ cents an hour for some of their track labor.

"That latter statement seems unbelievable, but it is true. These conditions exist on many roads where the men are not under contract. Furthermore, some companies use these low-paid men to replace men who are members of craft organizations and entitled to schedule rates of pay. So far as maintenance of way men are concerned, this is done by laying off the higher paid men and doing the work with 'extra gang' laborers at disgraceful wages."

There is little evidence that the carriers attempted to comply with the wage standards of NRA. Two years later (May 27, 1935) the United States Supreme Court declared the NRA unconstitutional.

The fortunes of maintenance of way workers reached their lowest ebb during 1933. Hours worked by these employes on Class I railroads in the United States decreased from 956 million in 1929 to about 374 million in 1933, a reduction of some 582 million hours. At the same time, their total earnings fell from $430 million in 1929 to $163 million in 1933, a difference of $267 million. On December 13, 1933, President Fljozdal sent a telegram to President Roosevelt appealing to him for aid in relieving distressing conditions and reading in part:

"As executive head of the Brotherhood of Maintenance of Way Employes, I am being overwhelmed with protests from these railway workers regarding continued force reduction and further decreases in weekly work periods. . . . Many receive five and six dollars per week or less and relief from public welfare agencies is being denied on grounds that they are employed men. . . . With more than a billion dollars of deferred maintenance of way work and money available at reasonable interest rates for the performance of this work we insist there is no justification for the starvation employment levels being imposed upon the railway employes in our department. . . . Immediate relief is essential if unbearable human misery is to be prevented."

The telegram met with a sympathetic response from the President, and he discussed the critical situation in detail with a committee of Brotherhood representatives. The thought of endeavoring to place railroad workers under the National Industrial Recovery Act had been considered, but after later conferences with the Director and the General Counsel of NRA, it was decided that this would not be feasible because of the many complications that would probably arise in attempting to establish an NRA code for railroad workers.

Government officials pointed out that a code could not be formulated for one group of employes only but would have to cover all workers in the railroad industry.

As the year 1934 began, it seemed apparent that the turning point had been reached and that the nation had at last begun the long journey over the road to recovery. But the low earnings of many workers were a formidable obstacle in the progress toward more normal economic conditions. Conditions had thus far improved little for maintenance of way workers.

"As a result of inadequate wage rates, part time employment and the 10 per cent wage deduction, thousands of railway workers are failing to earn sufficient to keep body and soul together," Fljozdal said in January, 1934. ". . . On important Class I railroads thousands are earning less than $10 a week, from which the railroads deduct 10 per cent. On some prominent roads maintenance of way men are receiving less than $6 a week. These conditions have grown worse in recent weeks rather than better. . . .

"On November 15 employment on Class I railroads, according to the Interstate Commerce Commission, has dropped 32,588 as compared with the middle of September. The work period of those remaining in service had likewise been further reduced. . . . Some of the employes remaining in service are working as little as two days a week."

As the year progressed, however, a gradual improvement in conditions could be noted. By May, 1934, there were 52,000 more employes in maintenance of way service than in March, 1933, the lowest point in employment during the depression, and the total compensation of maintenance of way workers had increased by $5.6 million a month. More men were engaged in maintenance of way work than at any time since the latter part of 1931, and their total compensation was greater than for any month since November of that year.

Notwithstanding the severe retrenchments they had made, the financial plight of many carriers was still serious, and on February 15, 1934, the railroads in the United States served notice of their wish to reduce basic rates of pay by 15 per cent on and after July 1, 1934. The railroad Brotherhoods countered with a request for an increase of 10 per cent in basic wage rates.

While negotiations were in progress during March, President Roosevelt expressed the wish that the wage-deduction agreement be extended at least six months. On April 26, 1934, an agreement was reached providing: (1) That basic rates of pay would not be disturbed until changed upon notice; (2) that the 10 per cent deduction would be reduced to 7½ per cent on July 1, 1934, to 5 per cent on January 1, 1935, and eliminated entirely beginning April 1, 1935; and (3) that no notice of a change in basic rates of pay would be served by either party prior to May 1, 1935.

Early in the year, three bills of great importance to railroad workers were introduced in Congress. A so-called "Flagging Bill," requiring that track and bridge crews consist of a foreman and at least three men who had passed examinations for flagging, died with the adjournment of Congress. On June 21, 1934, however, President Roosevelt signed the amended Railway Labor Act, and on June 27, 1934, he signed the first Railroad Retirement Act, providing annuities for retired railroad workers.

The Railway Labor Act of 1934 added two important provisions to the 1926 Act: (1) It gave greater protection to railroad workers in joining organizations of their choice and selecting representatives without interference or coercion on the part of the management. (2) It established a National Railroad Adjustment Board of four divisions to hear and decide controversies growing out of grievances or the interpretation or application of agreements concerning rates of pay, rules, or working conditions.

The Act also created a National Railroad Mediation Board of three members, instead of the five members under the 1926 Act. Maintenance of way workers were placed under the jurisdiction of the Third Division of the National Adjustment Board, and A. F. Stout, National Legislative Representative of the Brotherhood, became its first member on the board.

The Railroad Retirement Act became effective August 1, 1934, and permitted retirement on and after February 1, 1935. Retirement at age 65 was compulsory unless the employer agreed to continue the employe in the service for successive periods of one year each to the maximum age of 70.

Railroad workers between age 50 and 65 and with 30 years

of railroad service could retire on a reduced annuity (one-fifteenth reduction for each year under age 65) or on a full annuity if they were retired by an employer by reason of mental or physical disability.

The railroads promptly challenged the Retirement Act in the courts. On October 24, 1934, a Federal district court held it to be unconstitutional (the United States Supreme Court upheld the ruling of the lower court by a 5 to 4 decision on May 6, 1935).

In the meantime, conferences had been under way to improve the Canadian National Railways' Pension Fund. This plan had been in effect in one form or another since 1906, when it was known as the "Grand Trunk Act." The cost of the pension program was borne entirely by the company, but the employes felt that the pensions provided were insufficient. In June, 1934, an agreement was reached between representatives of the carriers and the standard railway labor organizations in Canada providing for a new Canadian National Contributory Pension Plan to become effective January 1, 1935. Under this new plan, the employes were to make contributions to the fund and would receive larger pensions than the old plan gave them.

At the 25th regular convention of Grand Lodge in Detroit, Michigan, beginning September 10, 1934, President Fljozdal was able to report an improvement in economic conditions both in the United States and in Canada. Maintenance of way forces had been increased somewhat since the low point reached in 1933, but the problems of part-time and uncertain employment continued to be serious.

"When our Convention was in session three years ago," President Fljozdal said in his report, "we were in a depression no one thought would become so serious or last so long. We have seen unemployment in the United States grow until we had an army of idle wage earners estimated by some authorities to have been fifteen million. Employment conditions in Canada were equally bad, although the number of unemployed was not as great.

"We have witnessed our captains of industry and finance, apparently bewildered with the deplorable economic and financial conditions confronting the country . . . incapable of providing a satisfactory remedy or solution.

"Eventually we saw the present Federal administration assume office in Washington and adopt a program for economic recovery that was remarkably in line with the program advocated by organized labor. Upon the adoption of this economic program we have experienced an improvement in our general social and economic conditions. . . . We are not yet 'out of the woods,' but we are on the way in both the United States and Canada."

In connection with important Federal legislation that had been passed, President Fljozdal reported that ever since the 1928 convention, the Brotherhood had maintained a National Legislative Representative in Washington, D. C. A number of the railroad Brotherhoods had had legislative representatives in Washington for years, and the assignment of a Brotherhood representative to the Washington scene had become imperative to round out the organization's legislative activities in the Federal field.

The convention adopted a resolution to expel from membership in the Brotherhood all persons who were members of the Communist party, and gave serious consideration to the problems of jurisdictional disputes and the contracting of maintenance of way work by the railroads, which had increased during the depression.

The laws of the Death Benefit Department were changed to provide death benefits ranging from $50.00 after 12 months' continuous good standing to $500.00 after 120 months, except that new or reinstated members who had attained age 50 at date of joining or reinstatement could accumulate benefits ranging from $25.00 after 12 months' continuous good standing to a maximum of $150.00 after 72 months.

President Fljozdal and Secretary-Treasurer Milliman were unanimously re-elected.

The 15 per cent deduction from wages in Canada was scheduled to be reduced to 10 per cent effective December 1, 1934, but the railways served notice well in advance of that date that they wished to continue the full deduction of 15 per cent. An agreement was reached in November, 1934, that the deduction would be handled as follows: Effective January 1, 1935, and continuing until April 30, 1935, 12 per cent would be deducted from the employes' pay checks. Beginning May 1,

1935, and thereafter, 10 per cent would be deducted. After July 1, 1935, a thirty-day notice could be served by either party of their wish to change this percentage.

Deferred maintenance of tracks, bridges, and structures by the railroads and the effect of this policy on employment conditions in the maintenance of way department had been given serious consideration at meetings of Grand Lodge and system officers and at the 1934 convention. A Track and Bridge Inspection Bill, sponsored by the Brotherhood, was introduced in Congress on January 7, 1935, to require the railroads to maintain tracks, bridges, and appurtenances thereto in safe and suitable condition and providing for adequate inspection of these facilities. This bill was opposed not only by the carriers but also by the Interstate Commerce Commission because of certain of its provisions, particularly the establishing of a group of inspectors outside the jurisdiction of the Commission, and it failed to win the necessary support in Congress.

In the wake of the depression, a general sentiment throughout the country in favor of social insurance providing old-age and unemployment benefits had rapidly gained impetus. Early in 1935, more than 500 bills on this subject were introduced in Congress and 43 state legislatures. A similar movement was taking place in Canada.

During the summer, rumors prevailed that the Association of American Railroads planned to make some 600 consolidations of various kinds in an economy move. Estimates of the number of employes who would be displaced should such consolidations be made ran as high as 250,000. This potential danger to the jobs of railroad workers spurred the railroad Brotherhoods to increased activity to seek a solution to this menacing problem.

Immediately after the United States Supreme Court declared the Railroad Retirement Act of 1934 unconstitutional, two new railroad retirement bills were introduced in Congress, one to provide for a retirement system, the other to levy an excise tax on employers and an income tax on employes to finance the system. Congress passed the Railroad Retirement Act of 1935 on August 19 and the Carriers' Taxing Act of 1935 a few days later. President Roosevelt signed both bills on August 29. Again the carriers sought to have the two acts declared illegal by the courts, although the drafters of the acts had sought to overcome the deficiencies cited by the courts in the 1934 act.

On August 14, 1935, just 15 days before he signed the two railroad retirement bills, President Roosevelt had approved the Social Security Act, providing for old-age benefits, unemployment insurance, and Federal grants to states for old-age assistance and welfare and rehabilitation purposes. Only the unemployment insurance provisions of the Act applied to railroad workers. Thus the nation embarked on an entirely new program of aid to the aged, the unemployed, and the needy, and in this respect the year 1935 became a momentous one for workers in the United States.

"The year just closed has been a successful and profitable one for our Brotherhood," President Fljozdal said in January, 1936. "In our united efforts to increase our membership, we have seen a gain of approximately 10,000 new members. . . .

"Since our last triennial convention we have extended our representation to cover a substantial number of roads. . . . At this time there are but two major railroad systems in the United States on which we do not have representation. These are the Pennsylvania and the Santa Fe. . . .

"Still further progress in protecting the interest of our members was realized during the past year in our successful opposition to railroad terminal consolidations that were proposed and undertaken under the Emergency Railroad Transportation Act. . . .

"During the past year we have seen the enactment of legislation providing for the regulation of buses and trucks . . . that will re-act to the mutual welfare of railway management and railway workers. . . .

"Our achievements of 1935 should be an inspiration for us to work for bigger and better things in the present year."

The Emergency Railroad Transportation Act was scheduled to expire June 16, 1936. Originally intended to expire June 16, 1934, the Act had been extended for an additional year by proclamation of the President and to June 16, 1936, by a resolution of Congress. The chief executives of the railroad Brotherhoods sought a way to prevent the detrimental effects that might follow the expiration of those provisions of the Act protecting the interests of railroad workers in consolidations or coordinations of railroad facilities. A bill had been introduced in Congress to provide the necessary protection to the workers after the Act expired, but President Roosevelt suggested that an agreement be reached instead.

After five grueling months of negotiations, an agreement known as the Washington Job Protection Agreement was signed on May 21, 1936, by representatives of the railroad Brotherhoods and the participating carriers to provide allowances for employes affected by coordinations; that is, when two or more railroads unify, consolidate, merge, or pool their facilities or operations.

The short work week, with its resultant loss in earnings, was another issue of major importance, and at a meeting of Grand Lodge officers and General Chairmen on June 15, 1936, a resolution was unanimously adopted providing that on systems where the short work week was still in effect, notice would be served on the management requesting that employes be permitted to work a full week beginning July 1, 1936. General progress along this line was not made, however, until in 1937.

The efforts of railroad workers to obtain a retirement system met with another setback when the District Court of the United States for the District of Columbia, in a decision dated June 30, 1936, declared unconstitutional the Carriers' Taxing Act of 1935 and that portion of the Railroad Retirement Act of 1935 which required the railroads to supply the Board with information.

The railroads were now well on the way to recovery from the effects of the depression, and Class I carriers in the United States had a net railway operating income of $667 million in 1936. Despite the upturn in business conditions, however, millions of workers were still unemployed.

Meanwhile, President Roosevelt had been returned to office by a plurality of approximately 11 million, the largest ever given to a presidential candidate, in an overwhelming vote of confidence, just as in Canada the year previously the Liberal Party had won a sweeping victory. The movement for social reform had now become deeply rooted.

As the year ended, Grand Lodge and system officers met to lay plans for celebrating the Brotherhood's golden jubilee in

1937. "Our entrance into the year 1937 is of unusual significance to the members of our Brotherhood," President Fljozdal said in January, 1937. "It marks the fiftieth year of our Organization's existence and this Golden Jubilee will be appropriately recognized and celebrated throughout the United States and Canada.

"Many things have happened since John T. Wilson and that small group of Section Foremen met . . . one Sunday afternoon in 1887. . . . Yes, many things have happened. The 12-hour day then in effect has been forgotten. So has the 10-hour day that took its place. . . . Gone too are the wages of 80 and 90 cents a day for Trackmen, $40 a month for Foremen and 15 cents an hour for Carpenters. Gone are the long weary days and nights of continuous work at wrecks and other emergencies without overtime pay. . . .

"It took a lot of loyalty, hard work, courage and patience on the part of our early dues-paying pioneers to obtain these first improvements. They were real crusaders in those early days. No such sacrifices are required today. No longer must we meet organizers behind a stack of ties, or hold secret meetings in hidden places. A paid-up card is no longer the signal for dismissal. . . . Today we are reaping the harvest of their earlier courage and determination.

"By a unanimous vote [of Grand Lodge and system officers] it was decided that 1937 would be set aside for special celebration and for new accomplishments. . . . Much remains yet to be done and it is our job to do it. Fifty years from now, when 1987 rolls around, it must not, and will not, be said that we failed in 1937 to keep faith with those who started the movement in 1887."

Plans for the golden jubilee year included an intensive membership drive, the publishing of a brief history of the Brotherhood serially in the "Journal," and a rather extensive program to improve the earnings of maintenance of way workers.

Affairs in Canada had now reached a crisis. At a meeting held in Montreal in December, 1935, a decision had been reached by the railway labor organizations to seek an early end to the deduction from wages. Negotiations held later with the railways failed to bring about a settlement, and at the request of the employes a Board of Conciliation was appointed under the Industrial Disputes and Investigation Act.

The Board began hearings on November 23, 1936, but in spite of a convincing array of facts presented by the employes showing the injustice of continuing the 10 per cent deduction, the majority report of the Board recommended a plan that was wholly unsatisfactory to the employes for eventually ending the deduction. In a strike vote that followed, Canadian workers voted almost unanimously not to accept the Board's report. No recommendation of the Canadian government through a Board of Conciliation and Investigation had ever before been so thoroughly rejected.

On March 29, 1937, representatives of the railways and their employes reached an agreement providing for a graduated reduction of the 10 per cent deduction at the end of each two-month period, beginning February 1, 1937, until the deduction had been completely eliminated by April 1, 1938.

In the United States, meanwhile, on March 4, 1937, fourteen standard railroad labor organizations, including the Brotherhood, had launched a national movement requesting the following: (1) A general wage increase of 20c an hour; (2) a guarantee of full-time employment for all regularly assigned forces; (3) a guarantee of two-thirds of full-time employment for all stand-by forces; and (4) that the proceedings be handled in joint national conferences.

Conferences between the national committees began on June 3. By the end of June, when the negotiations had reached an impasse, the Mediation Board proffered its services. As a result, a mediation agreement was reached on August 5, 1937, granting a wage increase of 5 cents an hour effective August 1, 1937. The taking of a strike ballot had been authorized on July 2, and the employes had voted to strike if a satisfactory settlement could not be reached.

The agreement also contained a provision that share-the-work practices however established would be terminated on request of the General Chairmen, no such request to be made prior to September 1, 1937. It was the stated purpose of this provision to bring about regular employment to such forces as were required by each carrier. Negotiations after September 1 on various individual systems resulted in agreements guaranteeing more stability of employment to maintenance of way workers.

Another important accomplishment during the golden jubilee year had been completed some months before. For some time, negotiations had been under way to bring about the reaffiliation with the Brotherhood of maintenance of way men on the Pennsylvania Railroad. At a convention on March 10, 1937, representatives of the local lodges of the rival organization on that system voted unanimously to return to the jurisdiction of the Brotherhood. Thus, after more than fifteen years of non-affiliation, this major system again amalgamated with the Brotherhood.

While these important matters were being handled, the railroad Brotherhoods were also engaged in conferences seeking to straighten out the confused situation with respect to the Railroad Retirement Act of 1935. The court decision of June 30, 1936, declaring the Act illegal had been appealed and was pending before the Uuited States Supreme Court. Although the outlook was not too hopeful, there was some indication that the carriers might be amenable to the negotiation of an agreement on a mutually satisfactory retirement system.

Early conferences accomplished little, and on December 28, 1936, President Roosevelt suggested that representatives of the two groups renew their efforts to reach an agreement with the advice and assistance of the Railroad Retirement Board. On February 18, 1937, an agreement was signed that led directly to the establishment of a sound retirement system. This agreement has been called one of the most significant in American labor-management relations.

The parties agreed to establish a retirement system for the railroad industry based on the principles set forth in the memorandum of agreement. In addition, they agreed on two basic points: (1) The railroads agreed that they would never raise the question of the constitutionality of the system; and (2) the employes agreed that they would not depart from the principle of an equal tax burden on employers and employes to support the system. The memorandum of agreement also provided that pending litigation pertaining to the constitutionality of the Railroad Retirement Act of 1935 and the Carriers' Taxing Act of 1935 would, subject to the approval of the Attorney General, be disposed of in such a manner as to carry out the purposes of the agreement.

The two groups prepared joint drafts of bills to amend the Railroad Retirement Act of 1935 and the Carriers' Taxing Act of 1935. These bills were later passed by Congress and became law on June 24 and June 29, 1937, respectively.

The Railroad Retirement Act of 1937 permitted retirement at age 65 (but no compulsory retirement age was established) or after age 60 on a reduced annuity if the applicant had 30 years of creditable railroad service. Totally and permanently disabled employes became eligible for full annuities if they had attained age 60 or had 30 years of service.

One of the most important provisions of the Act, in that it permitted the immediate retirement of older workers, was the crediting of railroad service prior to January 1, 1937 (the 1934 and 1935 Acts had contained a similar provision). When, however, prior service was included, no more than 30 years' service could be counted. The amount of the annuity was to be based on creditable railroad service and average monthly earnings not exceeding $300.00. Average monthly earnings during the years 1924-1931 were to be applied to creditable service prior to January 1, 1937. The system was to be financed by taxes applying equally to employers and employes.

In presenting his report to the 26th regular convention of Grand Lodge, which met in Detroit, Michigan, beginning September 13, 1937, President Fljozdal said: "This report . . . will go down in [the] history of this organization as one of . . . the finest reports from the standpoint of accomplishment that has ever been presented to a convention of our organization."

The progress of the Brotherhood had indeed been impressive. Its success was reflected in a substantially higher membership. The number of paid-up members had increased approximately 44 per cent since the 1934 convention.

President Fljozdal reported that since the last convention the Brotherhood had extended its representation on 55 railways consisting of about 46,000 miles of line. Agreements were then in effect on 47 of these roads, but negotiations were pending on the remaining eight.

He also pointed out the further progress that had been made

in securing the payment of the time and one-half rate after eight hours' work. A rule containing this provision had been negotiated on 72 roads.

The delegates took action approving union-management co-operation, the principle of time and one-half pay after eight hours' work, government ownership of railroads, non-partisan political action, the union shop, vacations with pay, a shorter work week without reduction in pay, regional uniformity of working agreements, and efforts to secure a federal track and bridge inspection bill.

The delegates re-elected President Fljozdal and Secretary-Treasurer Milliman.

The Track and Bridge Inspection Bill had, however, become bogged down in Congress. A new bill, revised to overcome objections to the earlier version, had been introduced, but there appeared little hope that it could be successfully progressed. The Interstate Commerce Commission still declined to give its unqualified approval to the bill. The Chairman of the Commission suggested that this was a type of legislation that could better be enacted by individual states, despite the fact that it affects interstate rather than intrastate commerce. He also apparently failed to consider the veritable hodgepodge of laws wholly lacking in uniformity that would result if each state attempted to adopt its own regulations.

In March, 1937, the President of the Association of American Railroads expressed a wish to meet with the representatives of the railroad Brotherhoods then having legislation pending in Congress in order to explore the subjects on which they were seeking Federal legislation. A number of conferences on the Track and Bridge Inspection Bill followed between committees representing the railroads and the Brotherhood.

As a result of these conferences, in May, 1937, representatives of the Brotherhood submitted to the carriers' committee a twelve-point program outlining the basic reasons the Brotherhood had sought passage of the bill. The carriers' committee appeared to be favorably impressed by the Brotherhood's program and promised to bring the suggestions of the Brotherhood to the attention of all railroad presidents.

General Chairmen were instructed to confer with their managements on this twelve-point program in an attempt to bring about a greater measure of job security and some degree of stability of employment in the maintenance of way department. By the end of 1937, some progress had been made on a few roads, but the attitude displayed by the managements on a number of roads toward this program was disappointing.

A new economic crisis, however, now demanded the attention of the organization. A serious business slump, beginning in August, 1937, and continuing into the summer of 1938, had given a temporary setback to the nation's efforts to emerge from the depression. It is estimated that more than 10 million workers were unemployed by the spring of 1938. The net railway operating income of Class I railroads in the United States declined from $590 million in 1937 to $372 million in 1938.

The inexorable repercussions of the business recession were soon apparent to railroad workers. On May 12, 1938, the carriers in the United States served a notice requesting a 15 per cent reduction in wages effective July 1, 1938. Railroad workers prepared to resist the wage cut by a nationwide strike if necessary.

"The financial troubles of the railroads were not caused by wages and cannot be cured by wage reductions," President Fljozdal said. "The immediate problem of the railroads grows out of their need for more business. Back of this lies the fact that the railroads have permitted themselves to run hopelessly into debt and they can never be placed on a sound financial basis, in our opinion, until they reorganize for the purpose of scaling down their top-heavy debt structure."

National conferences in July and early August and the intercession of the Mediation Board failed to bring about a settlement. A strike vote had been taken, and the cooperating railroad Brotherhoods authorized a strike to begin at 6:00 p.m., September 30, 1938, after the railroads announced their intention to reduce wages by 15 per cent on October 1.

In view of the emergency, President Roosevelt appointed an Emergency Board to investigate the dispute in accordance with the Railway Labor Act and the strike was postponed. On October 29, 1938, the President released the Board's report, which held that the financial distress of the carriers was as yet a short-term situation, that the wages of railroad workers were not high in comparison with those in other comparable industries, that a horizontal wage reduction would not meet the financial needs of roads in the worst shape, and that a wage reduction would run counter to the trend of wage rates in industry generally. A short time later the carriers withdrew their wage-cut request in accordance with the Emergency Board's recommendations.

Although overshadowed for the time being by the wage dispute crisis, several other happenings of great importance to railroad workers had taken place. On June 25, 1938, President Roosevelt signed the Railroad Unemployment Insurance Act providing a system of unemployment insurance for railroad workers (beginning July 1, 1939), who up to that time had been covered by the unemployment insurance provisions of the Social Security Act.

Another important act of Congress had been the passage of the Fair Labor Standards Act of 1938 (commonly called the Wage-Hour Act) placing a floor under wage rates and a ceiling on the length of the work week. Railroad workers were covered by the minimum-wage provisions of the Act but not by the limitation on hours. A minimum wage of 25¢ an hour was established for one year, 30¢ for the next six years, and thereafter not less than 40¢. Industrial boards established under the Act could, however, raise the minimum hourly wage for a particular industry to 40¢ an hour before the expiration of the seven-year period.

The minimum-wage section of the Wage-Hour Act brought wage increases to thousands of railroad workers, many of them section men in the south and southwest, where wage rates were as low as 15¢ to 18¢ an hour. Early in 1939, the Railway Labor Executives' Association requested that the Administrator of the Wage-Hour Act create a committee to investigate wages in the railroad industry with the view of establishing a minimum wage of 40¢ an hour for railroad workers. Many thousands of railroad workers were receiving wages below the 40¢ figure.

The carriers throughout the United States generally applied the minimum wage provisions of the Wage-Hour Act. The Atlantic Coast Line Railway, however, endeavored to absorb the difference between the 20¢ an hour it had been paying its trackmen and the minimum wage under the Wage-Hour

Act by charging them with such items as house rent, fuel, ice and water, repairs, replacement and tax on water wells and pumps, transportation by motor car to and from work, time paid for but not worked because of rain, travel time paid for, special police protection, special medical care not covered by Relief Department membership, and retirement and social security taxes.

The Brotherhood and the Wage-Hour Administrator cooperated in suits brought against the railway company by employes affected to recover these deductions. The court decisions (rendered in 1940) were an overwhelming victory for the interested employes and the Brotherhood. A sum of approximately $260,000.00 was recovered for these low-paid workers.

The 1937 convention had instructed that uniform national rules governing working conditions be drafted to be used in future negotiations with the carriers. After the preliminary work had been done on a regional basis, a National Rules Committee met in February, 1939. On March 7, 1939, the committee completed its work of drafting 66 national rules, which were later adopted at a meeting of Grand Lodge and system officers in July, 1939.

After six years of effort by Canadian railway workers, a law closely following the Washington Job Protection Agreement of 1936 in the United States was passed by the Canadian parliament in June, 1939, "to provide for the payment of compensation by the employing companies to railway employes who are deprived of employment or adversely affected by cooperative measures undertaken by the Canadian National Railway Company and the Canadian Pacific Company pursuant to the provisions of the Canadian National-Pacific Act."

During the six-year period since President Roosevelt assumed office in 1933, the government of the United States had adopted many important measures, not only to bring the nation out of the depths of the depression but to improve the economic condition of the worker. In a Labor Day statement, Secretary of Labor Frances Perkins summarized the progress that had been made:

"The wage earners of the United States can observe Labor Day this year secure in the knowledge of the gains they have made since 1933. The Roosevelt Administration has had among its objectives good working conditions and relative continuity of income and opportunity for our people, reasonable profits for business, opportunity for investment in new and expanding industries and good wages throughout the Nation.

"Aid has been extended to the unemployed, to crippled business and financial interests, to hard pressed home owners, to the victims of depressed labor standards and to the destitute.

"Thus we have seen in a few years tremendous new enterprises started by the Federal Government, working in cooperation with State governments, charged with the responsibility of carrying on Nation-wide economic and humanitarian programs hitherto not tried in our country.

"We have seen a public works program to give work to the unemployed and a work relief program inaugurated. We have seen launched a much needed and long delayed social security program on a vast and varied scale which already has had fine achievement in the general welfare. Special aid to widows, children, the aged, needy and handicapped groups in our population has been extended as well as regular provision by insurance protection to aged wage earners and unemployed to compensate for their wage losses or loss of earning capacity.

"We have seen the formulation of a program to promote the welfare of wage earners through shortening of hours of work and through increasing minimum wages and purchasing power of the lowest income groups of our employed people.

"By recognition of the principle and benefits of collective bargaining and by providing the opportunity for employment of the unemployed in public work the lot of wage earners has been greatly improved.

"We have seen also the effective efforts to restore and improve our whole economic setup, to protect the savings and investments of the people, to stabilize the income of farmers and to strengthen the country as a whole by building sounder financial foundations."

But as America finally began to emerge from the depression, the world tottered on the brink of disaster. After a comparatively quiescent period of some twenty-one years, the simmering cauldron of strife had again begun to boil in Europe. Since 1933, the peoples of Europe had lived under the ominous threat of war. A series of crises beginning in 1938 culminated in the invasion of Poland by Germany on September 1, 1939. Two days later England and France declared war on Germany. On September 10, 1939, the Prime Minister of Canada issued a proclamation that a state of war existed between Canada and the German Reich.

Thus began World War II, which lasted for six years, eventually engulfed the United States, and swept from one end of the earth to the other, profoundly changing the course of world events.

↑ *Above: Today, the modern Jordan standard type spreader-ditcher is a composite machine used in railway construction and maintenance as a spreader, ditcher, ballast plow, ballast and roadbed shaper, snow plow, and ice cutter.*

Right: The primitive equipment used to build the grade of America's railroads many years ago. →

↑ Above: Note the smooth efficiency with which jointless track, a modern innovation, made by welding ordinary rail together, end to end, is being laid by workmen.

Left: In contrast, note the cluttered scene during the early days of railroad construction. ←

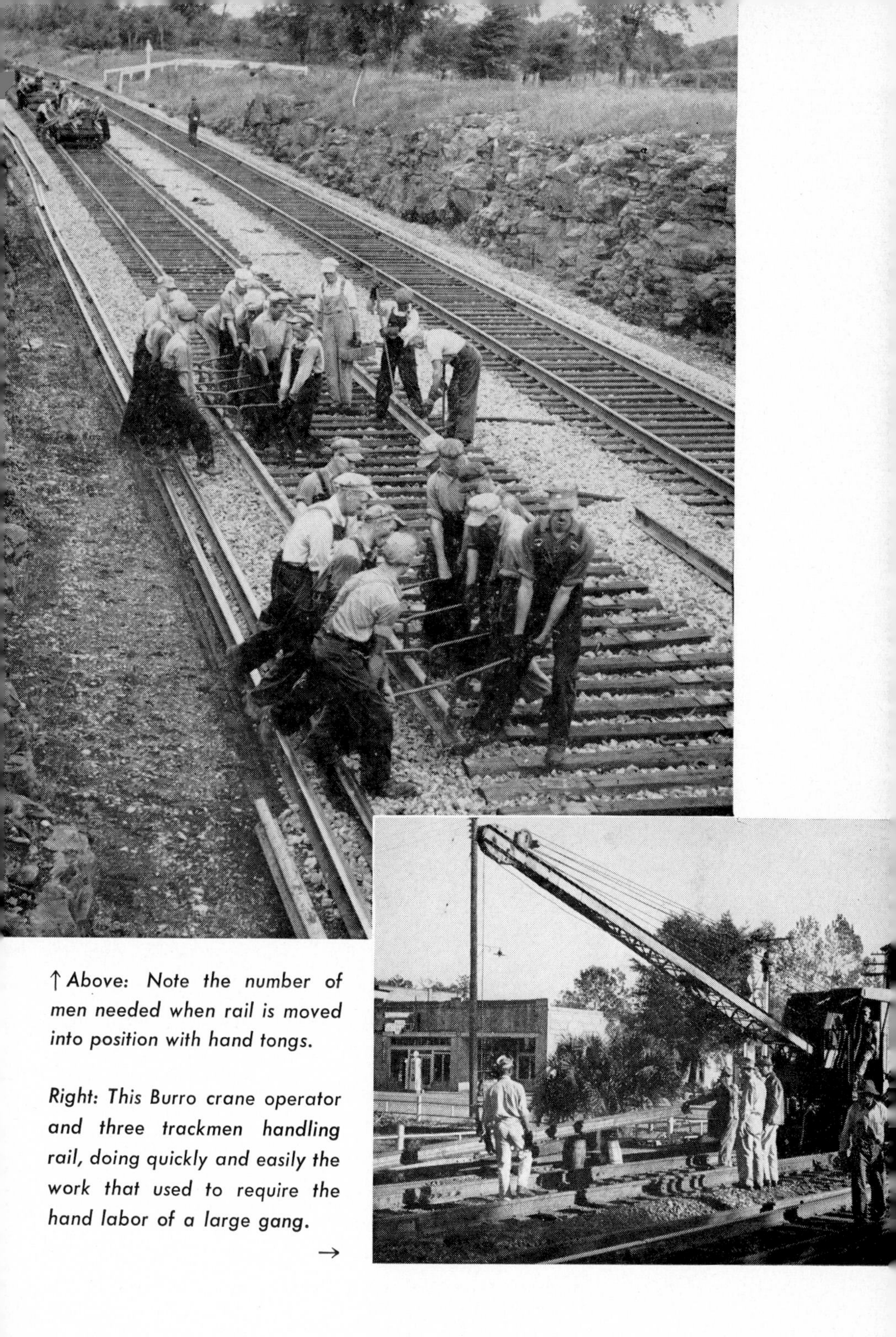

↑ *Above: Note the number of men needed when rail is moved into position with hand tongs.*

Right: This Burro crane operator and three trackmen handling rail, doing quickly and easily the work that used to require the hand labor of a large gang.

→

↑ *Above: A rail-laying gang at work. After the old spike holes have been filled with wooden plugs, the ties will be resurfaced by the adzer in the background.*

Left: A workman is shown resurfacing ties with the old hand adzer.
←

↑ *Above: The power-operated spike puller, which removes spikes quickly and easily, has speeded up the maintenance and renewal of America's rail lines.*

Right: The claw bar was once standard equipment for removing spikes. →

↑ *Above: The one-man power wrench tightens track bolts uniformly, making the track stronger and better riding.*

Left: Compare this complicated machine with the simple hand tool being used here. ←

Above: A gaging machine in operation. Note that holes are being bored to position the tie plates to assure that when the track is laid the rails will be the proper distance apart.

Left: This maintenance crew on the Chesapeake & Ohio at Thayer, West Virginia, drive steel spikes to make the rails secure and safe. ←

Above: To begin the modern motif, two workmen distribute spikes ahead of the spike driver.

Right: This modern one-man mechanized spike driver completes the evolution and is commonly used in large rail-laying jobs. The use of modern equipment such as this has revolutionized maintenance of way work. →

Above: After the spikes have been inserted in the holes, workmen drive them home with power tools, an intermediate step in the evolution from hand to machine.

Above: A weed burner in action. Mechanical mowers and chemical sprays are also used to control weeds along the right of way, work formerly done with hand scythe and scuffle hoe.

↑ *Above: The self-propelled track liner shifts track into place with a sideward thrust, replacing hand labor.*

Right: Note the number of men needed in the picture to line track by hand.

→

↑ *Above: one of the mechanical devices used to remove ties in the process of mechanization, helping maintenance of way workers to reach new heights in efficiency.*

Left: The removal of ties by the use of hand tongs is a tedious job.
←

↑ *Above: The power track jack is being used to raise track in a surfacing operation.*

Right: The picture illustrates the use of hand jacks under the alert eye of the foreman.

→

↑ *Above: Dirt extracted from railroad ballast is thrown aside by an endless belt as the specialized machine extracts, cleans, and replaces ballast while it slowly moves along the track.*

Left: Another type of ballast cleaner also cleans foul ballast in the shoulders which prevents proper drainage and causes soft and uneven track.

←

↑ *Above: A gang of men surface track with hand tools under the direction of their foreman.*

Right: Workmen use power tools to tamp ballast under ties.

→

Right: This modern mechanical tamper requires the services of a skilled operator.

→

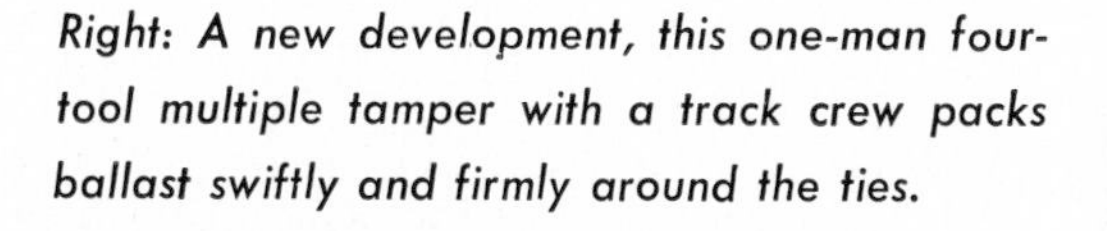

Right: A new development, this one-man four-tool multiple tamper with a track crew packs ballast swiftly and firmly around the ties.

→

↑ *Above: National champion handcar team from the Pennsylvania Railroad—Brotherhood Day at the Chicago Railroad Fair—1949.*

Right: Section crew on the Chicago and North Western Railroad ride an open motor car to work.

→

Right: One of the latest model gang motor cars equipped with electric lights, a windshield, and a top.

→

CHAPTER VII

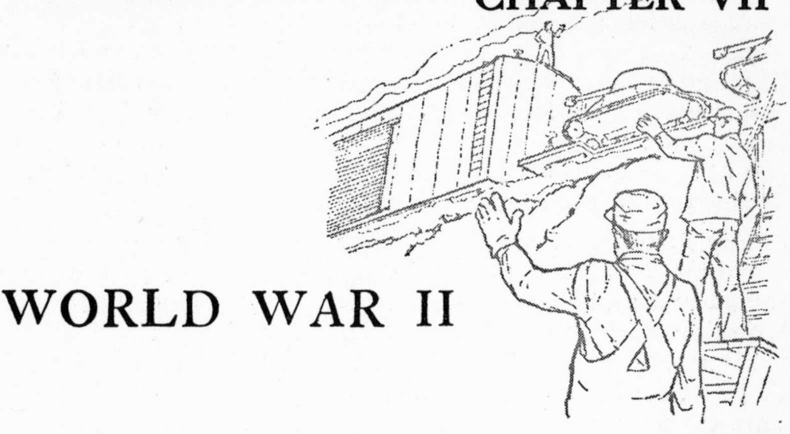

WORLD WAR II

THE impact of the war on economic conditions in both the United States and Canada was immediate. Industrial production in the United States rose to an all-time high by the end of 1939, and as business revived and expanded, employment increased. The volume of traffic on the railroads soon reached the highest point in nine years.

By the summer of 1940, the success of the German armies in Europe brought the American people to a realization of the nation's dangerous state of unpreparedness. As the war continued, plans calling for the expenditure of billions of dollars by the United States were evolved to aid the countries at war with the aggressor nations in Europe and to provide for the defense of America.

The bombing of Pearl Harbor, Hawaii, by the Japanese on December 7, 1941, made the United States an active participant in the war and resulted in a mobilization of manpower, resources, and industrial production unprecedented in the nation's history.

Profiting by experience, the railroads did not repeat the mistakes which brought about government control in World War I. Instead, they pooled and coordinated their facilities in such a way as to enable them to meet the tremendous wartime transportation needs of the nation efficiently and effectively. Anticipating a boom in rail traffic, in the fall of 1939 the Association of American Railroads announced plans of the carriers to start work on a large-scale equipment program. As a matter of fact, the expansion program was already under way. Reports from locomotive builders indicated that the backlog of unfilled orders at the close of July, 1939, was double that of the same period a year ago.

The fortunes of the Brotherhood, too, had improved considerably. In an optimistic report to a meeting of Grand Lodge and system officers on November 27, 1939, President Fljozdal said: "During the past year, our organization has continued to go forward and we are in a postition to report at this time that our great and highly essential Brotherhood is in the best shape it has been in for many years. We have the highest membership today that we have had at any time since October, 1922, and the highest percentage of membership in the history of the railroad industry. We estimate that when full reports are in covering dues paid to October of this year we will have . . . twice as many members as we had at the low point of the depression in the first months of 1933."

In successfully weathering the critical period of the 1920's and the dark years of the business depression, the Brotherhood had displayed a stamina and an impregnability that assured it a place among the strongest labor unions in the United States and Canada.

As general business conditions improved, the Brotherhood continued its efforts to improve the wage rates of maintenance of way workers. The minimum wage under the Wage-Hour Act of 1938 had increased to 30¢ an hour on October 24, 1939, but it was scheduled to remain at this figure until October, 1945, unless a committee established under the law for a particular industry recommended that a minimum wage not in excess of 40¢ an hour become effective before 1945. On November 2, 1939, the Wage and Hour Division of the United States Department of Labor appointed a twelve-member board (four representing the public, four the employers, and four the employes) to study the wage situation and formulate a minimum wage scale for the railroad industry. Vice President

T. C. Carroll was appointed as one of the employes' representatives on the board.

The committee did not begin public hearings until February 14, 1940. During the hearings, representatives of the railroads spent nine days in opposing any minimum wage in excess of 30¢ an hour. For seven of these nine days they concentrated their attack against any higher minimum rate in the maintenance of way department. Although the committee completed its work on May 8, 1940, it was not until March 1, 1941, that the Wage-Hour Administrator made effective the recommendation of the committee that a minimum rate of 36¢ an hour be established for Class I carriers and of 33¢ for Class II and smaller carriers.

In the spring of 1940, the Brotherhood joined with other non-operating railroad Brotherhoods in a national movement that had long been urged by railroad workers. On May 20, notices were served on railroad managements in the United States requesting two consecutive weeks' vacation with pay each year. In replying to the request, many railroad managements proposed a 10 per cent reduction in pay to offset the cost of a vacation plan.

Conferences on individual railroads took considerable time, complicated as they were by the carriers' counter-proposal, and the movement was still in the conference stage when the 27th regular convention of Grand Lodge met in Quebec, Province of Quebec, Canada, beginning July 15, 1940.

President Fljozdal's report reflected the continued progress that had been made in negotiating agreements with railroad managements. The Brotherhood then held agreements on about 93 per cent of the Class I mileage in the United States and on practically the entire mileage in Canada.

Considerable progress had been made also, he said, in securing the time and one-half rate after eight hours' work. This rule had been obtained in agreements on 192 railroads covering approximately 70 per cent of the mileage in the United States (including Class II and Class III carriers and switching and terminal companies).

The delegates took action on many important questions and approved the following: a movement to obtain the union shop on the railroads; cooperative action among railroad labor organizations on individual railroad systems through General Chairmen's associations; a Federal work program and a Federal old-age pension to relieve unemployment; time and one-half pay after eight hours' work on all systems; union-management cooperation; the inauguration of a wage increase movement; amendments to improve the Railroad Unemployment Insurance Act; a movement to obtain the five-day week; and efforts to bring about greater stability of employment. The convention condemned the growing tendency of the railroads to contract maintenance of way work.

On the morning of July 17, President Fljozdal announced to the convention that he would not be a candidate for re-election to the office of president. "Thirty-five years ago," he said, "this Brotherhood honored me by selecting me as General Chairman of the railroad upon which I was then employed. In the years that have passed since that day in 1905, my debt of gratitude has been increased manifold by additional honors. . . .

"Beginning with our 1922 convention, you have chosen me on six consecutive occasions as your leader—in the capacity of chief executive of this organization. . . . It is with a mingled feeling of relief and regret that I now inform you that I am no longer to be considered as a candidate for the office of president. I have decided that this position of great responsibility should now be placed in other and younger hands."

President Fljozdal had successfully led the organization through some of the most critical years in its history, and the convention unanimously adopted a testimonial conferring upon him the honorary title of "President Emeritus," and expressing the gratitude of the membership for the eminent service he had rendered to the Brotherhood.

"Your constant fairness, your unquestioned integrity and your signal ability as the executive officer of this Brotherhood have commanded our admiration and confidence, and your unfailing courtesy and kindness have won our deep and undying respect and personal affection," the testimonial said. "For more than thirty-five years you have been an active officer of this Brotherhood. . . . During all this public career no man, whether friend or foe, has ever raised his voice to question your integrity, fairness, courage or your honor."

The convention elected Elmer E. Milliman, who had served as Grand Lodge Secretary-Treasurer since 1922, to succeed Fljozdal as President, and A. Shoemake to succeed Milliman as Secretary-Treasurer.

Milliman was born in Mount Morris, New York, on November 22, 1890. He had studied engineering and served as a telephone company engineer before he went to work for the Delaware, Lackawanna & Western Railroad. He soon became a general foreman in the maintenance of way department. At that time, only the five transportation Brotherhoods had any semblance of an organization on that system. When the edict of Director General of Railroads McAdoo during government control in World War I gave railroad workers the right to organize, Milliman promptly began a campaign to organize maintenance of way workers on the D. L. & W., and they elected him their first General Chairman.

Milliman served on the committee that negotiated the national agreement with the Federal Railroad Administration in 1919, and at the next Brotherhood convention (1922), the delegates recognized his undeniable ability and elected him Grand Lodge Secretary-Treasurer. He had held this position continuously since that time, helping to guide the organization through the disastrous years that followed.

"It must be clear to every member that grave and serious times confront us," Milliman said in his first message to the membership as Grand Lodge President. "The war and defense problems of the United States and Canada now occupy the minds and hearts of all of us. . . .

"I am thoroughly sensible to the needs and requirements of all of you and also realize the many problems with which you are confronted. I know much injustice, inequality and unfairness exists. I trust and hope that I will never fail to persuade myself that your difficulties and burdens are my first concern and with God's help it will always be my earnest desire to serve and labor in your behalf."

On September 16, 1940, the Selective Training and Service Act of 1940, the first law calling for peace-time military conscription of manpower in the United States, became effective. The Brotherhood took the necessary action to ensure that the seniority and re-employments rights of railroad workers who entered military service were protected in accordance with this act and similar Federal laws subsequently enacted.

The following month (October 10, 1940), President Roosevelt signed a bill passed by Congress making important changes in the Railroad Unemployment Insurance Act, including a higher benefit scale, an increase in the maximum benefits payable in a benefit year, and a reduction in the waiting period before benefits became payable.

In the meantime, the 1940 political campaign in the United States had been gathering momentum. President Roosevelt's fine record during the depression years and his strong advocacy of an adequate preparedness program made his re-election almost a certainty, in spite of the fact that no previous President of the United States had ever served more than two terms. At the November election, the voters cast precedent aside and returned him to office by a plurality of almost 5 million votes.

By the latter part of 1940, it had become apparent that the railroads generally were unwilling to grant the employes' request for paid vacations; nor had they shown any inclination to form a national conference committee to negotiate this dispute. In response to a strike ballot issued on February 15, 1941, railroad workers voted overwhelmingly to suspend work if a satisfactory settlement could not be reached. The National Mediation Board proffered its services and mediation proceedings began on March 19.

Meantime, the Wage and Hour Administrator under the Fair Labor Standards Act of 1938 had signed an order on February 12, 1941, making effective March 1, 1941, the recommendation of the railroad industry committee that minimum hourly rates of 36¢ and 33¢ be established for railroad employes on Class I and Class II railroads, respectively. Although this order provided some relief from low wages to almost 56,000 railroad workers, rapidly changing economic conditions made a movement for a general wage increase imperative.

Apparently in anticipation of a request from their employes for higher wages, on June 9, 1941, a number of carriers served notice of their wish to make drastic changes in agreement rules that had been in existence for many years. The following day, the non-operating railroad Brotherhoods served a uniform notice on railroad managements requesting a wage increase of 30¢ an hour and a minimum hourly wage of 70¢.

The railroad Brotherhoods had tentatively agreed to enter into an arbitration agreement in the pending vacation dispute, but the request of the carriers for sweeping rules changes had so complicated the situation that the Brotherhoods decided it would be futile to attempt to arbitrate the vacation issue. Moreover, the employes' request for a wage increase had now entered the picture.

Railroad workers insisted that higher wages were more than justified because their productivity had increased remarkably during recent years; the carriers were in a highly improved financial condition; the cost of living had increased; and the grossly inadequate wage and living standards of railroad workers had rapidly deteriorated during the emergency conditions compared to those of workers in other industries.

On July 25, 1941, national conferences began on all the questions in dispute; i.e., vacations with pay, the carriers' request for rules changes, and the wage increase notice. The conferences ended on August 5 when it became apparent that no settlement could be reached. Mediation proceedings failed to develop any basis for settlement, and when a large majority of the workers again voted to strike, a suspension of work was order to begin on September 11, 1941. The strike was postponed, however, when President Roosevelt appointed an Emergency Board to investigate all the issues involved.

The Brotherhoods promptly and emphatically rejected the Board's recommendation, made to the President on November 5. For maintenance of way employes and certain other classes, the Board recommended a temporary wage increase of 9¢ an hour (except on short lines), effective September 1, 1941, and ending December 31, 1942; a vacation of six working days each year; and a minimum wage of 45¢ an hour, except on short lines, where a minimum wage of 40¢ an hour was recommended. The Board recommended no specific wage increase for employes of short lines, except that which might result from the establishment of the 40¢ minimum hourly rate, and suggested that the wage-increase issue be handled on these lines through the process of collective bargaining.

Because of the vigorous protest of the employes, President Roosevelt instructed the Emergency Board to reconvene on November 28 to hear re-arguments. The Board proposed a mediation settlement of the issues in dispute, and offered its services as a mediation board. As a result, a wage agreement was signed on December 15, 1941, applicable to all roads represented by the Carriers' Conference Committee, providing that the wage increase of 9¢ an hour effective September 1, 1941, would be increased to 10¢ an hour effective December 1, 1941, and that this latter amount would become a permanent addition to basic wage rates. The agreement also established a minimum hourly rate of 46¢ an hour on the roads concerned, effective December 1, 1941. It also provided that the carriers' request for rules changes would be withdrawn and that there would be a moratorium on changes in rules (not to include rates of pay) for a period of eighteen months from December 1, 1941.

A vacation agreement signed on December 17, 1941, granted an annual vacation of six consecutive work days with pay, beginning with the year 1942, to each employe who rendered compensated service on not less than 160 days during the preceding calendar year.

The agreements of December 15 and 17 disposed of the wage and vacation disputes on approximately 93 per cent of the mileage in the United States. The problem remained of bringing about the acceptance of the provisions of these agreements on the remaining roads (more than 80 in number), most of which were so-called short lines.

Other occurrences during the year had been temporarily obscured by these rather dramatic happenings. Early in the year, railroad workers won a significant victory when a three-judge Federal court at Washington, D. C., unanimously decided that the Interstate Commerce Commission had been mistaken in holding that it had no authority to require protection and compensation for railroad workers adversely affected by abandonments. The court held that railroad employes who lose their jobs through abandonments should be protected and compensated the same as those who are affected by mergers and coordinations. (This decision was sustained by the United States Supreme Court on March 2, 1942.)

On July 29, 1941, an agreement unique in the history of the railway industry was reached between Canadian railways and their employes. This agreement negotiated in accordance with an order of the Canadian government, established a wartime cost of living bonus effective June 1, 1941, to be automatically adjusted at intervals of three months when the cost of living changed 5 per cent or more. The cost of living in August, 1939, was to be used as a base for these adjustments. The government's order was not compulsory but was intended more as a guide or formula for meeting changing conditions.

In October, the Canadian government announced a general system of price and wage controls designed to prevent runaway wartime inflation in the Dominion. Under this program, persons selling goods or rendering services were to be governed by maximum prices established during a designated base period. Cost-of-living wage bonuses were to be granted to workers on a basis similar to that already established for the railway industry. This action by the Canadian government created considerable interest in the United States, where government officials were considering means to curb the deterioration in the living standard brought about by the continued rise in living costs.

In the south, meanwhile, a rival organization had forced the Brotherhood into the courts. This organization, the "United Transport Service Employes of America", appeared on the Florida East Coast Railway in 1940 soliciting membership particularly among colored railroad workers. The U.T.S.E.A. finally sought the services of the National Mediation Board in a representation dispute with the Brotherhood over the right to represent maintenance of way workers.

The Mediation Board announced on November 12, 1941, that the Brotherhood had won the election. Thereupon, the U.T.S.E.A. entered suit in a Federal court alleging improper handling by the Mediation Board and intimidation and coercion by the Brotherhood and a number of maintenance of way employes. The court's decision exonerated the Board, the Brotherhood, and the employes concerned of all charges, and this rival organization failed to proceed with its announced intention to appeal from the court's decision.

The entry of the United States in the war in December, 1941, made imperative the full utilization of all the available manpower, resources, transportation facilities, and industrial production of the nation. To assure that the nation's transportation facilities would be used to the fullest extent and to the best possible advantage during the war, on December 18, 1941, President Roosevelt created the Office of Defense Transportation by Executive Order. During the course of the war, the O.D.T. issued many orders and engaged in numerous activities to coordinate transportation facilities and expedite the movement of the tremendous volume of traffic handled by the railroads.

As the war progressed and as millions of workers entered military service, the manpower situation became acute. A program of the War Manpower Commission and the O.D.T. to freeze railroad employes to their jobs was objected to by the railroad Brotherhoods. "We are opposed to freezing any worker in his job," said a statement by the Railway Labor Executives' Association. "It is unnecessary and will destroy production, wipe out free labor and inevitably result in abandoning our system of free enterprise, ideals of human freedom and democratic processes."

The Association's statement contained a detailed outline of methods for meeting the nation's manpower needs without the necessity for job freezing. The War Manpower Commission, however, proceeded with its program in areas of critical labor shortage.

As the manpower situation became more serious, the railroads in the United States insisted that because of the shortage of workers they be permitted to use war prisoners, some 125,000 relocated Japanese in this country, and Mexican nationals to relieve the manpower shortage, particularly in the maintenance of way department. The Brotherhood contended, however, that the problem of the carriers was not a shortage of labor but a shortage of wages, and that it resulted from low wages, unfair overtime rules, and highly unsatisfactory commissary conditions.

Although the organization succeeded in preventing the use of war prisoners or relocated Japanese in the maintenance of way department, on April 29, 1943, the government of the United States entered into an agreement with the government of Mexico permitting the temporary migration of Mexican workers for railroad service in the United States. The use of these workers ceased, however, when the war ended.

The inability of the United States to take retaliatory measures on the Japanese following the bombing of Pearl Harbor and its reverses in the Far East in the succeeding months, combined with the urgent necessity for furnishing the implements of war to its military forces and those of its allies at widely scattered points throughout the world, made the productive capacity of America a vital factor in World War II. To prevent interruption of war production by strikes or lockouts, President Roosevelt created by Executive Order a National War Labor Board of twelve members, representing industry, labor, and the public, to bring about the settlement of labor disputes through peaceful means for the duration of the emergency.

As the peoples of the United States and Canada set about the grim task of winning the war, the railroads were called upon to do a stupendous job in meeting the transportation needs of the two countries. The hauling of immense quantities of raw materials to the great industrial centers, the distribution of the finished products to ports and harbors for shipment to far-distant battlefields, and the transportation of troops and their equipment, placed an unprecedented burden on the railroad industry. The rationing of gasoline and the restrictions on the manufacture of automobiles made the public greatly dependent on the railroads for transportation.

The efficient job done by the railways of the United States and Canada in meeting the consuming needs of a wartime economy is one of the sagas of World War II. The freight hauled by Class I railroads in the United States increased from 333 billion revenue ton miles in 1939 to 638 billion in 1942 and to 737 billion in 1944. From the standpoint of passenger service, the revenue passenger miles of Class I railroads increased from about 22½ billion in 1939 to approximately 53½ billion in 1942 and to 95½ billion in 1944. The railways in Canada met the emergency conditions with similarly outstanding efficiency.

Railroad workers played a vital role in the impressive job done by the carriers during the war. The following figures illustrate the tremendous gain in the productivity of maintenance of way workers during the war years.

UNITED STATES

Year	Number of Maintenance of Way Employes	Gross Ton-Miles * (000,000)	Maintenance of Way Employes per Billion Gross Ton-Miles
1925	389,114	1,023,370	380
1930	343,474	1,006,505	341
1935	205,679	766,873	268
1941	231,752	1,188,712	195
1942	257,624	1,493,354	173
1943	267,348	1,628,750	164
1944	286,403	1,658,449	173
1945	292,532	1,532,275	191

CANADA

Year	Number of Maintenance of Way Employes	Gross Ton-Miles * (000,000)	Maintenance of Way Employes per Billion Gross Ton-Miles
1926	45,484	86,921	523
1930	42,734	77,579	548
1935	31,167	63,983	487
1941	35,402	119,226	297
1942	36,354	128,439	284
1943	38,985	139,777	278
1944	38,663	145,741	265
1945	40,247	140,978	285

* Excludes locomotives and tenders.

The greater number of maintenance of way workers per billion gross ton-miles in Canada than in the United States does not necessarily indicate a lesser efficiency on their part, but rather reflects more difficult conditions of climate and terrain, and other factors.

In releasing a report early in 1942 on the increased productivity of railroad workers, prepared by the Statistical Department of the Brotherhood, President Milliman pointed out that American railroads were making huge profits with fewer employes. "With a reduction of 31.4 per cent in total workers and a drop of 21.6 in total wages," the report said, "the railroads handled 6.2 per cent more business. . . . The labor cost last year was 25.7 per cent lower than when we were in the first World War 25 years ago."

As has already been outlined, the Administrator of the Wage-Hour Act had issued an order making effective March 1, 1941, minimum wage rates of 36¢ and 33¢ an hour on Class I railroads and short lines, respectively. In April, 1942, the Administrator issued an order establishing another minimum wage committee to make a further study of wages in the railroad industry. Hearings before this committee were held on April 28. When, however, this committee unanimously recommended the establishment of a minimum wage of 40¢ an hour in the railroad industry (which an order of the Wage-Hour Administrator made effective August 31, 1942), this minimum figure had in most instances already been surpassed through the processes of collective bargaining. The average straight-time hourly earnings of maintenance of way workers on Class I railroads in the United States averaged 58.7¢ during 1942.

American labor had agreed generally that during the war there should be no strikes. The procedure under the Railway Labor Act, however, made it almost mandatory that a strike vote be taken and a date for a strike set before the President of the United States could declare that an emergency existed and appoint an Emergency Board to investigate the dispute. To obviate the necessity for this procedure, on May 21, 1942, the President signed an Executive Order establishing a National Railway Labor Panel consisting of a chairman and eight members. The chairman of the Panel had the power to assign three members of the Panel to sit as an emergency fact-finding board when an unadjusted dispute threatened to interfere with the prosecution of the war, even in the absence of a strike vote. This Panel functioned for the railroad industry in much the same manner as the National War Labor Board, appointed earlier by the President to settle labor disputes in industry generally.

On June 18, ten of the non-operating railroad labor organizations, including the Brotherhood, submitted to this Panel pending disputes arising from the refusal of certain railroads to accept the wage increase and vacation agreements of December, 1941. Hearings began on August 10, 1942, before an Emergency Board selected from the Panel. The report of this Board, made to the President on September 14, 1942, was a complete victory for the Brotherhoods.

The Board recommended: (1) that the Class I railroads and short lines included in the dispute before the Board grant the basic wage increase provided by the agreement of December 15, 1941, effective December 1, 1941; (2) that a basic minimum wage rate of 46¢ an hour be established for all Class I roads, and 43¢ an hour for Class II and Class III carriers, effective December 1, 1941; (3) that the roads concerned accept the terms and conditions of the vacation agreement of December 17, 1941.

As the war progressed into 1942, the cost of living and the prices of commodities had continued to climb steadily upward. An Executive Order issued by the President on April 11, 1941, establishing the Office of Price Administration and Civilian Supply had been only moderately effective in controlling prices. To prevent the disastrous effects of an uncontrolled inflation, on October 3, 1942, President Roosevelt signed an Executive Order, following authority vested in him by an act of Congress, establishing an Office of Economic Stabilization to control prices and wages during the war emergency. Within a few months, the wage control policies of the administration precipitated a serious controversy between the government and railroad workers.

By this time, the rapid increase in living costs and other economic factors had made a further increase in wage rates for railroad workers imperative. On September 25, 1942, the Brotherhood joined with other non-operating railroad labor organizations in the United States in a national movement to obtain a wage increase of 20¢ an hour and a minimum wage of 70¢ an hour. In addition, for the first time in the history of collective bargaining negotiations on the railroads, the labor organizations requested the establishment of a union-shop agreement on a national basis under which a railroad worker would be required to join and retain membership in the standard labor organization by which he was represented.

The injection of the union-shop issue in the wage-increase request was not at all accidental. It had been included in the September 25 notice after repeated demands from members of the railroad Brotherhoods, who felt that all workers who receive the protection of a labor union and share in the benefits it obtains should help to bear the cost of providing this protection and obtaining these benefits. The failure of the Brotherhoods, after years of continual effort, to prevail upon a minority of the workers they represented to become members, had brought about convention action favoring a union shop.

Meantime, representatives of the employes and the railroads had been unable to agree on the application of certain provisions of the Vacation Agreement of December 17, 1941. After conferences in the summer of 1942, it was agreed that the disputes would be submitted for decision to a referee to be selected by the National Mediation Board. The Board appointed Dean Wayne L. Morse, a member of the National War Labor Board, who had served as chairman of the Emergency Board which had investigated the wage and vacation dispute in 1941. On November 12, 1942, Referee Morse issued a lengthy award outlining in detail his decisions on the disputed points. This award has become the basis for the accepted application of various portions of the Vacation Agreement.

Mediation proceedings during January, 1943, failed to bring about a settlement of the employes' wage-increase and union-shop request of September 25, 1942, and on January 13, 1943, President Milliman sent a telegram to President Roosevelt reading in part:

"Following the outbreak of war the railroad workers represented by the Brotherhood of Maintenance of Way Employes gave you their pledge to refrain from strikes for the duration. In making that pledge in behalf of our organized craft I intended then, and desire now, to keep the promise so made as evidence of our deep gratitude to you personally for all you have done for our low paid group and also because we realized then, and realize now, that the efficient and uninterrupted operation of the railroads is indispensable to our war effort and, therefore, to the preservation of the American way of life. However, the railroad maintenance of way wage situation has become so intolerable that certain of our members are threatening drastic action and unless prompt relief from the now existing substandard wages is assured, I am convinced that, in spite of my no strike pledge and in spite of efforts that will, of course, be put forth by the officers of our Brotherhood, these workers may take matters into their own hands and engage in a series of unauthorized strikes which, if once started, may spread like a prairie fire throughout the entire railroad industry. . . .

"The [wage increase] dispute is now dragging along in mediation with carrier representatives trying to take it out of the hands of your Railroad War Labor Panel and place it on the already overburdened docket of the War Labor Board in order to delay further the increases in present substandard wages that must be granted and granted promptly if labor chaos is to be avoided in the Railroad Industry."

Milliman pointed out as an example of the critical situation two instances in which railroads were hiring employes through dummy contractors and paying them 75¢ an hour for track work while regular trackmen on these roads were receiving from 46¢ to 58¢ an hour. "As a result of this kind of action," he said in his telegram to the President, "our men are highly enraged, and justly, and are threatening to strike. . . . I am afraid we cannot control the situation much longer."

Because of the government's price control and wage stabilization program, the question of whether the National War Labor Board (established for industry generally) or the National Railway Labor Panel (established for the railroad industry) had final jurisdiction over the wage dispute had now become of paramount importance. On February 4, 1943, President Roosevelt issued an Executive Order upholding the contention of the employes that the National Railway Labor Panel had jurisdiction, and on February 20 the chairman of the Panel appointed an Emergency Board to investigate the controversy. This Board began hearings on March 1.

After forty-four days of public hearings, the Emergency Board made its report to President Roosevelt on May 24, 1943. The Board recommended that wages be increased by 8¢ an hour retroactive to February 1, 1943, but it made no recommendation as to a minimum hourly wage. It also recommended that the railroad labor organizations withdraw their request for a union shop agreement, taking the position that their request if granted "would compel the carriers to violate clear provisions of the Railway Labor Act." These provisions, incidentally, had been written into the Act in 1934 at the request of the railroad Brotherhoods to prohibit the formation or continued sponsoring of company unions by the railroads as had been the case in so many instances since 1922.

At the time the Board's report was sent to the President, there was little indication of the dramatic events to follow which converted the wage-increase recommendation of the Board into a highly controversial issue for the remainder of the year. Although disappointed by the Board's recommendations on both the wage and union-shop issues, the Brotherhoods were prepared to accept the report. On June 22, 1943, however, Judge Fred M. Vinson, Director of Economic Stabilization, issued an order to the effect that the 8¢ hourly increase "shall no become effective," and directing the Board to reconsider its recommendations in the light of a memorandum opinion to be filed by him. In his memorandum, Director Vinson held that the increase did not conform to President Roosevelt's "Hold-the-Line Order" or to a directive issued by Director Vinson on May 12, 1943. He said, in effect, that the Board's report would have to be revised downward in keeping with the government's wage stabilization policy.

Judge Vinson's order dropped like a bombshell into a situation which up to that time had been comparatively placid, and brought a wave of violent protests from Brotherhood representatives and railroad workers alike. At hearings before the Emergency Board, representatives of the employes had pointed out that the wages of railroad workers had lagged behind those of workers in other industries.

Trackmen, the testimony showed, were paid an average of only 54¢ an hour in October, 1942, while unskilled labor in manufacturing industries throughout the United States received an average of 80¢ an hour. The disparity was much greater for some railroad workers who received wages ranging as low as 40¢ an hour. To tell railroad workers employed under these conditions that they could not receive the modest 8¢ hourly increase was to precipitate a reaction that arose with an intense spontaneity.

Thus the matter stood when the 28th regular convention of Grand Lodge met in Detroit, Michigan, beginning July 19, 1943. Reports to the convention by Grand Lodge officers revealed a record of remarkable progress. In the three-year period from April 1, 1940, to April 1, 1943, the membership of the Brotherhood had increased by 40,893. The Brotherhood then held agreements on 93 per cent of the total railroad mileage in the United States and on the entire mileage in Canada with the exception of one small railroad. The Santa Fe was the only major railroad system in the United States and Canada with which the Brotherhood did not hold an agreement.

The time and one-half rate after eight hours' work, the Grand Lodge President's report showed, was being paid on 88 per cent of the entire mileage in the United States.

The delegates reaffirmed action taken on many important issues at previous conventions and unanimously adopted a committee report establishing a procedure for forming and financing state legislative committees. President Milliman and Secretary-Treasurer Shoemake were re-elected by acclamation.

The wage controversy had now become a national issue of major importance. At the request of President Roosevelt, the carriers and the labor organizations held further conferences, and on August 7, 1943, they reached an agreement providing for a wage increase of 8¢ an hour and a minimum rate of 54¢ an hour, subject to government approval. The Economic Stabilization Director, however, refused to approve this agreement, and the controversy grew more strident. It even echoed in the halls of Congress, where a resolution was introduced expressing the opinion that the wage agreement of August 7 should be considered an appropriate and valid settlement of the dispute.

On October 16, President Roosevelt appointed a Special Emergency Board to reconsider the case and recommend wage adjustments that would conform to the government's stabilization policy. In a report filed with the President on November 4, 1943, the Special Board recommended increases in wages ranging from 4¢ an hour for the higher-rated employes to 10¢ an hour for those receiving less than 47¢ an hour.

The Economic Stabilization Director approved the Board's report, but the non-operating Brotherhoods refused to accept the report and invoked the services of the National Mediation Board. They had begun the circulation of a strike ballot on October 25, and a strike was called to begin at 6:00 p.m., December 30. On December 27, the President issued an Executive Order directing the army to take over the railroads "to avoid interruption of transportation by threatened strikes". On that same day, however, the Brotherhoods had already canceled the strike call, and conferences toward a settlement of the dispute were then under way in Washington.

On January 17, 1944, about sixteen months after the request had been filed, the seemingly interminable controversy was finally settled when an agreement having the approval of Stabilization Director Vinson and the Special Emergency Board was signed at Washington, D. C. The agreement provided wage increases ranging from 4¢ an hour for those employes receiving 97¢ an hour and over, to 10¢ for those receiving less than 47¢ an hour, retroactive to February 1, 1943.

Effective December 27, 1943, supplementary amounts (to be paid as the equivalent of or in lieu of claims for time and one-half pay for work performed in excess of 40 hours a week) were to be added to the increases effective February 1. The net result was that effective December 27 wages were increased by amounts ranging from 11¢ an hour for the lowest-paid employes to 9¢ an hour for the highest-paid.

While this dispute was in progress, President Milliman had pointed out to the membership of the Brotherhood the urgent need for action to combat the growing sentiment against labor unions on both national and state levels. He emphasized the handicap under which the Brotherhood attempted to carry on its legislative program because it then had no state legislative representatives, and he urged the cooperation of system and lodge officers and individual members in the "desperate battle of self-preservation confronting organized labor in a number of states".

"This situation is a serious threat in Congress as well as in many of the State Legislatures where particularly vicious anti-labor measures have been introduced and are being strongly pushed," he warned. "The present anti-labor trend in national and state legislation has stronger backing and is a more serious threat to organized labor than any such movement within the past twenty years."

During this time, a controversy between the Brotherhood

and Canadian railways had taken shape. On January 8, 1943, the Central Committee served notice on the Railway Association of Canada requesting:

"1. The elimination of existing wage inequalities through the establishment of rates of pay which will be more equitable in comparison with the rates paid employes in similar work on these same railroads in Canada; with employes of other railroads, not covered by our Agreement, but operating in Canada or in territory adjacent thereto; and with employes of similar or equal skill in other major and organized industries in Canada.

"2. The adoption of a vacation plan for an annual two weeks' vacation with pay beginning with the year 1943."

The railways had rejected the employes' request, and the Central Committee prepared the case for submission to the National War Labour Board of Canada in accordance with regulations established by the Canadian government.

One of the most serious problems confronting the Brotherhood for years had been its jurisdictional disputes with the Building and Construction Trades Department of the American Federation of Labor. Through the years, various organizations have claimed, at one time or another, practically all classes of maintenance of way work except that of crossing flagmen and watchmen. The organization has been compelled to carry on an almost constant resistance to the repeated efforts of other organizations to invade the jurisdiction of the Brotherhood. Other labor organizations, and particularly those established along craft lines, have tried persistently to claim work being performed by maintenance of way employes in spite of the fact that when the Brotherhood first affiliated with the American Federation of Labor (and each time its charter has been subsequently amended), it was given the exclusive right to represent all employes engaged in the building and maintaining of the tracks, bridges, buildings, and appurtenances thereto in the maintenance of way and structures departments of the railroads. Thus the Brotherhood was chartered as a semi-industrial organization rather than a craft organization. Most unions affiliated with the American Federation of Labor are chartered as craft organizations.

On May 21, 1943, the Brotherhood reached an agreement

with representatives of the building and construction trades providing basically that the building trades would have jurisdiction over work on any railroad property not located on the line of the railroad, and that the Brotherhood would have jurisdiction over all work located on the line of railroad coming within the jurisdiction of its agreement with the carriers.

At the time this agreement was signed, representatives of the Brotherhood confidently expected that it would definitely dispose of any future jurisdictional disputes with the building trades. The Brotherhood has tried to comply fully with the terms of this agreement. The building trades, however, have not; and they have since raised numerous jurisdictional disputes which would be automatically settled by compliance with the 1943 agreement.

Meanwhile, the non-operating Brotherhoods had met with difficulty in persuading the Columbus & Greenville Railroad to apply the provisions of the wage and vacation agreements of December, 1941. The carrier had refused to establish the minimum hourly rate of 46¢ or to comply with the terms of the Vacation Agreement. Instead, it had attempted to make unreasonable changes in rules covering working conditions. A strike which began on November 23, 1943, ended on December 8 when an agreement was signed establishing a basic minimum wage rate of 46¢ an hour and a vacation-with-pay plan containing the essential benefits of the national Vacation Agreement. The company withdrew its demand for rules changes.

As the war continued, the manpower shortage became more and more acute, and the railroads in many sections of the country desperately sought workers to keep the nation's rail transportation system functioning at top efficiency. A number of workers, particularly in regions where wage rates were low, had left the service of the carriers to seek more lucrative employment in other industries. The Railroad Retirement Board's report of personnel needs for January, 1944, showed that the railroads in the United States needed 98,639 workers, and that of this number 46,000 (almost 47 per cent) were needed in occupational groups represented by the Brotherhood.

Although considerable progress had been made in improving the working conditions of maintenance of way employes, more adequate rules covering work performed in overtime hours and on Sundays and holidays had long been an objective of the Brotherhood. A meeting of Grand Lodge and system officers held in February, 1944, authorized the inauguration of an overtime rules movement. On April 15, 1944, a notice was served on the managements of all railroads in the United States with whom the Brotherhood held agreements requesting four specific overtime rules, including double-time pay after sixteen hours of service.

After system conferences had been completed with little success, national committees representing the carriers and the Brotherhood were formed. Conferences between the two committees began on September 14, 1944, and ended on October 21. On that date a National Overtime Rules Agreement was signed containing uniform provisions for the payment of the time and one-half rate for work in excess of eight hours; the time and one-half rate for work performed on calls, with a minimum of four hours at the straight-time rate; the time and one-half rate for work performed on Sundays and seven specified holidays; and the double-time rate for work performed in excess of 16 hours in any twenty-four hour period.

This agreement was of great importance not only because it established a much higher degree of uniformity in rules governing the payment of overtime work, but because it brought about a substantial improvement in the overtime rules in most of the individual system agreements.

In the early part of the year, railway workers in Canada secured a partial settlement of their request of January 8, 1943, for adjustments in wage rates and a vacation of two weeks with pay. On March 1, 1944, pursuant to the "finding and direction" of the National War Labour Board of Canada, the Central Committee of the Brotherhood signed an agreement with the Railway Association of Canada providing for an annual vacation of six days with pay effective with the year 1944.

Railway workers in Canada, however, had still not received a general wage increase, although the cost-of-living bonus had been added to basic wage rates, effective February 15, 1944, in an amount equivalent to about 10¢ an hour. On July 31,

1944, the War Labour Board issued a decision granting a wage increase of 6¢ an hour to hourly-rated workers, 48¢ a day to daily-rated workers, $2.88 a week to weekly-rated workers, and $12.48 a month to monthly-rated workers. The decision granted back pay to maintenance of way employes from March 3, 1943.

Railroad workers in the United States had continually expressed dissatisfaction with the Vacation Agreement of 1941, which granted only six days' paid vacation each year and which was manifestly not in keeping with vacation policies generally established in other industries. On June 26, 1944, the non-operating railroad Brotherhoods served formal notices on railroad managements in the United States requesting annual vacations with pay of twelve, fifteen and eighteen consecutive days to be granted on the basis of length of service.

After almost eight months of intermittent conferences, a settlement was finally reached on this request. On February 23, 1945, national committees representing the carriers and the Brotherhoods signed a mediation agreement supplementing the Vacation Agreement of 1941 to provide an annual vacation of twelve consecutive work days, effective with the year 1945, for employes with five or more years of continuous service. The paid vacation of six working days for employes with less service continued in effect.

The tide of war had now definitely turned in favor of the allied nations. In Europe and in the Pacific, the military forces of the allies were drawing ever-tightening circles about the aggressor nations. At the 1944 election, the voters of the United States had again shattered precedent by returning President Roosevelt to office for the fourth successive time, and as the year 1945 began and the end of the war became more and more imminent, plans for peace and the rehabilitation of the lands shattered and made desolate by the war were already well under way.

Although the average straight-time hourly earnings of railroad workers represented by the Brotherhood on Class I railroads in the United States had increased from 47.9¢ in 1939 to 68.3¢ in 1945, the wage increases granted had been added to basic rates. Thus the inequalities in wage rates for the same class of work on the same road, from road to road, and between different sections of the country, were unaffected.

At a meeting of Grand Lodge and system officers in May, 1945, the report of a special committee appointed to analyze wage inequalities was given careful study. The meeting by unanimous action authorized a national movement to correct these inequalities and to establish a more equitable and uniform wage schedule on all systems. A national wage committee was appointed to study the over-all situation.

As a result of these preliminary moves, on June 25, 1945, formal notices were served on all roads with whom the Brotherhood held contracts in the United States requesting a basic minimum hourly wage of 75¢, a standard uniform wage scale, and eleven uniform rules governing working conditions. Not only did the carriers reject the employes' request in system conferences, but they displayed a reluctance to join in national handling, although this had become an established procedure since the wage-deduction agreement of 1932. On October 10, 1945, the Brotherhood invoked the services of the National Mediation Board.

At the time the Brotherhood served its notices, no other general movement affecting wages and working conditions was in progress. Shortly thereafter, however, other standard railroad labor organizations became active, and soon the railroads were confronted with a number of separate and dissimilar notices affecting practically all the 1½ million railroad workers then in the service. Because of the highly-complicated situation that resulted, on November 29, 1945, an agreement was reached between national committees representing the carriers and the non-operating Brotherhoods that all the requests made by these organizations would be converted into one uniform request for a wage increase of 30¢ an hour.

During this time, a simultaneous movement had been under way in Canada to correct gross inequalities in wage rates. A great deal of study had been given to the situation by the Central Committee, and in its notice of January 2, 1945, to the Railway Association of Canada, the Committee proposed a specific wage rate for each separate maintenance of way classification instead of a uniform over-all increase to be added to existing basic rates of pay.

When the Railway Association denied the request, the dispute was submitted to the National War Labour Board of Canada on March 31, 1945. Briefs and exhibits were subsequently filed with the Board in support of the employes' proposal. But weeks turned into months of delay, and on November 26, 1945, the Brotherhood filed a protest with the Board and urged that it take prompt action to furnish the relief so sorely needed by Canadian maintenance of way workers.

While these movements were in progress, the Brotherhood had suffered a defeat in its campaign to regain jurisdiction over maintenance of way workers on the Santa Fe System, the lone major line on which the Brotherhood did not hold an agreement. This movement began in June, 1944, after employes on that road had sent numerous letters and petitions to Grand Lodge requesting that they be represented by the Brotherhood.

Of the approximately 13,000 maintenance of way employes on the system eligible to vote, some 10,000 signed authorization cards for representation by the Brotherhood. The services of the National Mediation Board were invoked on December 18, 1944, but the Board failed to assign a mediator to the case until April 6, 1945.

In the meantime, the independent union on the Santa Fe, apparently sensing defeat, had affiliated with the "United Railroad Workers of America, C. I. O." A further delay was encountered over the question of whether Mexican nationals employed by the Santa Fe were entitled to vote. The Mediation Board held that they were. These delays served to take the edge off the Brotherhood's campaign, which up to that time had been progressing favorably, and it became clearly apparent that an election would have to be held to decide the issue.

The balloting of the employes began on May 28, 1945, under the direction of the Mediation Board and ended on June 30. An official certification of the ballot, released by the Board in July, 1945, showed that the Brotherhood had failed to win representation rights. The heavy vote cast for the Brotherhood, however, was very encouraging and showed the growing dissatisfaction among maintenance of way workers with conditions on the Santa Fe System.

As the summer of 1945 ended, the design of world affairs had undergone a decided change. Vice President Harry S. Truman had become President of the United States when Franklin Delano Roosevelt died unexpectedly on April 12, 1945. The capitulation of Germany on May 7, 1945, and the surrender of Japan four months later ended hostilities in World War II, and the nations of the world began the tremendous job of rehabilitation and the critically important transition from a wartime to a peacetime economy.

Wartime conditions had brought about drastic changes in rates of pay of maintenance of way workers and some improvements in agreement rules in both the United States and Canada. The general and principal changes, as referred to in this chapter, may be summarized as follows:

UNITED STATES

March 1, 1941—A minimum hourly rate of 36¢ for Class I carriers and of 33¢ for Class II and smaller carriers became effective on this date under the Wage-Hour Act.

December 15, 1941—An agreement signed on this date granted a wage increase of 9¢ an hour effective September 1, 1941, and an additional 1¢ an hour effective December 1, 1941, and established a minimum hourly rate of 46¢.

December 17, 1941—A national vacation agreement granted six days' vacation with pay each year, beginning with the year 1942.

August 31, 1942—A minimum hourly wage of 40¢ an hour became effective for railroad workers under the Wage-Hour Act. This government order, however, had already been superseded by the collective-bargaining agreement signed December 15, 1941, establishing a minimum hourly rate of 46¢.

January 17, 1944—An agreement signed on this date granted wage increases ranging from 4¢ to 10¢ an hour, retroactive to February 1, 1943; additional amounts to be added, effective December 27, 1943, to bring these increases to amounts ranging from 9¢ to 11¢ an hour.

October 21, 1944—A national agreement signed providing improved overtime rules.

February 23, 1945—National vacation agreement amended to provide an annual vacation of 12 days with pay to railroad workers with five or more years of railroad service.

CANADA

June 1, 1941—A cost-of-living bonus, to be adjusted periodically on the basis of living costs in August, 1939, became effective on this date.

February 15, 1944—Cost-of-living bonus added to basic wage rates in an amount equivalent to approximately 10¢ an hour.

March 1, 1944—An agreement signed on this date granted annual vacations of six days with pay beginning with the year 1944.

July 31, 1944—A wage increase of 6¢ an hour granted retroactive to March 3, 1943.

As the greatest conflict in the history of mankind drew to a close, railroad maintenance of way workers were able to view with considerable satisfaction the part they had played in helping to win the war. Not only had the maintenance of way department done an outstanding job in maintaining the tracks and bridges of the railway system under the heaviest rail traffic in history, but it had contributed liberally to the fighting forces of the two nations.

Figures by the Office of Defense Transportation showed that 304,000 workers had left their railroad jobs in the United States to enter the service of their country during World War II. Of this number, 68,000 (22 per cent) were employes from the maintenance of way and structures department. Maintenance of way workers in Canada had made a similar contribution toward victory.

Some of these workers had helped to operate railroads in foreign lands; others never returned from the battlefields. The delegates attending the 1946 convention of the Brotherhood paid a warm tribute to the servicemen from the maintenance of way department. But the Brotherhood sought to make a more substantial contribution to the welfare of veterans of World War II who were seeking to reestablish themselves in civilian life.

"Since V-E and V-J days," President Milliman told the convention, "it has been a popular pastime in both Canada and the United States to pay glowing tributes to our returning heroes. . . .

"It is, of course, the unanimous feeling of the delegates at this Convention that our report would not be complete, and would indeed reflect some lack of appreciation, if we failed to give expression to the gratitude that we feel to those who served their country so nobly during the recent war years. However, this Brotherhood wants its expression of gratitude and its tribute to these servicemen to be real. We want it to be sincere. We want it to be acceptable to them in that it will indicate something more on our part than a mere outburst of eloquence.

"Therefore, may I say on behalf of this Brotherhood and the delegates assembled here at this Convention, that in our opinion the most sincere and worth while way for the entire United States and Canada to show their appreciation to our returning servicemen is to see that they are now given good jobs, with regular employment, at good wages, and under fair working conditions, so that they may return to civilian life on an economic basis that will permit them to enjoy some of the security for which they have been fighting. . . . This will be our tribute for the service they have rendered, and this is the kind of gratitude they want to see."

In a telegram which President Milliman read to the convention, L. B. Schwellenbach, the United States Secretary of Labor, said: "Throughout this long period which imposed a steadily mounting strain on our transportation system, your union met each new demand with unfaltering service and devotion; as troops and fighting equipment moved in an endless stream, your union literally 'kept them rolling.' Equally important, you kept them rolling safely over road-beds that were burdened far beyond their normal capacity. It was a great job, magnificently done!"

A telegram in a similar vein from Humphrey Mitchell, Minister of Labour, Dominion of Canada, read: "I have watched the development of the Brotherhood of Maintenance of Way Employes and its struggle to its present eminent and constructive position in the international labor movement, which I know will maintain a high degree of true labor statesmanship as it has done in the past."

The war record of labor during the forty-four long, tense months following Pearl Harbor had been impressive. In production, the results had been almost miraculous. The output of munitions increased eleven-fold, from one-half billion dollars a month to 5½ billion at the peak, more than the rest of the world combined.

America virtually scraped the bottom of the barrel to secure needed manpower for industry and the armed forces. Millions of housewives took war jobs. Unions cooperated in helping to secure workers to relieve critical manpower shortages at various strategic points.

Work stoppages because of strikes averaged less than one-tenth of one per cent of the time worked during the war. And even these insignificant losses were more than offset by work on legal holidays.

The efficiency of workers in munitions industries climbed 72 per cent during the war; on the railroads by even more. Although the railroads were short both in equipment and manpower, railroad workers did almost the impossible in carrying a transportation load double that of prewar levels.

With the end of the war, the two nations turned their thoughts to the serious post-war problems that were certain to follow in a world torn and divided economically and politically. In a statement made on Labor Day, 1945, President Harry S. Truman said:

"Six years ago the workers of the United States, and of the world, awoke to a Labor Day in a world at war. The democracies of Western Europe had just accepted the challenge of totalitarianism. We in the United States had two years of grace, but the issue was squarely joined at that hour, as we now know. There was to be no peace until tyranny had been outlawed.

"Today we stand on the threshold of a new world. We must do our part in making this world what it should be—a world in which the bigotries of race and class and creed shall not be permitted to warp the souls of men.

"We enter upon an era of great problems, but to live is to face problems. Our men and women did not falter in the task of saving freedom. They will not falter now in the task of making freedom secure. And high in the ranks of those men and women, as a grateful world will always remember, are the workers of all free nations who produced the vast equipment with which victory was won.

"The tasks ahead are great, and the opportunities are equally great. Your Government is determined to meet those tasks and fulfill those opportunities.

"We recognize the importance and dignity of labor, and we recognize the right of every American citizen to a wage which will permit him and his dependents to maintain a decent standard of living."

CHAPTER VIII

THE AFTERMATH

THE paramount question both in the United States and Canada as the war ended was whether the sudden conversion from an economy geared for a maximum production of all the materials of war to the more moderate needs of peace, would result in depressed business conditions. Those who took a pessimistic view of the immediate economic situation in the two countries, overlooked the tremendous shortage of all types of products used in everyday living, created by the strict rationing of essential materials during the war.

Some letdown was to be expected as the world shook off the after-effects of an overexpanded wartime production; nevertheless, the early post-war years became a period of great business activity as industry sought to fill the needs of a populace clamoring for products that had become extremely scarce or even non-existent.

By 1947, when the return to peace-time production had been completed, 60 million employed workers in the United States produced an immense volume of goods and services. Prices rose rapidly during the post-war boom, and after Congress removed the price controls imposed during the war, the specter of inflation menaced the economic future of the nation. In Canada, too, the cost of living continued a steady upward trend after the war.

The net railway operating income of carriers in the United States dropped somewhat in the years immediately following the ending of the war, and a gradual but steady reduction in the maintenance of way work force took place, stimulated by the use of modern machinery for performing various work operations previously done by hand. The number of maintenance of way employes decreased from 292,532 in 1945 to 256,748 in 1946 and to only 226,994 in 1950.

The reduction in the number of maintenance of way workers employed on railways in Canada was not so drastic. From 40,247 in 1945, the number of workers decreased to 37,944 in 1946, but by 1950, this figure had increased slightly to 38,878.

As the year 1945 closed, the joint request (November, 1945) of the non-operating railroad Brotherhoods for a wage increase of 30¢ an hour had reached a stalemate. The services of the National Mediation Board had been invoked when national conferences between representatives of the railroads and the employes brought no progress. The Board announced on January 19, 1946, that it had been unable to bring the parties into agreement, and on January 26, the national committees agreed to submit the dispute to an Arbitration Board of six members. President Milliman served as one of the two labor members on the Board.

In a report to the 1946 convention, Milliman emphasized that a careful study of the situation had been made before the Brotherhood dropped its separate requests and joined in the movement for a uniform wage increase. The wage increase demand, he pointed out, was justified for three principal reasons: (1) Compared to employes in other industries, the non-operating railroad workers had been the victims of a steadily growing wage inequity; (2) the railroad industry was in the most prosperous condition in its history; and (3) the rising cost of living made a wage increase necessary to avoid a substantial reduction in living standards.

The Arbitration Board began its hearings on February 18, 1946, and on April 3 it announced its award, granting a wage increase of 16¢ an hour to the employes concerned, to be effective January 1, 1946, under the terms of the arbitration

Bridge and building workmen set a scaffold to repair a building.

↑ *Above:* Bridgemen work at dizzy heights in maintaining this railway bridge.

Right: Workmen repair the surface of a tunnel —one of the many skills required of maintenance of way men. →

Above: A bridge gang overhauls a highway overpass.

Right: One of the mammoth steel structures (over the Mississippi River at Memphis, Tennessee) maintained by steel bridgemen on the Frisco System.

→

Above: Two views of the million-and-a-half dollar Missouri Pacific freight terminal at St. Louis built by maintenance of way bridge and building forces. This mammoth structure covers more than three city blocks.

Above: A bridge under construction on the Great Northern Railway to be maintained by maintenance of way workers. The job of lowering the 37-ton girder took three and one-half hours.

Above: Painting a water tank—only one of the many skilled jobs of the maintenance of way painter. Tomorrow he may be an interior decorator or paint a depot.

Above: Bridge and building mechanics often work in high places in maintaining railway bridges. Proud of their skill, they know that their work must pass each rigid test to safely support the giant locomotives and heavy trains.

Above: Two water-service mechanics inspect a "stand pipe" where the locomotive takes on water—an important item in railroad operation requiring ***skilled mechanics.***

Above: More than 600 delegates representing subordinate lodges in all parts of the United States and Canada attended the Thirty-first Regular Convention of Grand Lodge in Montreal, Quebec, Canada, June 16 through 23, 1952.

ɔove: A Louisville & Nashville freight train crossing Red ʋer bridge near Sloan, Kentucky.

Right: A passenger train winds its way through the gorge along the rapids.

→

5925

Above: D. W. Hertel, the author, reviewing the History's original manuscript before final printing.

Left: Lights on as a locomotive wending its way through the mountains, prepares to enter a tunnel.
←

Through the valley—a picture of grace and serenity as this passenger train rounds a curve along a placid stream. A summer scene along the Canadian Pacific Railway.

agreement. The employes, however, felt that the award was insufficient. In a special opinion accompanying the award, the labor members of the Board said:

"With great reluctance we have joined with the [neutral] members of the Board . . . in making an award which . . . is made wholly arbitrarily, is not based on the evidence before the Board, and is made without consideration of the equities of the employes' claim. . . . We have joined in such an award solely because the only alternatives left to us by the attitude of other members of the Board were to have the proceedings end in failure to make an award, or to have the amount awarded subjected to a further arbitrary reduction below the amount considered proper by the [neutral] arbitrators . . . in order to induce the carrier representatives to join in it. . . . If the correction of inequities as of the close of the war were calculated on even the lowest possible basis reconcilable with the evidence . . . [it] would require an award granting the employes' request in full."

On April 15, 1946, the non-operating Brotherhoods, wholly dissatisfied with the Board's award, filed a formal notice on all railroads that were parties to the arbitration proceedings and the award (acceptance of which was compulsory), requesting a further increase of 14¢ an hour. In filing this notice so soon after the Arbitration Board had rendered its award, the Brotherhoods were acting entirely in accordance with the provisions of the Railway Labor Act. As a matter of fact, inasmuch as they were compelled to accept the Board's award, this was the only way in which they could proceed to obtain an additional wage increase. In early May, 1,200 representatives of the Brotherhoods met in Chicago and authorized the distribution of a strike ballot to determine the wishes of railroad workers in the event a satisfactory settlement could not be reached.

At a conference on May 22, President Truman told a committee representing the Brotherhoods that he would not attempt to change the award of the Arbitration Board. He suggested, however, that railroad workers were entitled to an additional increase of 2½¢ an hour, but he emphasized that this was all that was permissible under the government's current stabilization policy. On May 25, 1946, an agreement was reached between the participating carriers and the Brotherhoods providing for an additional wage increase of 2½¢ an hour effective May 22, 1946.

The representatives of the engineers and the trainmen, however, refused to accept a proposal by the President to settle their dispute with the carriers, and a strike of these two organizations, postponed from its original date of May 18, began on May 23. For two days, the movement of trains was virtually at a standstill, but the strike ended on May 25 when an agreement was reached between the carriers and these two groups of employes. The government had seized the railroads on May 17 and placed them under the control of the Office of Defense Transportation, but they were returned to private ownership on May 26.

In the meantime, an extremely serious situation had arisen on the Toledo, Peoria and Western Railway. This road had been placed under government control on March 22, 1942, because of a strike then in progress. When the road was returned to private ownership, effective October 1, 1945, the management flatly rejected a proposal of the employes that wages and rules negotiated during government control be continued in effect. Instead, the management insisted upon terms that were wholly unreasonable and arbitrary. The ensuing strike, which began on October 1, 1945, developed into a bitter conflict and was the longest in the history of the railroad industry. Eighteen and one-half months later, after the tragic death of the president of the road, a settlement was reached on April 20, 1947.

Under the terms of the agreement ending the strike, the employes retained the rules in effect during government control, including the application of the vacation agreement, were granted the 1946 wage increase of 18½¢ cents an hour, and were restored to the service with seniority unimpaired.

Early in 1946, maintenance of way workers in Canada secured action at last on their request for a rectification of gross inequalities and injustices in wage rates, pending since March 31, 1945. On March 13, 1946, the War Labour Board of Canada began hearings on this dispute. On June 12, 1946, the Board issued a decision granting an increase of 2¢ an hour, effective February 16, 1946, except in certain classified yards, where hourly increases of 3¢, 4¢, and 5¢ were granted to section men.

Because of the intense dissatisfaction among Canadian maintenance of way workers with the Board's award, the Central Committee filed a new request on July 23, 1946, for an additional increase of 20¢ an hour. "It is inconceivable that such an award could have been handed down," the Secretary of the Committee said. "We are again forced to present our demands the relief."

The protests from Canadian railway workers reached such volume that the War Labour Board decided to reopen the case, and suggested that the Brotherhood join with the other railway labor organizations in Canada in the national handling of the wage question. On August 23, 1946, an agreement was reached with the Canadian National Railways and the Ontario Northland Railway, providing for a wage increase of 8¢ an hour for maintenance of way workers, retroactive to June 1, 1946, in addition to the increase granted effective February 16, 1946. A similar agreement was signed with the Canadian Pacific and other railways in Canada on October 31, 1946.

Meantime, an editorial in the "Journal" warned that the floodgates of inflation were about to be opened because of the apparent reluctance of Congress to continue price controls. "Inflation, the greatest enemy of the wage earners, is about to be given more leeway," the editorial commented. "This is a dangerous policy at this time—one from which the common people will suffer most. . . . Labor will soon find itself back where it was before the movement for increased wages started, and will have to demand more increases. . . . It is passing strange that the Administration was able to hold the wage line in the face of mounting prices during the war, but now that peace has come (in the military sense) it is unable to hold the price line."

Unfortunately, this prediction came true, and after Congress removed price controls, the rapidly soaring cost of living forced workers to seek additional wage increases.

On July 15, 1946, when the 29th regular convention of Grand Lodge, one of the largest in the history of the Brotherhood, met in Detroit, Michigan, the reports of Grand Lodge officers reflected the continued progress of the Brotherhood. Since the 1943 convention, President Milliman reported, agreements had been secured or extended on 47 railroads. The report of Secretary-Treasurer Shoemake showed that the membership of the Brotherhood had increased more than 21,000 in the three-year period.

The convention increased the initiation fee for new members from $3.00 to $5.00, re-elected President Milliman and Secretary-Treasurer Shoemake, and took action condemning the substandard conditions arising out of the carriers' policies with respect to board and commissary companies, camp outfits, and employment agencies; and favoring union-management cooperation, an annual wage for maintenance of way workers, uniform working conditions, a joint national movement in Canada to correct gross inequalities in wage rates as compared to those in the United States, stability of year round employment, and compensation for recognized holidays.

The Convention also increased Grand Lodge dues from $2.50 to $3.00 a quarter. This was the first change in Grand Lodge dues, insofar as the general fund is concerned, since 1922, when Grand Lodge dues were reduced from $2.00 to $1.50 a quarter. Following the 1925 convention, Grand Lodge dues had been increased from $1.50 to $2.50 a quarter, but the increase of $1.00 a quarter had been added by referendum vote of the membership to be used to maintain the new Death Benefit Department.

A two-year fight to obtain liberalizing amendments to the Railroad Retirement and Unemployment Insurance Acts ended on July 31, 1946, when President Truman signed the so-called Crosser bill. The Crosser amendments to the Railroad Retirement Act provided for the payment of monthly survivor annuities; broadened the scope of disability benefits, including a new provision for an occupational disability annuity; increased minimum retirement benefits; and raised the retirement tax to pay for the increased benefits. Amendments to the Railroad Unemployment Insurance Act lengthened the period during which benefits were payable and added a new and highly important feature to the Act. Effective July 1, 1947, benefits became payable for time lost because of sickness or injury on the same basis as for time lost because of lack of work.

Another bill sponsored in Congress by the standard railroad labor organizations and approved by the President on August 2, 1946, brought refunds of approximately $5½ million to railroad workers in ten states for unemployment insurance tax deducted from their wages under the Social Security Act before the passage of the Railroad Unemployment Insurance Act.

President Milliman had warned the membership of the Brotherhood in 1943 of a developing anti-labor attitude among state legislatures. This trend became clearly apparent at the November, 1946, elections when the states of Arizona, Nebraska, and South Dakota adopted amendments to their state constitutions, patterned after a similar amendment adopted by Florida in 1943, prohibiting any provisions in a collective bargaining contract which requires union membership as a condition of employment. Thus began a concerted movement by employers to secure the enactment of similar laws in all states under the misleading title "right to work". The union shop movement of the railroad Brotherhoods was later to be seriously hampered by these laws.

Twenty railroads, most of them short lines, had refused to apply the arbitration wage award of 16¢ an hour, effective January 1, 1946, or the additional 2½¢ wage increase effective May 22, 1946. A strike vote was taken on the roads concerned, and the non-operating Brotherhoods called a suspension of work to begin October 28, 1946. The strike was postponed, however, when President Truman appointed an Emergency Board on October 25 to investigate the dispute.

In its report to the President on December 4, the Board decided that fourteen of the twenty carriers concerned should conform to the established pattern of an 18½¢ an hour wage increase, and that negotiations on the six remaining roads should be carried out under conditions outlined in the Board's report.

On the last day of the year, tragedy struck suddenly. President Milliman entered the hospital on December 26 for a diagnosis of an ailment that had been troubling him. Five days later he died while undergoing a serious operation. Hundreds of his friends and associates attended his funeral on January 3, and messages of sympathy were received from all parts of the United States and Canada.

"The untimely passing of Elmer E. Milliman deprives our Brotherhood and the American labor movement of a great leader, a man with great promise for the years to which he had every reason to look forward," the "Journal" said. "He was a man of sterling quality with a fine character. . . . His devotion to his fellow man and to his Brotherhood never faltered during his long years of service as a Grand Lodge officer. . . . He was constantly thinking of the welfare of the Brotherhood membership and their needs as railroad workers. . . . If any man ever gave a fuller measure of service and devotion to mankind than Elmer E. Milliman, it would be difficult to find him."

The officers of Grand Lodge met in Detroit on January 4, 1947, and elected A. Shoemake, Grand Lodge Secretary-Treasurer, to fill the office of Grand Lodge President, and Vice President T. L. Jones to fill the office of Grand Lodge Secretary-Treasurer, until a special election could be held in accordance with the Grand Lodge constitution.

Acting President Shoemake was born in Calhoun County, Mississippi. After entering railroad service in the maintenance of way department he held various important offices in the Brotherhood. From 1925 to 1929 he served as subordinate lodge secretary-treasurer and Joint Protective Board member on the St. Louis-San Francisco System Federation, from 1929 to 1934 as Vice General Chairman on that system, and thereafter as its General Chairman until his election as Grand Lodge Secretary-Treasurer in 1940. In this office he had served the Brotherhood for six years with efficiency and distinction.

At their meeting on January 4, the Grand Lodge officers adopted a resolution proposing that all system divisions and subordinate lodges of the Brotherhood be given an opportunity to contribute to a fund to be used for the erection of a monument to the memory of President Milliman.

In a special election held in Detroit, Michigan, on February 14, Vice President T. C. Carroll became the eighth President of the Brotherhood. Son and grandson of section foremen on the Southern Railway, President Carroll was born in a section house at Donalds, South Carolina, on May 22, 1894. After completing high school, Carroll entered railroad service as a clerk in a roadmaster's office on the Seaboard Air Line. Later, he held various jobs as brakeman and conductor and as section foreman on several railroads before entering the service of the Louisville and Nashville Railroad as an extra gang and yard foreman in Kentucky. While engaged in this work, he was elected General Chairman for the Brotherhood on the Louisville and Nashville System in October, 1919.

As a member of the Grand Lodge Executive Board from 1922 to 1925, he took an important part in straightening out the tangled affairs of the Brotherhood and in formulating the policies that helped to revive the organization in the critical years following the 1922 convention. He was elected as a Grand Lodge Vice President in 1925 and held that office continuously for more than twenty-one years until his election as Grand Lodge President. During these many years he helped to guide the destiny of the Brotherhood—at conventions of Grand Lodge, on negotiating committees, as a member of many of the policy-forming bodies of the organization. A recognized leader of men, Carroll brought to the presidency many years of rich experience in labor-management relations and a deep belief in the justice of the maintenance of way worker's struggle to improve his conditions, a program to which he has dedicated himself completely.

"I embark upon my new duties with profound pride in being chosen to carry on the work of the distinguished leaders who brought our Brotherhood to the forefront of the labor movement," President Carroll said in a message to the membership of the Brotherhood. "Carrying on in the tradition of leadership of Elmer Milliman and his predecessors will be no easy task.... Ours is the task of building a better standard of living for all maintenance of way workers and their families—to bring more income, more comfort and greater security into their homes. . . . As I take over the duties of President, I am thinking of these homes and the things we can and must do to make these homes better places in which to live. . . .

"I pledge myself to a program of justice and progress, constructed upon the fundamental aim of achieving better conditions for our membership and, at the same time, protecting those already gained through years of struggle and sacrifice."

In the years that followed, President Carroll was able to

continue with unusual success the Brotherhood's program of progress and to fulfill his pledge to the membership of better conditions in the maintenance of way department.

On February 12, two days before the new President assumed office, a strike had been called on the Georgia and Florida Railroad because of the failure of that road to comply with a notice served by the Brotherhood on June 15, 1946, requesting a wage increase of 18½¢ an hour, the amount recommended by the Emergency Board in the general wage movement of 1945-1946. The road was admittedly in poor financial condition, a fact which the management emphasized continually to the employes during the strike. A compromise settlement, accepted by the employes, brought the strike to an end on March 6.

In the meantime, rising living costs had canceled the effect of the last increase in wages and made another boost in wage rates imperative. Moreover, the wages of railroad employes still lagged behind those of workers in other industries and their efficiency and productivity had increased considerably. For these reasons, railroad workers maintained a persistent pressure on their Brotherhoods to begin a movement for higher wages. On March 25, 1947, the Brotherhood joined with other non-operating railroad labor organizations in the United States in a national notice requesting an increase of 20¢ an hour in basic wage rates.

Conferences between national committees representing the railroads and their non-operating employes came to an abrupt end on June 26, 1947. Failing to bring about a settlement in mediation conferences beginning on July 8, the Mediation Board proposed that the dispute be settled through arbitration.

Hearings before a six-man Arbitration Board, established under an agreement signed July 25, 1947, began on August 4. On September 2, the Board rendered its award granting an increase of 15½¢ an hour to the employes concerned, effective September 1, 1947, and an implementing agreement was signed by the two committees on September 3.

On April 8, 1947, members of the Central Committee of Canada met to discuss proposed changes in the Canadian agreements. A request for an annual vacation of 14 days with pay was then pending, notice having been served by the cooperating Brotherhoods on February 15, 1947. When conferences failed to produce a settlement of the dispute, the committee requested the intervention of the National Labour Relations Board. On June 30, 1947, a Conciliation Board released its report unanimously recommending vacations with pay of six, nine, and twelve days for Canadian railway workers effective with the year 1947. The Canadian railways, however, refused to accept the Board's recommendations.

The Brotherhoods completed plans to order a suspension of work beginning November 3, 1947, after 99 per cent of the workers had voted to strike. Negotiations had continued in the meantime, however, and on October 25, 1947, the basis of an understanding was reached granting 6 days' vacation with pay to employes with one year's service, 9 days' vacation to those with three years' service, and 12 days' vacation to those with five years' service. A formal agreement finally signed on January 9, 1948, contained the details for placing this understanding in effect beginning with the year 1948.

Another strike, lasting from May 30 to June 4, 1947, brought about a satisfactory settlement of the wage increase question on the Midland Terminal Railroad, located at Colorado Springs, Colorado.

Meanwhile, the anti-labor trend of legislation had become even more apparent. In June, 1947, Congress passed the Taft-Hartley Act over a Presidential veto. This Act placed many restrictions on labor unions, and it was immediately and almost unanimously condemned by labor organizations as a "slave labor act." Although the Taft Hartley Act does not apply to railroad workers in its general application, the railroad labor organizations have been just as critical of the Act as those it actually affects.

In the late summer, the "Journal" warned members of the Brotherhood against plans being promoted by certain "pension" groups to make fantastic amendments in the Railroad Retirement Act. Their activities financed by scattered contributions from railroad workers and from those on the annuity rolls, these groups sought changes in the Act which were wholly unfeasible. Activities of these pension groups have since increased. Although many of their proposals contain considerable merit, these groups ignore the detrimental effects these changes would have on the actuarial soundness of the retirement fund.

As the year 1948 began, a movement of railway workers in Canada was well under way to bring their wage rates to a more equitable level with those paid to railroad workers in the United States. On November 20, 1947, the Central Committee joined other standard railway labor organizations in Canada in serving a notice on railway managements requesting a general wage increase of 35¢ an hour. When conferences with the railway managements failed to produce any offer of settlement on their part, the Brotherhoods appealed to the National Labour Relations Board. At further conferences arranged by a conciliation officer, the railways refused to consider any increase in wage rates and on February 25, 1948, a Conciliation Board of three members was appointed to investigate the dispute.

The majority report of the Conciliation Board, rendered on May 3, recommended a wage increase of 7¢ an hour. A minority report, made by the employes' representative on the Board, recommended an increase of 20¢ an hour. At a meeting on May 4, representatives of the employes rejected the majority report of the Board and began the circulation of a strike ballot on May 20. The railways later offered to grant an increase of 10¢ an hour, but the negotiations were discontinued on July 5 when the employes rejected the offer.

Meanwhile, the Brotherhoods had called a strike to begin at 6:00 a.m., July 15. At conferences arranged by the Minister of Labour, an increase of 15½¢ an hour was proposed. This the Brotherhoods rejected. The deadlock continued until July 14, the day before the strike. At that time an understanding was reached that wages would be increased 17¢ an hour retroactive to March 1, 1948, and an agreement to this effect was signed with the railways on July 17.

While this wage movement was in progress, a strike had taken place on the Tennessee Railroad. In the Short Line wage decision of 1947, the Emergency Board recommended that the employes on this railroad be granted a wage increase of 15½¢ an hour, effective January 3, 1948. The employes on this road felt, however, that they were being discriminated against, since employes on other roads had been granted this increase retroactive to September 1, 1947. A strike which began on March 15, 1948, ended on April 24, 39 days later, when the company agreed to make the wage increase retroactive to September 1.

At this time, a crisis had arisen in the United States affecting three of the transportation organizations. The engineers, firemen, and switchmen had called a strike to begin on May 11, 1948, when their wage and rule negotiations with the carriers broke down. On May 10, President Truman authorized the seizure and operation of the railroads by the army. The government returned the roads to private ownership on July 9, after a basis for settling the dispute had been agreed upon.

Even before this dispute was ended, the non-operating railroad labor organizations had begun an important national movement. Although the 40-hour week had been accepted almost universally in other industries, the 48-hour week still remained in effect on the railroads. On April 10, 1948, these organizations served uniform notice on railroad managements requesting the following:

1. Forty-eight hours' pay for a 40-hour work week, Monday through Friday.
2. The time and one-half rate for Saturday service and the double-time rate for work on Sundays and holidays.
3. A general wage increase of 25¢ an hour.

The railroads countered with a proposal to change many existing agreement rules.

By late summer, the request had reached the national level. National conferences, which began on September 8, ended on September 17 when the carriers' committee made no offer of a settlement. On September 18, the non-operating Brotherhoods began the circulation of a strike ballot. The Brotherhoods rejected the suggestion of the Mediation Board that the controversy be submitted to arbitration.

The Mediation Board terminated its services on October 13, and on October 18, 1948, the President created an Emergency Board to investigate the dispute. The Board began its hearings on October 26 and concluded them on November 27. In its report to the President on December 17, 1948, the Emergency Board recommended:

(1) That basic rates of pay be increased 7¢ an hour, effective October 1, 1948.

(2) That effective September 1, 1949, a work week of forty hours, consisting of five days of eight hours each, be established for non-operating railroad employes (with certain exceptions) with two consecutive days off in each seven.

(3) That in connection with the establishment of the 40-hour week, all basic wage rates be increased by 20 per cent (exclusive of the 7¢ hourly increase) to provide the same basic earnings in forty hours as were paid for 48 hours.

(4) That in establishing the 40-hour week the time and one-half rate be paid for all work performed in excess of 8 hours a day and/or 40 hours in a week.

(5) That the request of the organizations for punitive pay for Saturdays and Sundays as such and for a minimum guarantee of 8 hours for service on Saturdays, Sundays, and holidays be denied.

(6) That the parties agree, before September 1, 1949, on changes in existing rules necessary to give effect to the 40-hour work week.

It was not until March 19, 1949, however, that national committees representing the carriers and their non-operating employes reached an agreement making effective the recommendations of the Emergency Board. Following the Board's report, conferences between the committees failed to produce an agreement. The carriers' committee accepted a suggestion by the employes that the members of the Emergency Board assist in reaching a settlement. The members of the Board were asked by the two committees to sit in on the conferences, not as arbitrators or mediators but as friends of the committees, to help bring about a settlement of the dispute. Finally, these former members of the Emergency Board were asked specific questions as to their intent and purpose in writing the Board's recommendations, and their answers materially assisted in bringing about the agreement of March 19.

"Since beginning my railroad career," President Carroll said in commenting on the forty-hour week agreement, "I have witnessed three revolutionary changes in the hours of service of maintenance of way employes—changes which were accompanied by weird predictions on the part of those who were opposed to the changes ranging from 'it can't be done,' or 'it is impossible to maintain the tracks and bridges with such short hours of work,' to the pessimistic prediction that it would bring bankruptcy to the railroads.

"When I first started work the hours of service were regulated by the rising and setting of the sun; otherwise, no definite hours were prescribed....When the 10-hour day came into effect, the employes felt that they had really accomplished a great economic change. . . . This was the first great change.

"The second and most revolutionary change . . . came in 1919 when the . . . 8-hour day with overtime thereafter came into being. . . . The 8-hour day went into effect smoothly; dire predictions failed to come true and no railroad, to my knowledge, has ever claimed that it went into the hands of receivers or became bankrupt because of the 8-hour day. . . .

"I have [long] dreamed . . . of the day when the 40-hour week with 48 hours' earnings would be established for the maintenance of way department employes. Thank God, I have lived to see that dream come true! On March 19, 1949, a historic agreement was signed at Chicago, Ill., between the 16 non-operating organizations and the carriers' conference committee representing about 99 per cent of the total railroad mileage in the United States. This agreement provides that September 1, 1949, the 40-hour week with 48 hours' pay and two consecutive rest days each week, will be put into effect. In addition, we secured an across-the-board increase in pay of 7 cents per hour effective October 1, 1948. Thus, the third change has been brought about.

"It is true that workers in other industries achieved the 40-hour week earlier; but, in most instances, they did not preserve their 48-hour earnings. . . . We on the railroads . . . secured the shorter week without loss of earnings. . . . I think . . . we have great cause for celebrating the most progressive, outstanding and important rules change in the history of the railroad industry."

As this important case was being progressed, two strikes took place, one in Canada and the other in the United States.

Conditions on the Newfoundland Railway in Canada from the date of its construction some 40 years previously had been deplorable. Although living costs in Newfoundland were much higher than in Canada or the United States, the wages of railway workers were extremely low, generally about 60 per cent of those paid by Canadian railways. The railway was operated by the Commission Government and all requests for increased wages or improved working conditions had to be submitted by the railway management to the Commissioner of Public Utilities for approval.

On June 15, 1948, nine of the international organizations holding contracts with the Newfoundland Railway, including the Brotherhood, requested a wage increase of 15¢ an hour and an adjustment of the cost-of-living bonus. When conferences with the general manager of the railway and the Commissioner of Public Utilities failed to produce any appreciable results, the nine organizations distributed a strike ballot. Ninety-eight per cent of the employes (100 per cent of the maintenance of way men) voted to strike.

The strike began at 11:00 a.m., on October 11, 1948, and for almost five weeks rail transportation on the island was completely halted. The strike was well conducted, however. The employes engaged in no violence or demonstrations, but simply remained off company property. The strike ended when an agreement was reached adding the cost-of-living bonus of 8½¢ an hour to basic wage rates, effective November 12, 1948, and increasing all wages by an additional 10¢ an hour, retroactive to June 16, 1948.

The second strike on the Georgia and Florida Railroad began on September 27, 1948 (the first strike[1] had lasted from February 12, 1947, to March 6, 1947) because of the inability of the employes to obtain a satisfactory settlement of their request for increased wages. Originally called to begin on July 14, 1948, the strike was postponed until September 27 because of the financial condition of the railroad and the management's promise to try to complete a refinancing survey that would make a settlement of the dispute possible. The employes returned to work on October 3, 1948,

[1] p. 204

after an agreement had been reached granting a wage increase of 12¢ an hour.

On July 9, President Carroll sailed from New York to represent the Railway Labor Executives' Association at conferences of the International Transport Workers' Federation in various foreign countries, and at a convention in Oslo, Norway. The purpose of the conferences was to strengthen the international bonds of unity between nations here and abroad and to erect a barrier against the infiltration of communism.

On June 23, 1948, President Truman approved amendments to the Railroad Retirement and Unemployment Insurance Acts passed by Congress. The amendments to the Retirement Act increased most annuities by a flat 20 per cent, and guaranteed that an employe or his survivors would never receive less than the taxes he had paid plus a small amount in lieu of interest. Instead of the flat 3 per cent payroll tax on employers under the Railroad Unemployment Insurance Act, a sliding scale of contributions was substituted, the rate of the tax, up to a maximum rate of 3 per cent, depending on the amount of money in the unemployment insurance fund.

At the general election in November, 1948, the voters in the United States re-elected President Truman in an unexpected victory over his Republican opponent, and the Democratic party began the 17th year of its national administration.

As the year closed, the "Journal" announced that plans were under way to erect a new international headquarters building at Woodward Avenue and California Street, Highland Park, Michigan, within the Detroit metropolitan area. Not only had the old building become inadequate for the offices of Grand Lodge, but the continued expansion of Wayne University in the vicinity of the old building made condemnation of the site by the city of Detroit imminent.

During the year, the Brotherhood lost for the second time an attempt to secure representation rights on the Santa Fe System. In spite of this second defeat within the space of a few years, however, it was clearly apparent that the maintenance of way men on the Santa Fe had become restive and were dissatisfied with the representation given them by the C. I. O. organization, and that their return to the Brotherhood after many years of non-affiliation was only a matter of time.

By the early part of 1949, the reduction in forces on railroads in the United States had become a serious problem. The number of maintenance of way employes in railroad service dropped from 292,532 in 1945 to 256,060 in 1948 and to 224,067 in 1949. In spite of the fact that the net railway operating income of Class I railroads in the United States exceeded $1 billion in 1948 and that they had a net income of approximately $700 million for that year, heavy force reductions had been put into effect.

Maintenance of way workers on Canadian railways had fared somewhat better. Although the number of maintenance of way men in Canada decreased from 40,247 in 1945 to 37,944 in 1946, this figure increased to 39,237 in 1949.

The securing of a greater stability of employment for maintenance of way workers had now become a matter of utmost concern. The general practice of the carriers in reducing forces during the winter months and increasing them during the summer, and of gearing the number of maintenance of way workers to the fluctuating income of the railroads, had created a day-to-day job uncertainty that affected the morale of the workers and caused an unusually large labor turnover in the maintenance of way department. It had become clear that some effective means were needed to place maintenance of way employment on a more even level.

Another long-standing grievance of railroad workers was the failure of the railroads to provide basic safety and protective equipment on track motor cars, used to transport thousands of railroad workers, most of them maintenance of way men, and tools and materials, to and from their headquarters and points of work, and from job to job over the lines of the carriers. The employes ride these cars in all kinds of weather. They use them if they are called out at night in an emergency. They use them to patrol track—particularly in bad weather. The average distance over which these cars are operated has been increased considerably in recent years by the lengthening of territories under the jurisdiction of maintenance of way gangs.

Numerous accidents resulting in serious injury and death to many railroad workers have occurred because track motor cars were not adequately equipped to provide for the safety and protection of the employes. Travel in dusk or in darkness or through tunnels becomes a serious hazard to workers riding on track motor cars not equipped with adequate electric headlights and taillights. No estimate can be made of the health and safety hazards encountered by railroad workers who must ride on open-deck motor cars without any protection from the elements.

Because many carriers had not provided this equipment, in spite of the repeated requests of the employes, the Brotherhood began in 1949 the sponsorship in state legislatures of bills requiring that track motor cars be equipped with electric headlights and taillights, windshields, windshield wipers, and canopies or tops. Although these bills are basic safety measures, most railroad managements have vigorously opposed their enactment, contending that electric headlights are not needed and that windshields and tops are "luxury equipment."

Nevertheless, during 1949 and in subsequent years through 1954, twenty-six states have passed track motor car laws. Unfortunately, however, these state laws are not uniform and not all of them require full equipment. Although all twenty-six laws require electric headlights on motor cars, only seventeen require windshields, thirteen require windshield wipers, and ten require tops.

When the 30th regular convention of Grand Lodge met in Detroit, Michigan, beginning June 20, 1949, the delegates took decisive action on many of the vital problems then confronting the Brotherhood. Like its members, Grand Lodge found itself caught in the spiral of mounting prices, and the convention voted to increase Grand Lodge dues from $3.00 to $3.50 a quarter. A portion of this added revenue was to provide a subscription for every member to the newspaper "Labor", published weekly by the standard railroad labor organizations. Ten cents per member was to be placed in a special fund to be used for state and provincial legislative activities. The remainder was to be retained in the general fund.

The funds provided for the operation of the State Legislative Department since its establishment in 1943 had proved to be inadequate. Although the funds provided by the increase in dues were still modest in amount, they did make it possible to expand the work of the legislative department and to extend its activities to all provinces in Canada.

"Once every three years it is our privilege to meet together and take an inventory of our Brotherhood, to strike a balance and review the record of the past three years," President Carroll told the convention. "Ours is the task of evaluating what has been accomplished and charting our future course. The plans and policies we formulate and enact here may well have a vital bearing on the lives and fortunes of over 350,000 maintenance of way workers and their families.

"We must realize that ours is indeed a great responsibility and that we must face it with a high resolve and a firm determination to do the very best that we can for those who rely on us for guidance and leadership.

"Although the years have not always been kind to us, the long history of our Brotherhood presents a record of almost constant growth, progress and accomplishment of which we may well be proud. Despite the great loss we suffered just a few months after our last convention in the sudden and untimely death of our beloved leader, the late President Elmer E. Milliman, the plans he had laid so well and the inspiration of the able leadership he had given us helped us carry on and achieve during the past three years the greatest gains in our history."

President Carroll outlined the progress made since 1939 in increasing wage rates in the maintenance of way department in the United States and Canada. The following figures are representative:

AVERAGE EARNINGS

	CANADA		UNITED STATES	
	1939	1948	1939	1948
CLASSIFICATION	(per mo.)	(per mo.)	(per mo.)	(per mo.)
Bridge and Building Foremen	$151.98	$244.80	$187.68	$293.76
Section Foremen	121.79	216.24	144.84	250.92
	(per hr.)	(per hr.)	(per hr.)	(per hr.)
Carpenters and Bridgemen	$ .614	$ 1.05	$ .72	$ 1.24
Trackmen	.429	.89	.45	.96

Similar gains had been made by other maintenance of way classes.

The report of Secretary-Treasurer Shoemake reflected the continually growing membership and the increasing financial stability of the Brotherhood.

The delegates unanimously re-elected President Carroll and Secretary-Treasurer Shoemake. Among the resolutions adopted were those approving uniform rules governing working conditions; a standardization of rates of pay; longer vacations with pay; increased benefits under the Railroad Retirement and Unemployment Insurance Acts; the inauguration of a national movement to stabilize employment; the elimination of unsafe and unsanitary conditions on the railroads; union-management cooperation; the union shop; legislation to place all forms of public transportation on an equal competitive basis; and the erection of a monument in memory of Leo E. Keller. Following similar action taken at previous conventions, the delegates condemned the growing practice of the railroads in letting to outside contract work coming within the scope of the Brotherhood's agreements with the carriers.

A few days before the convention was called to order, railway workers in Canada had begun a movement to obtain the 40-hour week. On June 16, 1949, the Brotherhood and other non-operating unions filed a joint request on the managements of Canadian railways for a wage increase of 7¢ an hour and a 40-hour week with the same pay as for 48 hours. In a counter movement, the Railway Association of Canada served notice on July 8 of its wish to make extensive changes in rules governing working conditions after deploring the fact that the employes were again seeking wage increases.

Negotiations between committees representing the railways and their non-operating employes having failed to bring about a settlement, the Brotherhoods filed a request with the Minister of Labour that the issue be submitted to conciliation. Hearings before a Board of Conciliation began on January 10, 1950. Formal hearings ended on March 10, but it was not until April 11 that the Board rendered its report.

The employes promptly rejected a formula recommended by the Board for the establishment of a 44-hour week. "The use of the terms 'novel and costly', and 'radical social experiment', as applied to the five-day, 40-hour week [by the Board of Conciliation]," said a letter addressed to the Minister of Labour by the cooperating Brotherhoods, "well illustrates the majority Board members' archaic and reactionary approach to the matter. They have ignored almost entirely the substantial progress which has been made by Canadian industry in this connection . . . The representatives of the employes view the majority recommendations of the Board as eminently unsatisfactory."

The Brotherhoods distributed a strike ballot in the latter part of June and called a suspension of work to begin on August 22. A mediator appointed by the Federal government sought to bring about a settlement of the dispute in conferences starting on August 18, but the strike began on August 22 as scheduled when a settlement could not be reached. The strike was orderly and peaceful, but all trains and telegraphic services were at a complete standstill. The strikers stood their ground in spite of attacks from the press and other sources.

On August 29, 1950, the Parliament convened in a special session, and the railway strike was the first order of business. The next day, Parliament passed an act providing that a wage increase of 4¢ an hour would be made effective immediately, that every railway would resume operation and every employe on strike would be required to return to the service, and that negotiations would be resumed. This act of Parliament had the effect of forcing the first compulsory arbitration in the history of the Federal law.

When subsequent negotiations between the railways and their employes failed to produce a settlement, the government appointed an Arbitrator to decide the dispute. The Arbitration Award, rendered on December 19, 1950, provided for an increase of 7¢ an hour (3¢ an hour more than the employes had received when they returned to work following the strike), retroactive to September 1, 1950, and a 40-hour week with 48 hours' pay, effective June 1, 1951. Although conferences between the two committees began immediately after the award, it was not until the latter part of January, 1951, that a "master agreement" was negotiated providing that existing agreements would be revised to give effect to the 40-hour week. On May 23, 1951, the Central Committee of the Brotherhood signed Wage Agreement No. 12, finally disposing of a dispute which had lasted almost two years. The final settlement of this controversy was a vindication of the employes' contention that their request was just and reasonable.

In the United States, meanwhile, a movement to stabilize employment in the maintenance of way department had been unanimously approved at a meeting of the International Association of Grand Lodge and System Officers in early May, 1950. On May 15, 1950, General Chairmen served notices on their respective managements requesting:

(1) That a normal force be restored in the maintenance of way department based on the average number of maintenance of way workers in the service during the ten-year period from 1940 to 1949;

(2) That maintenance of way employes be retained in the service on a ratio that approximated 20 per cent of the total number of employes in the railroad industry;

(3) That employes on the payroll on January 15 of each year be given full employment that year;

(4) That those on the payroll March 15 be guaranteed 8 months' employment; and

(5) That those in service on April 15 be guaranteed 6 months' employment.

The importance of this attempt to bring about some degree of stability of employment in the maintenance of way department is shown by employment figures for 1948 and 1949. In September, 1949, employment of maintenance of way forces had dropped to 225,000, 55,000 (19½%) less than in September, 1948. In October, 1949, employment decreased to less than 200,000, 75,000 (27½%) less than in October, 1948.

The railroads retaliated with a request to change many agreement rules, and some railway managements contended that the proposal did not properly come "within the purview of the Railway Labor Act".

"Despite the charges that our request is not within the purview of the Railway Labor Act and that the proposal is not workable," said President Carroll, "we maintain that our formal notice is in keeping with Section 6 of the Act. . . . The request to stabilize maintenance forces is not new. This topic has been discussed with railroad management over the conference table many times, and attempts were made to convince them that such a program would be beneficial to both the company and its employes. On several properties, the General Chairmen have attempted unsuccessfully to induce their managements to inaugurate such a program. . . .

"The reluctancy of the railroads to give favorable consideration to our request, particularly the question of joining with other roads in forming a National Carriers' Conference Committee, is alone responsible for the delay in the prosecution of our case. . . ."

Although the carriers in the Eastern Region eventually appointed a conference committee and some three years later a report of the discussions between the two committees was referred to the General Chairmen and the management on individual systems for further negotiations, no program of a tangible nature to stabilize employment has as yet been evolved from the employes' request of May 15, 1950. Carriers in other regions have not evinced a willingness to join with their maintenance of way employes in trying to find a solution to this important problem.

As the first half of the twentieth century ended, political tensions throughout the world had increased, and the fear of war had become a frightening incubus to the peoples of all nations, many of whom had not as yet repaired the ravages of World War II. When the Communists of North Korea invaded the Republic of Korea (South Korea) on June 24, 1950, the intervention of the United Nations again made both the United States and Canada active participants in warfare.

Although the hostilities in Korea were on a definitely limited scale, the apprehension that the conflagration, once started, might spread, became a distinct threat to world peace and security.

CHAPTER IX

BEYOND THE HALF CENTURY

WITH the advent of hostilities in Korea, the government of the United States, apprehensive of the results of this new conflict, began an extensive long-range defense program. These highly-expanded activities and the surge of heavy buying that followed as consumers anticipated possible shortages in critical materials, brought on a new upward swing in the inflationary cycle. The consumers' price index of the Bureau of Labor Statistics, United States Department of Labor, which stood (on the adjusted basis) at 171.9 in 1950 (1935-39=100), had soared to 185.6 by 1951. This rapid increase in prices precipitated a new crisis in the battle of wages versus living costs.

Meantime, in answer to repeated demands from their memberships, the non-operating railroad labor organizations in the United States had begun another movement to obtain union-shop agreements in the railway industry. It will be recalled that in 1943, a Presidential Emergency Board had rendered the opinion that the negotiation of union-shop agreements between the unions and the carriers would be in violation of the language of the Railway Labor Act. At a meeting of the Railway Labor Executives' Association on January 20, 1950, a committee had been appointed to draft an amendment to the

Act permitting union-shop agreements in the railroad industry. A bill to this effect was introduced in Congress in March, 1950.

As has been pointed out previously, the language of the Railway Labor Act of 1934 which prohibited union-shop agreements and the check-off of dues had been placed in the Act at the request of the railroad labor unions. One may now wonder why these same labor unions apparently changed their policy between 1934 and 1950 in seeking an amendment to the Act which would permit the union shop and the check-off; i.e., the deduction by the railroads of union dues from the employes' wages.

Actually, there was no change in policy on the part of these unions. Their action in 1934 was one of necessity to cope with a situation that had been built up in the railroad industry since 1922. Following the return of the railroads to private ownership after World War I, many railroads sponsored the formation of company unions and a check-off of dues for these unions. These unions were under the control of the railroad companies and were in no sense bona fide collective bargaining agencies for railroad workers. It is estimated that in 1934, 700 agreements representing more than 20 per cent of the total number of agreements in the railroad industry were in effect between the railroads and so-called company unions. This deprived many railroad workers of the right to bargain collectively with their employers.

It was this situation which caused the railroad Brotherhoods to seek a change in the language of the Act in 1934. Unsuccessful in their attempts to secure a provision in the Act applying only to company unions, the unions accepted of necessity the broader language of the Act which had the effect not only of prohibiting the formation of company unions but of preventing the Brotherhoods from seeking union-shop agreements and check-off provisions.

Since 1934, the railroad unions have been compelled, under the provisions of the Railway Labor Act, to treat the non-member worker in identically the same manner as they treat the union member insofar as wages and working conditions are concerned, even to the extent of handling individual grievances for non-members. After sixteen years of experience under the 1934 amendment to the Railway Labor Act, the unions found that between 10 and 20 per cent of the workers, classed by the unions as "free riders," were willing to receive all the benefits without contributing to the support of the unions.

As a result, mounting pressure for a union shop from within the ranks of the railroad Brotherhoods culminated in this movement to obtain an amendment to the Act permitting the negotiation of union-shop agreements with check-off provisions in the railroad industry. Federal legislation applying to employes in other industries (the Wagner Act and the Taft-Hartley Act) approved the principle of the union shop. Thus, railroad workers were denied by Federal legislation a privilege granted to other industrial workers.

The reaction of railroad management to the proposed amendment was immediate and completely adverse. Lobbyists for the railroad industry sought to create sentiment against the bill among members of Congress, and witnesses for management appeared before Congressional committees to testify against the bill. It is difficult to select from the maze of evidence presented by the carriers' witnesses any tangible or persuasive reason for their opposition to the bill. The only logical conclusion that can be drawn is that they were not primarily interested in the "rights" of individual workers, as they insisted, but in perpetuating the problem of non-membership, which had been a continual source of dissatisfaction among organized railroad workers.

The railroad Brotherhoods insisted, on the other hand, that a union-shop agreement did not infringe on the basic rights, privileges, or liberties of any worker. Moreover, that in requiring each employe to fulfill his obligation to his fellow workers through union membership, the union-shop is the very essence of American democracy, and that it would tend to promote more harmonious personal relationships between railroad workers and thereby increase their efficiency and productivity.

The controversy over the bill soon developed into one of the most difficult legislative battles ever waged by the railroad Brotherhoods. President Carroll took an active part in supporting the bill, and he assumed the chairmanship of a group of officers of the various organizations working to secure its passage. It is generally recognized that his courage and determination when the outlook appeared the most hopeless helped to bring about the bill's eventual enactment.

The Senate approved the bill on December 11, 1950, and the battle shifted to the House of Representatives. Numerous changes had been made in the personnel of the House at the November, 1950, elections, and opponents of the bill sought desperately to prevent its passage before the imminent adjournment of the 81st Congress. Had they succeeded, the Brotherhoods would have had to start their difficult and discouraging campaign anew when the 82nd Congress convened. Because so many Congressmen had gone home for the Christmas holidays, opponents of the bill were able to block its passage on December 21, 1950. Although a majority of House members were on the floor of the House that day, for four hours opponents of the bill, led by members of the House Rules Committee, refused to answer the roll call, thus resorting to what was termed a "sit-down strike" against the bill. Finally, many members of the House found it necessary to leave to make arrangements for transportation to their homes. When it became apparent that the sit-down strike had effectively blocked action on the bill that day, arrangements were made to hold the bill over until January 1, 1951. Meeting for the first time in history on New Year's Day, the House passed the bill by a vote of almost 6 to 1. President Truman signed the bill on January 10.

The Railway Labor Act as amended permitted the negotiation of agreements requiring employes to become members of the union representing their craft or class within a certain period of time after the effective date of a union-shop agreement, or the date of their employment, and under certain specified conditions. It also stipulated that such agreements may provide for the deduction of union dues, initiation fees, and assessments from employes' wages.

Meanwhile, several other important occurrences had taken place. On August 25, 1950, President Truman signed an Executive Order placing all the principal railroads in the United States under the control of the Secretary of the Army, effective August 27. This action was precipitated by a threatened strike of the transportation Brotherhoods. The order prohibited railway labor from striking, but at the same time it made no provision for settling the disputes over wages and rules which had created the critical situation.

"The railroads are accumulating, while under government operation, the largest profits in their history," said President Carroll in voicing an opinion shared by the other railroad Brotherhoods. "These profits are not seized by the government but go into the coffers of the owners. Nothing is seized except the rights of the employes. . . .

"If the government is compelled by circumstances, and for the general welfare of the nation, to resort to such drastic action . . . then in fairness to all, that same authority . . . should, at the same time, provide proper and adequate methods of hearing and adjudicating . . . the dispute that brought the seizure."

Government control and operation of the railroads did not end until May 23, 1952, after the controversial issues had been settled.

By the fall of 1950, rapidly changing conditions made another request for higher wages imperative. Since October, 1948, when the last general adjustment in the wages of non-operating railroad employes had been made, the injustice of the wage levels established at that time had been increased by the general upward movement of wages in other industries, augmented by conditions existing since the beginning of the Korean war. Substantial increases in wages were needed to improve the real wages and the living standards of these employes, which had been greatly impaired from 1946 to 1950 and were being reduced still further by mounting living costs. By the end of 1950, the cost of living had reached an all-time high.

On October 25, 1950, the Brotherhood and other non-operating unions joined in a national movement in the United States to obtain a wage increase of 25¢ an hour. When conferences on individual systems failed to produce a settlement, national conferences began on January 9, 1951, and concluded on January 19 when no basis for a settlement could be reached. The Mediation Board began mediation proceedings on January 25, but by February 24 it became apparent that the committees were hopelessly deadlocked.

On February 26, a representative of the President of the United States began conferences with the parties to the dispute in an effort to effect a settlement. After a nightlong session, which began at 3:00 p.m. on February 28 and lasted until 6:00 a.m. on March 1, the two committees reached an agreement. This agreement granted a wage increase of 12½¢ an hour, effective February 1, 1951, to the employes affected. It also contained an escalator clause providing that beginning April 1, 1951, quarterly cost-of-living adjustments would be made in wage rates. Wages were to be increased or decreased by 1¢ an hour for each one-point change in living costs above an arbitrary index of 178.0 (but wages could not be reduced below the rates established as of February 1, 1951).

During the conferences, the carriers had insisted that the employes agree to a three-year moratorium on rules changes. The agreement contained no moratorium on rules changes, but did provide for a term contract on wages until October 1, 1953; except that if the government's wage stabilization policy permitted an annual improvement factor in wage rates, the contract could be reopened on July 1, 1952, for further consideration.

The threat of uncontrolled inflation had now become serious. From an index figure of 128.6 in 1945, the cost of living had increased gradually during the post-war years. Following the crisis in Korea in 1950, it rose sharply to an index figure, as previously stated, of 185.6 in 1951. In a radio broadcast over a national network on March 7, 1951, President Carroll flayed the failure of Congress to take effective steps to control the situation. He spoke in behalf of one million railroad workers, whose unions were cooperating with the United Labor Policy Committee, representing more than fifteen million skilled workers.

"Whether it is because of the discouragement inherent in the very law under which they operate—or whatever the reason," Carroll said, "there just hasn't been, in our considered opinion, the will to do on the part of those charged with holding down prices. . . ." Citing the failure of the Defense Production Act of 1950 to control food prices effectively, Carroll said that "Congress, which is responsible for the laws under which inflation can be controlled, must correct its mistakes in the present control law."

Congress failed, however, to take adequate steps to check the inflationary tendency of the nation's economy, and by the end of 1951, rising living costs had increased the wages of non-operating railroad workers by 11¢ an hour under the escalator clause in the March 1, 1951, wage agreement.

In the meantime, the Brotherhood had successfully concluded a short strike and had won a victory over a rival organization. On April 20, 1951, maintenance of way employes of the Meridian & Bigbee River Railroad had joined other railroad workers in a strike in protest against the refusal of the management to apply the 40-hour week and wage agreement of March 19, 1949. Although the strike had not been authorized by the Brotherhood, the employes were justified in their action. They returned to work in a few days, and on April 25 the company agreed to apply the agreement.

In November, 1950, the Brotherhood had begun its third attempt in recent years to win representation rights on the Atchison, Topeka & Santa Fe System. By the middle of December, a majority of the employes had signed certificates of authority for representation by the Brotherhood, and the services of the National Railroad Mediation Board were invoked. On April 30, 1951, the Board certified the Brotherhood as the bargaining agency for the 13,000 maintenance of way employes on the Santa Fe System. On June 2, Brotherhood representatives who had participated in the strenuous campaign gathered in Kansas City, Missouri, for a victory dinner to celebrate the uniting with the Brotherhood of the maintenance of way workers on the last non-affiliated major railroad system in the United States.

Following the passage of the union-shop amendment to the Railway Labor Act, the cooperating railroad Brotherhoods immediately sought to negotiate union-shop agreements with railway managements. Effective February 1, 1951, the Brotherhood signed its first union-shop agreement with the Tennessee Railroad Company, a short line railroad. Most railroad managements, however, still opposed the union shop, and on February 5, 1951, formal requests were made to the carriers by the Brotherhoods for the negotiating of union-shop agreements.

The railroads continued their opposition to the negotiating

of these agreements, however, and on May 23, 1951, the cooperating Brotherhoods filed an application for mediation services with the National Mediation Board. The protracted conferences continued through the summer. On July 9, the Great Northern Railway Company became the first major system to sign a union-shop agreement with the Brotherhood. By September, union-shop agreements had been signed with two other major railroads, the New York Central Railroad and the Baltimore & Ohio Railroad, and with fifteen other smaller lines. But most railroad managements remained adamant in their refusal to sign such an agreement.

In late October, the Mediation Board stated that it had exhausted every means to bring about a settlement, and on November 15, President Truman created an Emergency Board to investigate the dispute. On February 14, 1952, the Board made a report to the President reading in part: "On the merits of the proposal before us, viewed in fair perspective and in light of the national policies determined by Congress, we find no sound or substantial basis for withholding the union shop and check-off from these 17 organizations any longer; we believe that in the framework of the dispute before us the arguments in favor far outweigh those in opposition to the proposal before us."

Meantime, in October, 1951, Grand Lodge had moved its offices to the new headquarters building at 12050 Woodward Avenue, Highland Park (Detroit), Michigan. Ground for the 98 x 112-foot two-story brick and stone structure had been broken by Secretary of Labor Maurice J. Tobin on April 27, 1950. President Carroll directed that the new building, completed at a cost of $600,000.00, be dedicated as follows: "To the memory of those who spoke without fear, who were persecuted and ridiculed because of their love of human liberties. These liberties, our heritage, we pledge to uphold for all mankind."

On October 30, 1951, the Brotherhood held open house in its new home. At 12:00 noon, Governor G. Mennen Williams of Michigan and President Carroll laid the cornerstone in an unusual ceremony which completed the structure. In a niche behind the cornerstone, various mementos and documents of the Brotherhood were sealed in a copper box.

In dedicating the new building, President Carroll said: "This building brings to full fruition the dreams of many men and the completion of plans begun many years ago." The founding fathers of the organization, Carroll said, had "laid the foundation upon which our present structure has been builded over these many years. . . . One hundred years from now this building will still be standing if it is not destroyed by an invading foe, or Providence . . . as . . . a monument to the dreamers and planners of the past. . . . It has been built without borrowing one penny."

Grand Lodge Secretary-Treasurer A. Shoemake presided at the dedication ceremonies, attended by several hundred Brotherhood officers and members and their families, and by railroad officials and officers from other unions. "I believe this will go down in the history of the Brotherhood as one of the highlights," Shoemake said. "We know that there have been many problems, many difficulties and many heartaches to bring this organization thus far; we are hopeful and prayerful that this organization will render service to humanity in a way that will bring a blessing to many people in the maintenance of way department."

The ceremonies were climaxed by an evening banquet at which Governor Williams was the principal speaker.

On the same day the new building was dedicated (October 30, 1951), President Truman signed an important bill amending the Railroad Retirement Act to provide considerably increased benefits. The President's signature culminated a difficult fight extending over many months to have needed changes made in the Act which were stoutly opposed by railroad managements.

The amendments to the Act increased pensions and annuities by 15 per cent; increased survivor benefits by 33⅓ per cent; provided a new benefit for husband or wife aged 65 or over, amounting to 50 per cent of the employe's benefit, up to a maximum of $40; guaranteed that railroad retirement benefits would at least equal social security benefits; allowed credit for service after age 65; transferred to the coverage of the Social Security Act workers who leave railroad service after less than 10 years' service; and contained a provision for a financial interchange between the Railroad Retirement

Account and Old Age and Survivors' Insurance (Social Security Act) so that the latter would neither gain nor lose from the separate existence of the railroad retirement system.

With the passage of the amendments, Congress established a joint congressional committee to make a complete study of the Act and related problems. The voluminous report of the joint committee on "Retirement Policies and the Railroad Retirement System," completed and issued in 1953, contains a history of the railroad retirement system and a full analysis of the many aspects of its operation.

In the spring of 1952, another strike of maintenance of way workers occurred, this time on the Copper Range Railroad, a short line. The employes had met with difficulty in having the carrier apply the agreement of March 19, 1949 (40-hour week and wage increase). When the company refused to accept the conditions of the wage agreement of March 1, 1951, the employes were authorized to suspend work beginning at 7:00 a.m., March 7, 1952. A mediation agreement settled the dispute on April 24, 1952, and the employes returned to work on April 25.

When the 31st regular convention of Grand Lodge met in Montreal, Quebec, Canada, beginning June 16, 1952, President Carroll and Secretary-Treasurer Shoemake presented reports outlining great progress by the organization. The accomplishments of the Brotherhood were reflected in the fact that the delegates to the convention represented a paid-up membership of more than 200,000.

"Since last we met in Canada twelve years ago," President Carroll told the convention, "we have enjoyed a steady upward . . . growth and expansion in our activities and services to our people. . . . Our march of progress during this period and especially during the last six years has always been onward . . . and upward.

"Today we hold agreements with every railway operating in the Dominion of Canada, with every Class I railway carrier in the United States and . . . with several hundred Class II, III and switching terminal railways. . . .

"We have made great progress in securing for our people better wages and working conditions. Just a few months after our last convention—September 1, 1949—the 40-hour week became a reality in the United States (40 hours' work with 48 hours' pay). In Canada similar provisions became effective June 1, 1951. In addition to the 40-hour week we have secured substantial wage increases for our people."

The delegates re-elected President Carroll and Secretary-Treasurer Shoemake unanimously and took action on many important current questions.

They approved:

1. Further efforts to obtain liberalizing amendments in the Railroad Retirement and Unemployment Insurance Acts.

2. A declaration that Congress should take action to bar the illegal entry of "wetbacks" into the United States from Mexico.

3. Efforts to re-establish the cooperative spirit and mutual working arrangement that existed between the various standard railroad labor organizations after the wage negotiations of 1931.

4. A movement to secure 7 paid holidays and longer vacations with pay.

5. The compilation and publishing of a history of the Brotherhood.

6. Continued efforts to secure representation on short lines and switching companies where the Brotherhood had not been established.

7. Union-management cooperation.

8. A continuation of joint national movements on wages and working rules by the cooperating railroad labor organizations.

9. Efforts to bring about an increase in wages commensurate with the savings derived by railroads as a result of technological changes in work methods and increased productivity.

10. A program to secure the passage of state or Federal legislation to correct unsafe and unsanitary conditions under which Brotherhood members must work and live.

11. Basic working rules adopted in 1939.

12. Continued efforts to stabilize employment.

13. Price controls and the stabilization of wages on a basis comparable to price rises.

14. Uniform working rules and standardized rates of pay.

15. The uniform regulation of all forms of public transportation.

They disapproved:

1. The substitution of automatic crossing protection for the manual operation of gates at highway crossings by watchmen.

2. The contracting of maintenance of way work by the railroads.

3. The seizure of railroads in the United States by the government in labor management disputes.

Trouble now began to loom in Canada. Extra gang laborers on Canadian railways, except those employed on a general year-around basis, had never come under the provisions of the Brotherhood's wage agreements. As a result, the railways had followed the practice of hiring "temporary" extra gang laborers at wage rates far below those paid to section men, and working them under deplorable conditions.

Late in 1951, the Canada Labour Relations Board certified the Brotherhood as the bargaining agency for all extra gang laborers employed on railways covered by Wage Agreement No. 12. On March 28, 1952, the committee broke off negotiations with the Railway Association of Canada when the association refused to apply the provisions of Wage Agreement No. 12 to these employes. On May 22, the Minister of Labour appointed a Conciliation Board to hear the dispute.

At hearings before the Board beginning on September 11, 1952, the Brotherhood requested standard wage rates for extra-gang men, a 40-hour work week, the time and one-half rate after eight hours' service and on rest days and holidays, the establishment of seniority rights and pension rights, and recognition of these workers as bona fide employes. The railways had continually denied all these requests. Approximately 10,000 employes were involved in the dispute.

On October 9, 1952, the Conciliation Board rendered a report unanimously recommending that an agreement covering temporary extra gang laborers be negotiated on the basis of specific proposals contained in the report. Wage agreement No. 13, signed on February 24, 1953, as a result of the Board's report, reduced the work week of these employes from 60 to 48 hours (the Board had recommended a 50-hour week) with pro rata pay for the ninth hour of service, gave them seniority, vacation, and pension rights, and established other rules governing working conditions similar to those enjoyed by other classes of maintenance of way employes. It also increased to 90¢ and 95¢ an hour, effective March 1, 1953, wage rates that had been as low as 60¢ an hour.

As a sidelight to this case, it is interesting to note that following the successful Canadian Pacific strike in 1901, the Brotherhood had requested that temporary extra gang laborers be included in the agreement negotiated at that time. This the railway company refused to do. Thus, after a lapse of more than fifty years, an agreement had finally been negotiated for this class of employes.

While this matter was being handled, another case involving other classes of maintenance of way workers in Canada was being progressed. On July 3, 1952, seventeen cooperating railway labor organizations in Canada, including the Brotherhood, served a notice on railway managements requesting a wage increase of 45¢ an hour; a cost-of-living bonus of 1¢ an hour for each one-point rise in the cost of living index numbers in Canada; that all employes be required to become members of and maintain membership in the organization by which they were represented; that union dues, initiation fees, and assessments be deducted by the railways without cost to the Brotherhoods; and that the so-called "Emergency Clause" be eliminated from Supplement No. 2 to the "Master Agreement" dated January 30, 1951. This clause provided that in the event of war, the employes would return to a forty-eight hour work week.

Conferences between representatives of the Brotherhood and the railways began on July 7 but ended four days later when it became apparent that an agreement could not be reached. Conciliation proceedings ended without success on August 2, and late in September a Conciliation Board began hearings on the dispute. On November 24, the Board issued its report recommending a wage increase of 7 per cent plus 7¢ an hour, but denying the establishment of an escalator clause to gear wage rates to living costs. The report also denied the request of the employes for an agreement requiring union membership and a check-off arrangement.

On November 28, the chairman of the general conference committee of the employes notified the Minister of Labour that the Board's report could not be accepted, but he expressed the hope that a satisfactory agreement could be reached through conferences between representatives of the employes and the railways. On February 7, 1953, an agreement was signed granting an increase in wages of 7 per cent, plus 7¢ an hour, effective September 1, 1952, and establishing an arrangement under which the railways would deduct union dues from the wages of employes covered by the agreement. This agreement also abolished the so-called "Emergency Clause" permitting reversion to the 48-hour week.

The railroad labor organizations in the United States had anticipated that in view of the Emergency Board's report of February 14, 1952, no great difficulty would be encountered in negotiating union-shop agreements with railroad managements. The carriers, however, continued their refusal to establish conference committees to discuss the Board's report. After several months, carriers in the eastern region agreed to meet with a committee representing the employes. Conferences which began on May 6 continued intermittently until August 29, 1952, at which time a union-shop agreement was signed covering systems in that region substantially following the recommendations of the Emergency Board's report with some modifications.

Carriers in the western region, however, flatly refused to enter into a union-shop agreement. They reiterated this refusal at conferences held on September 30 and October 3. At approximately the same time, the Bureau of Information of the Southeastern Carriers refused by letter to form a carriers' conference committee and stated that although individual railroad managements would discuss the situation, they were unwilling to make any kind of union-shop agreement.

"There is only one conclusion that can be drawn," said President Carroll, "as to the motive for this bitter last-ditch resistance; these carriers want to keep the ranks of their employes divided so as to give the carriers a bargaining advantage in the negotiation of wages and working conditions. One carrier spokesman in substance told Congress that this is what they wanted to do. . . . Notwithstanding the many years of experience under the Railway Labor Act with its mandate for collective bargaining between freely chosen representatives of carriers and employes . . . reactionary carrier managements . . . are still not ready to accept the unions as having a legitimate place in the industry."

Despite the resistance of many carriers to union-shop agreements, particularly in the southeastern region, the Brotherhoods continued to sign these agreements with individual railroads until agreements requiring union membership had been signed on 280 railroads covering about 180,000 maintenance of way employes. Sixty-three carriers, however, employing some 30,000 workers adamantly refused to enter into a union-shop agreement.

In an effort to block the further spread of the union-shop movement, several carriers instigated the filing of lawsuits by a handful of employes under so-called state "right-to-work" laws. These laws prohibit the making of agreements requiring union membership as a condition of employment or continued employment. The amended Railway Labor Act, however, permits the making of union-shop agreements "notwithstanding any other provision of this act, or any other statute or law of the United States, or Territory thereof, or of any State." The question which must be decided by the courts in pending suits, therefore, is whether a state right-to-work law or the Railway Labor Act as amended by Congress has supersedure.

Meanwhile, the election of Dwight D. Eisenhower as President of the United States at the November, 1952, election had placed a Republican administration in the nation's capital for the first time in twenty years.

The wage agreement signed by the non-operating railroad Brotherhoods and railroads in the United States on March 1, 1951, provided that "if Government wage stabilization policy permits so-called annual improvement wage increases, the parties may meet with the President of the United States, or such other person as he may designate, on or after July 1, 1952, to discuss whether or not further wage adjustments for employes covered by this Agreement are justified." Shortly before July 1, the organizations concerned requested that the President arrange conferences as contemplated in the clause.

At preliminary hearings in December before a Referee appointed by the President, the parties were unable to reach an agreement. Formal hearings on the issues involved were held by the Referee in January, 1953. On March 18, 1953, the Referee issued an award granting a wage increase of 4¢ an hour to the employes concerned retroactive to December 1, 1952. This amount was added to and became a part of basic wage rates. At that time, the employes were receiving 13¢ an hour above basic rates under the cost-of-living escalator clause in the wage agreement. The addition of the 4¢ improvement-factor increase brought their current wage rates to a figure 17¢ above those effective February 1, 1951.

Because of a new method employed by the Bureau of Labor Statistics, United States Department of Labor, to calculate the cost-of-living index figures, it became necessary to revise the arbitrary index figure of 178.0 used for making cost-of-living wage adjustments under the wage agreement of March 1, 1951. Effective October 1, 1953, this index figure was changed to 107.0, and cost-of-living wage adjustments of 1¢ an hour were to be made thereafter for each .6 point change in the Revised Consumers' Price Index of the Bureau.

Meantime, the non-operating Brotherhoods in the United States had begun a national movement to obtain improved agreement rules and a health and welfare plan. Basically, the unions' uniform notice of May 22, 1953, requested the following: an improved rule covering vacations with pay, seven paid holidays each year, a health and welfare program, premium pay for all Sunday work, and a uniform system for granting free transportation. Following a practice they had previously adopted, a number of carriers served counter-proposals requesting thirty-one rules changes that would destroy many of the basic provisions of rules agreements. The carriers eventually withdrew all but 15 of these proposals.

After five months had passed and little progress had been made toward a settlement of the dispute, the Brotherhoods invoked the services of the National Railroad Mediation Board. At the request of the Board, national conferences began on November 3. The carriers contended that the issues of health and welfare and free transportation were not proper subjects for discussion under the Railway Labor Act. A week previously (October 26, 1953) the Brotherhoods had begun the distribution of a strike ballot because of the generally adverse attitude of railroad managements toward the request.

On November 4, the carriers filed a suit in the United States District Court of Illinois asking a declaratory judgment against the cooperating Brotherhoods to establish the principle that the Railway Labor Act does not require bargaining on the issues of health and welfare and free transportation. (The Court dismissed the suit on February 4, 1954. A later opinion by a higher court reversing the lower court's decision was immaterial, for conferences on a health and welfare program were then well under way between committees representing the railroads and the Brotherhoods. The decision of the appellate court was itself later reversed by a decision of the United States Supreme Court reaffirming the judgment of the lower court.)

On December 17, the Brotherhoods accepted a suggestion of the Mediation Board that the issue be arbitrated, but the carriers declined the proposal. On December 28, after a great majority of the employes had voted to strike if a satisfactory settlement could not be reached, President Eisenhower created an Emergency Board to investigate the controversy. The hearings before the Board, the most lengthy and protracted ever held in a dispute involving the non-operating railroad employes, began on January 19, 1954, and did not end until April 3. Two extensions of time were agreed upon to permit the Board to complete the hearings. Eventually it became necessary for the Board to go into full-day sessions to hear the vast amount of testimony introduced.

Twenty-six witnesses testified, most of them several times—8 for the employes and 18 for the carriers. The testimony of these witnesses and the statements of counsel for both sides filled 6,184 pages in 38 volumes of recorded evidence with approximately 1½ million spoken words. In addition, 82 exhibits were presented, 24 by the employes and 58 by the carriers. Some of these exhibits ran into hundreds of pages.

On May 15, 1954, the Board issued a lengthy report, a great portion of which required careful analysis and consideration by the parties to the controversy. The Board recommended that certain of the rules changes requested by the railroads be adopted with modification. With respect to the proposals of the employes, it specifically recommended a third week of vacation with pay after fifteen years of service, payment at the pro rata rate when one of the seven enumerated holidays falls on a work day, and a health and welfare plan under which the employes and employers would share the cost equally. Although the Board recommended that the employes' proposal concerning free transportation be withdrawn, it suggested that the causes for the dissatisfaction that existed among the employes because of the railroads' policies with respect to the granting of passes be explored, and that appropriate remedies be adopted in conferences between the representatives of both parties.

National committees representing the carriers and the Brotherhoods began conference on June 3 to discuss the application of the Board's report. An agreement signed on August 21, 1954, made liberalizing changes in the National Vacation Agreement, increased the maximum paid vacation to fifteen days after fifteen years of continuous service, granted pro rata pay for holidays falling on a work day, established a health and welfare plan to be financed equally by the railroads and their employes, and made several changes in rules governing working conditions. The most important rule change placed a time limit on the handling of claims and grievances.

Prior to the signing of the agreement, a group of railroads in the southeast had withdrawn from the conference in an unprecedented move because they were not willing to accept the provisions agreed upon for a health and welfare plan. Through the services of the National Railroad Mediation Board, several of these railroads later became parties to the agreement, but a handful still refused to accept the plan. Thus, the employes on these systems were denied the benefits provided by the agreement of August 21. As the year closed, the cooperating Brotherhoods continued their efforts to bring the few remaining carriers under the agreement.

After months of negotiations, the non-operating Brotherhoods and the railroads who were parties to the agreement of August 21 signed a policy contract with an insurance company on January 18, 1955, placing in effect a plan providing hospital, surgical, and medical benefits for railroad workers.

During this time, the Brotherhood had been involved in two important movements in Canada. One of these movements brought into focus an oppressive condition that had developed under the Industrial Disputes and Investigation Act; i.e., the growing policy of compulsory arbitration adopted by the Canadian government in labor-management disputes on the railways.

On November 2, 1953, the Brotherhood joined with other non-operating railway labor organizations in serving formal notice on the managements of Canadian railways requesting pay for eight statutory holidays, longer vacations with pay, eighteen days' sick leave each year, and premium pay for scheduled Sunday work. Negotiations between committees representing the railways and the Brotherhoods ended a few weeks later when the railways refused to make any concessions and the Department of Labour failed in its efforts to settle the dispute through conciliation. At the request of the Brotherhoods, the Federal government appointed a Conciliation Board to investigate the dispute.

Hearings before the Board, which began early in February, 1954, ended on March 3. In spite of a convincing array of evidence presented by the employes as to the reasonableness of their request, the Board rejected the employes' petition for an annual sick-leave allowance and for premium pay for Sunday work. In fact, the Board split three ways in its recommendations, differing on the employes' requests for paid holidays and for longer vacations with pay. The employes rejected the unsatisfactory and divided report of the Board.

"No two members of the Board have jointly subscribed to findings which might be held to constitute a report within the meaning of the Industrial Disputes and Investigation Act," the committee said. "In the absence, therefore, of a report as contemplated by the law, to which consideration could be given, the committee is of the opinion that the unions' obligations as to procedure under the law have been exhausted."

Nevertheless, the Brotherhoods resumed conferences with representatives of the railways and began the circulation of a strike ballot, returnable August 2, when no progress toward a settlement could be made. The employes approved a suspension of work by a vote of approximately nine to one if the issues in dispute could not be settled satisfactorily, and by the middle of August, a general strike of non-operating railway employes in Canada had become imminent.

At this juncture, the Prime Minister called representatives of the employes and the railways into conference and requested that the controversy be submitted to arbitration. He made it plain that if the employes set a date for a strike, Parliament would be called into special session to deal with the situation. As a matter of fact, he had already publicly stated his position, and the government had taken action to insure that Parliament could be speedily convened if necessary to prevent a shutdown of the railways.

It will be recalled that Parliament had been called into special session in August, 1950, because of a general strike of Canadian railway workers then under way. An Act passed by Parliament at that time ordering the workers to return to their jobs had ended the strike after nine days. Faced with a repetition of that situation, the employes decided they had little recourse but to accede to the wishes of the Prime Minister and submit their case to arbitration. Although the action of Parliament in 1950 was the first instance of compulsory arbitration, it had become increasingly apparent to the employes that the government intended to follow this procedure in future unsettled disputes between the employes and the railways.

The chairman of the employes' committee voiced their protest against "repression and discrimination" by the government. "There is, of course, no essential difference between compulsory arbitration, as contemplated by the government, and acceptance of arbitration under duress," he said. " . . . Those we represent are being deprived of their right to strike, which they have always held in common with other Canadian workers."

Meanwhile, delegates attending the 69th convention of the Trades and Labour Congress of Canada unanimously "deplored and condemned" this interference with the right to strike. "This departure from the traditional freedom of industrial workers has grave implications and potentialities for all other Canadian workers," declared a resolution adopted by the convention.

The Federal government appointed Gordon McGregor Sloan, Chief Justice of the Appeals Court of British Columbia, to arbitrate the dispute, and on November 19, 1954, Arbitrator Sloan rendered an award, effective January 1, 1955, which was binding on all parties. The award denied the employes' proposal for eighteen days' sick leave (they had not pressed their request for premium pay for Sunday work). Arbitrator Sloan did recommend, however, that the rules agreement be revised to provide for five paid statutory holidays each year and three weeks' paid vacation for employes having fifteen or more years of service. In a significant recommendation beyond his findings in the specific issues before him, the Arbitrator suggested that the Federal government pay the railways a subsidy for hauling western grain at low rates. He expressed the opinion that this loss in revenue was a prime factor in the disparity between working conditions of railway workers and employes in other industries.

As committees representing the railways and their non-operating employes met to reach an agreement making the provisions of the award effective, a mass meeting of railway workers from all crafts went on record as being "unalterably opposed" to compulsory arbitration. A committee formed at the meeting prepared to seek changes in procedures under the Industrial Disputes and Investigation Act that would relieve the onerous situation that had developed.

The second dispute involving Canadian maintenance of way workers, which was actually a combination of two movements separately begun, had by this time reached the final stage. In a notice dated November 9, 1953, the Brotherhood had requested substantial increases in rates of pay for temporary extra gang laborers. The purpose of this request was to eliminate the differentials between the rates of these employes and those of section men.

Within a few weeks, negotiations between the Central Committee and the railways had become deadlocked. Conferences continued into early 1954 with a Federal Conciliator presiding. When it became apparent that no basis for a settlement could be reached, the Federal government appointed a Conciliation Board to investigate the dispute.

By this time, the Brotherhood had filed another request with the Railway Association of Canada involving this same class of employes. On March 1, 1954, the Central Committee notified the Association of its wish to revise certain rules in Wage Agreement No. 13 covering temporary extra gang laborers. Among other rules changes, the Committee requested a forty-hour week, the time and one-half rate after eight hours' work, pay for eight statutory holidays each year, penalty payment for all Sunday work, a sick leave of eighteen days each year, and an increased vacation allowance.

When negotiations with the railways reached a stalemate, the government agreed to a request that the dispute be referred to the Conciliation Board that had been formed to investigate the wage-increase case then pending for temporary extra gang men. Thus, the Board assumed jurisdiction in both cases.

During subsequent hearings, representatives of the Brotherhood urged the Board to eliminate the inequities that had been established during the many years these employes were unorganized and had no collective-bargaining agency through which their accumulated grievances could be handled with the railways. They pointed out that there was no justification for maintaining the differential in pay between extra gang workers and section men, who often work side by side and under the same supervision. Moreover, that a drastic revision in agreement rules was necessary if these employes were to enjoy the same working conditions that applied to other classes of maintenance of way workers.

In a report rendered on October 22, 1954, the Conciliation Board denied the request of the employes for a forty-hour week for temporary extra gang laborers. It recommended, however, that the work week should have a maximum limit of 50 hours, with payment of the time and one-half rate for work in excess of the agreed number of hours on any day. The Board declined to recommend that the number of paid holidays each year be increased above four, or that sick leave be granted, but it did recommend three weeks' paid vacation after fifteen years' service (the previous maximum was two weeks). The Board also proposed other improvements in rules to bring the working conditions of temporary extra gang men more in conformity with those of section men.

With respect to wages, the Board proposed a minimum rate of 80¢ an hour for probationary employes and an adjustment in compensation of 7¢ an hour to produce the same income for 50 hours' work as the employes had previously received for 54 hours. The recommended 80¢ rate marked a definite advance for probationary extra gang men, for the railways had been free to hire these workers at whatever rate they wished to pay. This rate exceeded by 5¢ the minimum hourly wage established in the United States under the Wage-Hour Act, and it was the first instance in which a board established by the Canadian government had recommended a minimum wage in the railway industry.

Although disappointed at the Board's failure to recommend a forty-hour week or a substantial wage increase for temporary extra gang men, the Central Committee sought conferences with the Railway Association of Canada to make the Board's report effective.

Two other important occurrences had taken place in the United States meanwhile. On August 31, 1954, the President of the United States approved legislation passed by Congress amending the Railroad Retirement Act and the Railroad Unemployment Insurance Act, and late in the year the cost-of-living wage adjustment became a part of basic wage rates.

The most important amendments to the Railroad Retirement Act reduced from 65 to 60 the age at which widows may draw monthly annuities; permitted the payment of monthly benefits to a widowed mother at any age if she had in her care a disabled child, even though the child was past age 18; made provision for disregarding service after age 65 whenever this service would tend to reduce a person's annuity; provided that widows drawing railroad annuities of their own could get the full widow's annuity to which they were entitled on the basis of their deceased husband's employment; and changed the work restrictions for annuitants under age 65 who retired because of disability to provide that they may earn as much as $100 a month without forfeiting their annuity for that month (the previous maximum was $75).

Amendments to the Railroad Unemployment Insurance Act established larger unemployment and sickness payment through a generally higher benefit-rate schedule. They also provided that an employe's benefits would not be less than half of his regular pay for his last railroad job in the preceding year, up to a maximum of $42.50 a week in benefits. Under this provision, almost all employes could receive at least $30 a week. The amendments contained a restriction, however, that only employes who had earned at least $400 in the preceding year could receive unemployment and sickness benefits (formerly only $300 was required), and that no employe could receive more in each type of benefit (sickness and unemployment) in a benefit year than his total earnings in the preceding year.

Effective July 1, 1954, railroad employes and employers began paying railroad retirement taxes on employes' earnings up to $350 a month instead of $300, the previous maximum tax base. This meant that earnings up to $350 a month would be credited toward retirement benefits. At the same time, the tax base for contributions by the railroads under the Railroad Unemployment Insurance Act was increased from $300 to $350 a month.

At a meeting of the International Association of Grand Lodge and System Officers in Detroit, Michigan, from November 8 to 10, 1954, action was taken on many of the important issues before the Brotherhood.

The history of the joint rules movement of May 22, 1953, culminating in the agreement of August 21, 1954, and the withdrawal of a group of southeastern railroads from the national conferences, were reviewed. The stabilization of employment, union-shop agreements in the United States, the check-off of union dues in Canada, the contracting of maintenance of way work, the recent no-raiding agreement between the A. F. of L. and the C. I. O. in jurisdictional questions, were among the subjects discussed.

The escalator clause in the wage agreement of March 1, 1951, adjusting wage rates periodically on the basis of changes in the cost-of-living index figures in the United States, had been in effect since April 1, 1951. On December 3, 1954, an agreement was reached between national committees representing the railroads and their non-operating employes providing that effective as of that date the escalator clause would be canceled and all cost-of-living adjustments made under the March 1, 1951, agreement would be added to basic wage rates. Basic rates were thus increased by 13¢ an hour. This agreement, however, did not apply to the southeastern railroads who had withdrawn their authority from the Southeastern Carriers' Conference Committee prior to the signing of the agreement of August 21, 1954, covering a health and welfare plan and various rules changes.

"Another year will soon have passed and while we are already looking into the future, we might pause to take inventory of our accomplishments," President Carroll said in December, 1954. "The year 1954 has been a fruitful one for the maintenance of way employes on our nation's railroads, despite the fact that we were confronted with new obstacles which we were compelled to surmount. The agreement of August 21, 1954, resulting from the recommendations of a Presidential Emergency Board, contains many new benefits for the workers. It has been in effect since that date except on railroads that withdrew from national handling. . . . Amendments to the Railroad Retirement Act have also resulted in additional benefits to our people. . . .

"In promoting the proposal for a Health and Welfare Plan, we were confronted with serious opposition. First, our right to make this a subject for negotiation was questioned, and the carriers petitioned the courts for a declaratory judgment to prohibit the cooperating organizations from discussing the proposal. Later, a group of southeastern carriers withdrew authority previously granted the Carriers' Conference Committee to represent them in national handling. Despite the resistance, our committee refused to falter and negotiations continued with the result that an agreement was reached upon a Health and Welfare Plan. . . . This agreement is, in my opinion, the largest insurance coverage plan ever to be consummated for the welfare of a group of workers, and includes the most comprehensive coverage ever written.

"As we look back over the past twelve months, we can again say that we have made progress. We have attempted to meet every challenge in the true American tradition. . . . While we realize there will always be differences of opinion, we look forward to the day when there will be a common objective for both management and labor that, when met, will assure the security of both. We shall strive toward that end as we cross the threshold of the new year."

As the year 1954 ended, the world still tottered on the peak of uncertainty. Although hostilities in Korea had ended with the signing of an armistice in July, 1953, President Eisenhower warned that even though a truce had been won on one battlefield, peace had not been achieved throughout the world. A moderate tapering-off of the country's defense program following the Korean armistice had created some economic dislocations and an increase in unemployment during 1954. Heavy force reductions had reduced the average number of maintenance of way workers in railroad service in the United States from 225,430 in 1953 to only 184,743 in 1954.

But as the year 1955 began, the general economic picture had grown considerably brighter, and the Brotherhood and its members looked forward hopefully to the future as it prepared for its thirty-second regular Grand Lodge convention to be held in Detroit, Michigan, beginning June 20.

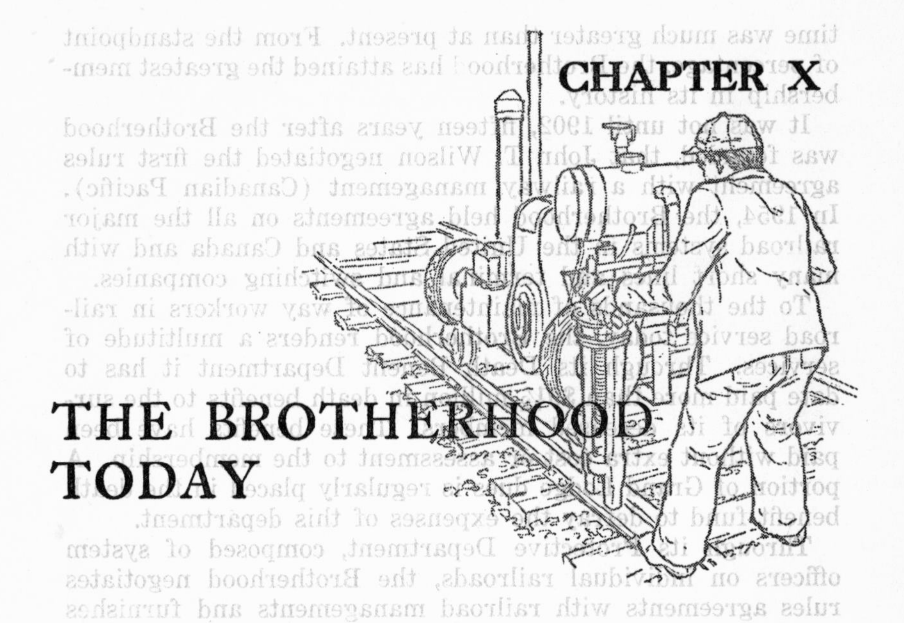

CHAPTER X

THE BROTHERHOOD TODAY

THE preparation of the conclusion is perhaps one of the most difficult tasks in writing a history of this nature. For the word "conclusion" in itself connotes a finality which is not final and the writing of "finis" to a story that is by no means finished. But the completion of this history requires the drawing of certain conclusions and a rounding out of some aspects of the Brotherhood's story that have not been fully told.

In the sixty-eight years of its existence, the Brotherhood of Maintenance of Way Employes, as will be noted from the preceding pages of this history, has not only grown tremendously in membership, but it has at the same time greatly expanded its jurisdiction and its service to railroad maintenance of way workers. From a few hundred members in 1887, the membership of the Brotherhood has increased to approximately 250,000 in recent years. This figure is surpassed perhaps by the lush era of World War I, but the number of maintenance of way workers in railroad service at that time was much greater than at present. From the standpoint of percentage, the Brotherhood has attained the greatest membership in its history.

It was not until 1902, fifteen years after the Brotherhood was founded, that John T. Wilson negotiated the first rules agreement with a railway management (Canadian Pacific). In 1954, the Brotherhood held agreements on all the major railroad systems in the United States and Canada and with many short lines and terminal and switching companies.

To the thousands of maintenance of way workers in railroad service today, the Brotherhood renders a multitude of services. Through its Death Benefit Department it has to date paid more than $9½ million in death benefits to the survivors of its deceased members. These benefits have been paid without extra cost or assessment to the membership. A portion of Grand Lodge dues is regularly placed in the death benefit fund to defray the expenses of this department.

Through its Protective Department, composed of system officers on individual railroads, the Brotherhood negotiates rules agreements with railroad managements and furnishes its membership with an opportunity to file and progress their claims and grievances arising out of the application of these agreements. Since the establishment of the National Railroad Adjustment Board (to which unsettled claims and grievances can be submitted for decision) under the amended Railway Labor Act of 1934, the Brotherhood has had a representative on the Third Division of the Board.

In addition, Grand Lodge maintains an office in Chicago, Illinois, where the Board is located, through which claims and grievances that cannot be settled on the system can be processed to the Board for decision. Favorable awards rendered by the Board in the great majority of maintenance-of-way cases submitted to it for adjudication have resulted in the payment of a vast aggregate sum of money to the claimants by the railroads involved.

In Canada, the Canadian Railroad Board of Adjustment No. 1 has functions similar to those of the National Railroad Adjustment Board in the United States, and unsettled claims and grievances arising on Canadian railways can be submitted to it for review.

Through affiliation with the Railway Labor Executives' Association, the President of the Brotherhood maintains constant contact with the chief executives of the other non-operating railroad Brotherhoods. At meetings of the association, cooperative action is decided upon in matters of mutual interest to members of the affiliated organizations. Joint national movements inaugurated by the non-operating Brotherhoods to secure higher wages or better working conditions for their members are progressed uniformly in accordance with a program adopted by the association; and opposition to wage reductions or other detrimental proposals of railroad managements affecting members of the non-operating organizations is on a cooperative basis.

Early in the life of the Brotherhood, John T. Wilson discovered that workers must take an active interest in political and legislative matters for sheer self-protection. The exploratory gropings of the young organization have since been considerably expanded. The Brotherhood is active in the national legislative field both in the United States and Canada, and national legislative representatives are stationed in Washington, D. C., and Ottawa, Ontario. Legislative representatives elected by subordinate lodge delegates look after the interests of the membership of the Brotherhood in each state and province. The activities of the Brotherhood's state and provincial legislative representatives and affiliation with Railway Labor's Political League by the President of the Brotherhood help to keep members of the Brotherhood well-informed politically.

No army can hope to give battle successfully without an efficient intelligence corps. To keep a precise finger on the pulse of constantly changing events and to diagnose their significance, the Brotherhood maintains its Statistical and Research Department. This department has continued and expanded considerably the research work begun in 1922.

Sixty-three years ago, Grand Chief Foreman John T. Wilson began publication of "The Foreman's Advance Advocate," the first official organ of the Brotherhood. Publication of the Brotherhood magazine under various names has been continued without interruption since that time. Today, a quarter of a million copies of the "Journal" are sent monthly to members of the Brotherhood in the United States and Canada. In addition, each member receives a copy of the weekly newspaper "Labor," the official voice of the standard railroad labor organizations.

It will be seen, therefore, that from its international headquarters in Detroit, Michigan, and through its 79 system divisions or federations and more than 1400 subordinate lodges, the activities of the Brotherhood today reach into every state and province and permeate the lives of all maintenance of way workers and their families.

In telling this story of the Brotherhood, little has been said thus far about the vast changes that have taken place in the methods of performing maintenance of way work. This is an important part of the Brotherhood's history. In the early days of the railroad industry, the work of building and maintaining the right of way and the bridges, trestles, buildings, and other structures of the railroads was done by hand with the aid of comparatively primitive tools. Maintenance of way workers traveled from place to place over the tracks by means of hand-propelled cars. As time passed, new tools and more efficient methods of performing the work were adopted. Within the past twenty years, technological advances through the use of machinery to perform much of the work formerly done manually have increased greatly.

A goodly part of daily maintenance work must still be done by hand, and the job of the average maintenance of way worker is still arduous. The technological revolution in the maintenance of way department, however, now requires a higher degree of skill and efficiency on the part of the workers, many of whom must operate complicated machines.

The old handcar on which maintenance of way workers once traveled and transported their tools and materials has long since been superseded by the track motor car powered by a gasoline engine. Ingeniously designed machines are now used to ditch the right of way, clean and spread ballast, tamp the ballast under ties, handle and lay rail, test rail for defects, adze ties, pull and drive tie spikes, tighten rail bolts, mow weeds, destroy weeds by chemical spray, pump concrete into soft spots in the right of way, and to perform many of the day-to-day tasks of the maintenance of way worker.

The extent to which railroads in the United States and Canada have converted to the use of machinery in the maintenance of way department is illustrated by figures given in Appendix G. During the seventeen-year period from 1937 to 1953, inclusive, the railroads bought 132,829 units of power equipment at a cost of more than $231 million. In the nine-year period from 1945 to 1953, inclusive, they purchased 85,072 machines of various types costing approximately $163 million. Seeking the highest degree of productivity and efficiency from their maintenance of way employes, the railroads have converted to the use of mechanized equipment to a degree that has had a profound effect on employment in the maintenance of way department.

In other ways, too, the railroads have sought to perform the work with fewer employes. The use of heavier rail and of ties and bridge timbers more adequately treated to prevent decay has increased the span of time between replacements. The installation of flashing lights and automatic gates at highway crossings and the construction of overpasses above highways have eliminated the jobs of many crossing watchmen. The use of automatic electric pumps to furnish water for the rapidly vanishing steam locomotive and the continuing conversion by the railroads to diesel power have reduced the number of coal chute and pumping equipment operators almost to the vanishing point. All these various factors have contributed to the severe decline in the number of maintenance of way employes now in railroad service. (See Appendices E and F.)

From time to time in the previous chapters of this history, reference has been made to the contracting of maintenance of way work, i.e., the performance of this work by arrangement between the railroad companies and contractors. This is one of the more serious problems that has plagued the Brotherhood and its members for many years. The jobs of maintenance of way workers depend on the amount of work to be performed in their department. Any reduction in the work eventually results in a reduction in the number of jobs. Instances have arisen where railroad employes were cut off in force reduction while their work was being done by employes of a contractor.

It is the long-established assertion of the Brotherhood that maintenance of way workers have the right to perform all work coming within the scope of its agreements with the railroads. Many agreements contain a rule providing that the railroads will let work to contract only under certain prescribed conditions, and then only through agreement reached with the General Chairmen in each instance. Some agreements outline the specific conditions under which work may be contracted. Difficulty has arisen chiefly under agreements which contain no rule prohibiting the contracting of work.

Maintenance of way workers are skilled craftsmen who have proved they are qualified to do any of the maintenance of way work that can be done by contractors. Many of the largest railroad bridges and structures in the country—some of them multi-million-dollar projects—have been built by maintenance of way forces. A rule in every agreement prohibiting the contracting of work has long been a goal of the Brotherhood. Numerous awards favorable to the Brotherhood in claims submitted to the Third Division of the National Railroad Adjustment Board involving the contracting of work are helping to eliminate this practice and to bring the Brotherhood closer to its goal.

Occasional reference has also been made in this history to the activities of rival unions. Since the early days of its history, the Brotherhood has been compelled to fight almost constantly against the efforts of these organizations to secure jurisdiction over railroad workers represented by the Brotherhood. Some of these rival unions have been created or supported by former members or officers of the Brotherhood. Others have been offshoots of labor unions established in other fields that were seeking to invade the railroad industry. Still others were formed by persons who neither had any practical knowledge of the railroad industry nor any actual ability to represent railroad workers effectively.

A detailed outline of the formation and the activities of these rival organizations would require a volume in itself. Most of them were short-lived. Some invoked the services of the National Railroad Mediation Board and forced the Brotherhood to join in balloting maintenance of way workers on various railroad systems to decide the question of representation; and several unsuccessfully sought court action in disputes over the representation of railroad workers.

Impotent and ineffective as they were, these rival organizations nevertheless succeeded in enlisting the support of some railroad workers, and in the aggregate they have cost the Brotherhood a great deal in time and money. Their activities have been more annoying than serious, however, and they have never been able to produce any tangible evidence of benefits which they secured for the railroad workers they purported to represent. Today, the great strength of the Brotherhood and its mounting success in effectively representing maintenance of way workers in both the United States and Canada have discouraged all but the most rash from seeking to form rival unions.

No attempt has been made in this history to treat the subject of strikes exhaustively or to give a complete list of strikes in the railroad industry or the maintenance of way department. As a matter of fact, contrary to the experience of labor unions in other industries, the progress of the Brotherhood, with one exception, has not depended in too great a degree on the winning of strikes. This one exception is the Canadian Pacific strike of 1901. The successful outcome of this strike and the subsequent negotiation of an agreement between the Brotherhood and the railway company, the first it signed with any railroad, gave a tremendous uplift to the Brotherhood and its members. A new era began when the railroads finally understood that the Brotherhood could use its economic strength effectively.

The reason for the lack of general strikes in the railroad industry is not difficult to understand. General railroad strikes are comparatively rare, due partly to the attitude of the government toward strikes in the railroad industry and partly to the deep-seated reluctance of railroad workers to engage in a suspension of work unless it is absolutely necessary. The uninterrupted operation of the railroads is so essential to the welfare of the public that the calling of a general strike on the railways in either the United States or Canada immediately paralyzes the economy. As a result, the Federal governments in both countries have adopted legislation intended to bring about the orderly and peaceful settlement of collective-bargaining disputes on the railroads. But this procedure does not always prevent crises from arising. When a general strike of railroad workers has become imminent or has actually begun, however, the government in either country has not hesitated to take action to prevent the strike or to bring it to an immediate end. As has been illustrated in this history, the government of the United States has on several occasions seized the railroads and placed them under the operation of the government to prevent or end strikes. The Canadian government ended the general railway strike of 1950 by an act of Parliament, and in 1954 the Prime Minister intimated that similar action would be taken if the employes set a date to begin a strike in an unsettled dispute over working conditions.

The situation has become of serious concern to railway workers, particularly in Canada. They feel that when governmental action takes away their right to strike, they are being deprived of the only recourse they have if management adamantly refuses to make needed improvements in wages and working conditions. Moreover, they contend that this attitude of government tends to destroy the basic purpose of collective bargaining and to make it only a formal step toward compulsory arbitration, and that there is a real danger that injustice may be perpetuated through a curtailment of the right to strike.

Although the Brotherhood has taken national strike votes on numerous occasions, it has called only one general strike of maintenance of way workers; i.e., the Canadian strike of August, 1950. All the other strikes in which it has participated have been on individual railroad systems. In the early years of the Brotherhood's history, maintenance of way workers generally stood alone in their strikes to obtain better conditions. Assistance from other railroad unions was more in the nature of moral support than actual participation in the strike. Even though the Brotherhood lost most of these early strikes, their effect is apparent in the gradually increasing willingness of the railroads to negotiate with representatives of the employes.

In more recent years, the Brotherhood has joined with other railroad unions in strikes on individual railroad systems, and most of them have been won by the employes. Each strike has been called only after negotiations with the management extending over many months had shown that the use of collective strength by the employes was the only recourse. The Brotherhood still believes as did its founder, John T. Wilson, that a strike should be used only as a last resort after all other means of bringing about a settlement of the dispute have failed.

It has not been possible in this history to give a detailed outline of the provisions of the Railroad Retirement and Unemployment Insurance Acts (United States). The Railroad Retirement Act provides old-age and disability annuities for railroad workers and benefits for their survivors. The Railroad Unemployment Insurance Act provides benefits for railroad employes who are not working because of loss of job, sickness, or injury.

Railroad workers first began their attempt to secure a national retirement system in 1932, but their bill died in Congress. The acts passed by Congress in 1934 and 1935 were the subject of adverse court decisions, and it was not until 1937, after the railroads and the Brotherhoods had agreed on the basic provisions of a retirement system, that Congress passed the Railroad Retirement Act of 1937, which is still in effect. In 1938, Congress passed the Railroad Unemployment Insurance Act, which superseded the unemployment-insurance provisions of the Social Security Act insofar as railroad workers are concerned.

Both of these acts have been subsequently amended to provide broader and higher benefits for railroad workers, their wives, and their survivors. Since 1937, hundreds of bills have been introduced in Congress seeking improvements in the railroad retirement system. Most of these proposals have been made by so-called "pension groups" who are in no way connected with the standard railroad Brotherhoods and have apparently given little consideration to the financial stability of the system. Many of these proposed changes have considerable merit, but actuarial studies have shown that their adoption would endanger the soundness of the system.

It is the wish of the chief executives of the railroad Brotherhoods that the highest benefits consistent with the future financial security of the system be provided under the Railroad Retirement Act, and they maintain a constant study of the operation of the system. At the same time, they feel it is imperative that the railroad retirement system be maintained on an actuarially sound basis and that any proposed changes in the Act must be considered from this viewpoint.

In concluding this story of the Brotherhood, some additional information should probably be given about the Central Committee of Canada, which has been frequently mentioned in previous chapters. The Central Committee had its beginning in May, 1918, when the system officers of the Brotherhood from all railways in Canada met to consider plans to secure an increase in wages, an eight-hour day, and standardized rates of pay and uniform rules governing working conditions on all railways in the Dominion. The meeting selected a subcommittee of system officers to conduct negotiations with the Canadian Railway War Board.

At a meeting in July, 1918, this subcommittee adopted the name "Central Committee for Canada of the Brotherhood of Maintenance of Way Employes." The first by-laws were adopted by the committee effective October 13, 1919. These by-laws as last amended effective September 1, 1953, provide:

"PREAMBLE

"The Central Committee for Canada is a Committee duly authorized by the Grand Lodge President and the Joint Protective Boards of the Brotherhood of Maintenance of Way Employes, on railways in Canada, for the purpose of negotiating rates of pay and working conditions for maintenance of way employes in the Dominion of Canada.

"COMPOSITION

"The Central Committee for Canada shall be composed of a Grand Lodge Vice-President, as assigned by the Grand Lodge President, and the General Chairmen and Vice-General Chairmen of the three system federations in Canada, namely: Canadian Pacific System Federation, Canadian National Eastern Lines System Federation, and Canadian National Western Lines System Federation; and in addition thereto, one active full-time System Federation officer who shall be elected by their respective System Federation Joint Protective Boards.

"Other railways in Canada, having 1,000 or more members and not represented by any of the above three system federations, shall be entitled to one representative on the Central Committee for Canada."

The national agreement signed by the Central Committee with the Canadian railways on March 7, 1919, is still in effect, although it has undergone considerable change during the intervening years. In comparison, the national agreement in the United States, signed with the United States Railroad Administration effective December 16, 1919, was terminated eighteen months later by decision of the United States Railroad Labor Board. Since that time, agreements covering rates of pay and working conditions in the United States have been negotiated and maintained for each railroad system instead of on a national basis, and the settlements obtained in national movements have been incorporated in the individual agreements. In Canada, however, any changes in rates of pay or working conditions are negotiated nationally by the Central Committee and incorporated in the master agreement covering practically all maintenance of way workers in Canada.

Although it is not the purpose of this history to attempt to answer the complex questions often asked about labor unions, the answers to several questions naturally emerge from this recital of the birth and growth of a labor union.

Are labor unions the product of beneficial laws? Could they survive in a more hostile atmosphere or under the oppression of a society less friendly to the worker? These questions are often asked. Manifestly, both labor unions and industry alike should thrive more under fair or favorable governmental regulations than under those that hamper their growth or confine their activities. Yet this story of the Brotherhood is a concrete example of the fact that the foundations of labor unions are rooted much deeper than the rather shallow footing of governmental fiat—that the power of faith and courage is difficult to assay. The hidden strength of labor unions is often seriously underestimated.

Are labor unions really necessary? Could not individual

employes obtain for themselves the benefits they derive through their union? The answer to these questions is obvious from the experience of the Brotherhood. Not one major concession affecting maintenance of way workers generally has ever been placed in effect by railroad managements of their own volition. Progress toward improving the worker's lot has been entirely at the instigation of the union.

Another question frequently asked is this: how democratic *are* labor unions? So far as the Brotherhood of Maintenance of Way Employes is concerned, this question scarcely needs answering to the reader of this history. At the regular conventions of Grand Lodge, the members of the Brotherhood through their chosen delegates have the opportunity to decide the policies of Grand Lodge and to elect its officers (they have similar rights at conventions of system divisions or federations or at meetings of subordinate lodges). Delegates to conventions of the Grand Lodge have not hesitated to voice the wishes of the membership they represent, both in adopting the laws to govern the Brotherhood and in selecting its officers.

In sixty-eight years the Brotherhood has grown from a visionary dream in the mind of a railroad section foreman to one of the most powerful railroad Brotherhoods in the United States and Canada. Today it has reached a high point in strength and in service to railroad maintenance of way workers. But what of the future? Following are some of the goals on its program: fairer wages; standardized rates of pay; uniform and improved agreement rules; greater job security and a guaranteed annual wage; a more liberal vacation agreement; safer working conditions; still higher employe productivity and efficiency; labor-management cooperation; a greater share of transportation business for the railroads.

Will the Brotherhood continue its progress? Will it attain its goals? To repeat and paraphrase the words of John T. Wilson, the founder of the Brotherhood:

"Having passed some of the most dangerous breakers in our infancy, having struggled through the most trying crises our nation has ever witnessed, having withstood the crucial test of time, why, then, should we not face the future with confidence?"

APPENDIX A

HISTORICAL DOCUMENTS

The agreement which became effective June 1, 1902, on the Canadian Pacific Railway was the first formal agreement ever signed by the Brotherhood with a railway company. The agreement quoted below, although it was effective June 1, 1903, contained the basic features of the 1902 agreement.

"RULES,
REGULATIONS AND WAGES
for
MAINTENANCE-OF-WAY EMPLOYES
of
CANADIAN PACIFIC RAILWAY COMPANY.

"TAKING EFFECT JUNE 1, 1903.

"RULES AND RATES.

"The following rules and rates of pay will govern the service of Permanent Maintenance-of-Way Employes on the Canadian Pacific Railway:

"SECTION 1. By 'Permanent Maintenance-of-Way Employes' is meant employes who take their orders from the Roadmasters and Bridge and Building Masters on such parts of the line as are open for traffic, and who have been in the Maintenance-of-Way service continuously for one year or more, or who have had one year's cumulative service during the three years immediately preceding, and same will hereinafter be referred to as 'Employes.' Laborers in extra gangs, unless those practically engaged all the year round, will not be ranked as 'Permanent Employes.'

"SEC. 2. Ten hours shall constitute a day's work, excepting for Switch Tenders, Track and Bridge Watchmen, Signalmen (except when employed as Telegraph Operators), Pumpmen and Pump Repairers. When required to work in excess of these hours time will be allowed for such excess at rate of time and a quarter until 10 p.m., and at rate of time and a half from 10 p.m. to 6 a.m. and on Sundays and Christmas day. If called or kept out after 10 p.m., a minimum allowance of three hours' straight time will be made.

"(a) The hours of Switch Tenders, Track and Bridge Watchmen, Signalmen, Pumpmen and Pump Repairers will be regulated by the Company, but they shall receive at least eight hours' continuous rest in each twenty-four hours.

"(b) In emergencies employes will not be required to work more than twenty-four (24) hours continuously without a rest of eight (8) hours.

"(c) Employes traveling on orders of the Company to and from work after regular hours outside of their regular sections will be allowed straight time. Bridge men traveling on their regular sections on orders of the Company to and from work, after regular hours will be allowed half time until 10 p.m. and straight time thereafter. When provided with boarding and sleeping cars to carry them to or from work, no allowance will be made. Employes when traveling from one section or division to another on account of promotion will not receive any allowance.

"(d) In computing time one hour will be allowed for thirty to sixty minutes. For less than thirty minutes no allowance will be made.

"SEC. 3. Employes will be promoted hereafter on their respective Superintendent's division in order of seniority, provided they are qualified. Employes may be transferred from one division to another for extra gang work, or on the opening of new lines, or when the necessary qualified men are not obtainable on the division.

"(a) Employes refusing promotion become junior to employes accepting such promotion.

"(b) An employe who is transferred from the Bridge and Building Department to the Roadmaster's Department, or vice versa, will lose his seniority standing.

"(c) Employes unable to read and write English (or French in the Province of Quebec) need not be promoted.

"(d) Employes leaving the service of the Company when their services are required, in event of re-employment, will rank as new men.

"(e) A list of all employes will be prepared for each Superintendent's division, and such lists will show the seniority standing of each employe. The lists will be revised from time to time to agree with length of service and promotions made, and copy will be furnished representative of employes. They will be open for correction on proper representation.

"(f) In the event of reduction in the number of men employed, those longest in service shall have preference of employment.

"(g) The position of Switch Tenders, Track and Bridge Watchmen and Signalmen is not one subject to the general rules for promotion, being intended to take care of men in any department who become unfitted for other service.

"SEC. 4. Employes suspended or dismissed will receive full and impartial hearings, and will be advised of decisions reached within fifteen (15) days from time of suspension or dismissal. Should investigation show suspension or dismissal was unjust, time will be allowed and employe reinstated. Appeals from decisions must be made in writing by the employe through his Roadmaster or Bridge and Building Master within fifteen (15) days after advised of such decision.

"SEC. 5. Leave of absence and free transportation will be granted to members of duly appointed committees for the adjustment of matters in dispute between the Company and employes, so far as is consistent with good service, within ten (10) days after request in writing has been made on the proper officer.

"SEC. 6. Employes taken off their regular sections temporarily to work on snow or tie trains, or other work, will be compensated for the board and lodging expenses they necessarily incur.

"SEC. 7. Employes required to attend to and light semaphore or switch lamps before or after their regular hours will receive therefor \$4.00 per month for six or less lamps and 50 cents per month per lamp for those in excess of six. Where lamps are located at a distance from employe's residence they will be attended to in regular working hours.

"SEC. 8. Employes called out for emergency work, outside of their regular working limits, requiring their absence beyond regular working hours, will be supplied with boarding cars when desirable and practicable.

"SEC. 9. The Company will keep section houses in good repair; the cost of repairs other than ordinary wear and tear will be charged to occupants.

"(a) Section houses shall be for the use of Foremen and their families, and, when necessary, for telegraph operators, and members of their permanent gangs. Their surroundings must be kept clean by occupants.

"(b) Where water is transported for use of section gangs, good water and suitable sunken tanks with pumps will be provided.

"SEC. 10. Employes will be granted leave of absence and passes or reduced rates in accordance with the current general regulations of the Company.

"(a) Opportunity and free transportation will be given employes for getting to their place of residence at week ends, when the Company's interests do not suffer thereby.

"(b) Employes will be granted free transportation and leave of absence three times each year. Such free transportation will not extend beyond their Roadmaster's or Bridge and Building Master's division and the leave of absence will not exceed two days, and then only when consistent with good service, and provided the Company is not put to additional expense.

"(c) Employes discharged through reduction in staff, when re-engaged within one year, will be granted free transportation to place of work over general division on which formerly employed.

"SEC. 11. Bridge and Building Gangs shall be composed of:

"1st. Foremen.

"2nd. Carpenters, who shall be skilled mechanics in house and bench work and have a proper kit of carpenters' tools.

Above: A present-day freight locomotive in use on the Baltimore & Ohio Railroad.

↑ *Above: The Southern Pacific's Sunset Limited crossing the Rio Grande into El Paso, Texas, enroute between Los Angeles and New Orleans.*

Right: A Denver & Rio Grande Western freight passing through Ruby Canyon near the Colorado-Utah border.

→

SOUTHERN PACIFIC

Grande
546

Above: The Burlington's California Zephyr, making daily trips between Chicago and San Francisco, pictured in Glenwood Canyon, Colorado.

"3rd. Bridgemen, who shall be rough carpenters, expert saw, axe and hammer men, and have a general experience in bridge work.

"4th. Bridge Laborers, who shall be strong, handy men, and who shall perform such work as may be assigned to them."

(NOTE: Rates of pay are not being listed in detail, but they ranged as follows:

TRACKMEN

Section Foremen: $1.85 to $2.60 per day.
Assistant Section Foremen in yards: $1.85 to $2.35 per day.
Sectionmen: $1.35 to $1.50 per day.
Foremen of Extra Gangs: $2.00 to $3.50 per day.
Assistant Foremen of Extra Gangs: $1.85 to $2.35 per day.
Section Foremen in charge of snow plows while in operation: $2.75 to $3.00 per day.
Laborers—Extra Gangs (permanent): $1.60 per day.
Signalmen: $1.25 to $1.50 per day.
Track Watchmen: $47.50 to $50.00 per month.
Switchtenders: $47.50 per month.

BRIDGE AND BUILDING MEN

Foremen: $2.50 to $3.25 per day.
Carpenters: $2.20 to $2.80 per day.
Bridgemen: $1.75 to $2.65 per day.
Foremen Painters: $2.40 to $3.00 per day.
Painters: $1.75 to $2.50 per day.
Drawbridgemen: $1.35 per day.
Blacksmiths: $2.25 per day (or railway shop rates in some instances).
Riveters: $2.75 to $3.00 per day.
Bridge Watchmen: $47.50 per month.

PUMPMEN

Pump Repairers: $60.00 to $80.00 per month.
Pumpmen: $40.00 to $55.00 per month.

"Above rules and rates will not be changed unless on sixty days' notice being given between the 1st day of May and the 1st day of November of any year."

Appendix A

The following agreement was one of the first (perhaps the first) signed by the Brotherhood with a major railway company in the United States.

"AGREEMENT
between
THE ATLANTIC COAST LINE RAILWAY
COMPANY
and
ITS MAINTENANCE-OF-WAY EMPLOYES.

"To Take Effect January 1, 1903.

"SCHEDULE OF WAGES
for
FOREMEN AND ASSISTANT FOREMEN EMPLOYED
in the
MAINTENANCE-OF-WAY DEPARTMENT, TO
INCLUDE SECTION FOREMEN, BRIDGE AND
TRESTLE FOREMEN, CARPENTER FOREMEN,
FOREMEN OF FLOATING GANGS
and
EXTRA GANGS, FOREMEN OF ROAD TRAINS,
PILEDRIVERS AND STEAM SHOVELS.

"Foremen who are now paid at the rate of $40.00 or less per month will have their rate of pay advanced $4.00 per month.

"Foremen who are now paid at the rate of over $40.00 per month will have their rate of pay advanced $3.00 per month.

"The daily rate to be based on the actual number of working days in each month.

"Time lost will not be paid for.

"The working hours from April 1 to November 1 will be from 6 a.m. to 6 p.m., and from November 1 to April 1, from 7 a.m. to 5 p.m.

"One hour will be allowed for dinner.

"Overtime will be paid for by the hour at the rate of 10 per cent of the day wage.

"Foremen will report, on the blank furnished for the purpose, all overtime made.

"The blank, properly filled out, must be sent to the Roadmaster or Supervisor for his approval within forty-eight (48) hours after such overtime is made.

"Whenever practicable the Company will furnish comfortable dwelling-houses for Section Foremen and will keep them in good repair.

"In case houses are not furnished, $5.00 per month will be allowed Section Foremen, in addition to their regular wages, for house rent.

"Preference in promotion or retention in the service shall be given to the foremen who have been longest in the service, provided they are, in the judgment of the proper officer of the Company, equal in merit, capacity and other qualification to other foremen in the service.

"When a foreman is disciplined by suspension or dismissal, he will be given a hearing within fifteen (15) days, if possible, and will be promptly notified of the action taken. Should the charges against him, in the judgment of the proper officer of the company, be unfounded, he will be paid full wages for the time suspended.

"When Section Foremen are taken from their sections to do extra work they will have all necessary expenses incurred for board and lodging paid by the Company.

"Foremen will be granted leave of absence and passes, or reduced rates, in accordance with the general regulations of the Company.

Appendix A

"SCHEDULE OF WAGES
for
MECHANICS, PAINTERS, PUMPMEN, WATCHMEN, SECTIONMEN AND OTHER LABORERS EMPLOYED IN THE MAINTENANCE-OF-WAY DEPARTMENT,
except
MASON FORCES.

"To Take Effect January 1, 1903.

"Employes who are now paid at the rate of less than 80 cents per day will be advanced to that rate.

"Employes who are now paid at the rate of 80 cents and over per day, with the exception of Carpenters, will be advanced ten (10) cents per day.

"The wages of Carpenters will be advanced twenty-five (25) cents per day.

"Rations for employes provided by the Company will be furnished at cost.

"The working hours, except for Pumpmen and Watchmen, from April 1 to November 1, will be from 6 a.m. to 6 p.m., and from November 1 to April 1, from 7 a.m. to 5 p.m.

"One hour will be allowed for dinner.

"The working hours of Pumpmen and Watchmen will be regulated by the head of their department.

"Overtime will be paid for by the hour at the rate of ten (10) per cent of the day wage.

"Overtime made by any of the men must be reported by the foremen on the blank furnished for the purpose. The blank, properly filled out, must be sent to the Roadmaster or Supervisor for his approval within forty-eight (48) hours after such overtime is made.

"When Sectionmen are taken from their sections to do extra work in cases of emergency, they will be provided with board and lodging by the Company.

"Employes will be granted passes, or reduced rates, in accordance with the general regulations of the Company.

Appendix A

"If any question of importance should arise in the operation of these schedules and the rules relating thereto, the General Superintendent of your respective divisions will see a committee of three of our own employes representing our own men for the purpose of considering such questions. The committee will have the right of appeal from the decision of the General Superintendent to the General Manager. Such committees will be required to get the necessary permission from the proper officer to leave their post of duty, and will be furnished transportation upon proper application.

J. R. KENLY, General Manager.

F. P. HAYGOOD, General Chairman for the Employes."

(NOTE: Before the signing of the foregoing agreement, many section men on the Atlantic Coast Line Railway worked for 56c a day.)

Laws of the Old Insurance Department

The Insurance Department established when the Brotherhood was founded was discontinued in August, 1913. In the intervening years, the laws of this department were amended and modified considerably from time to time.

Under the laws of the Grand Lodge constitution as revised and amended at the convention held in St. Louis, Missouri, in December, 1902, one of the oldest constitutions available in the files at Grand Lodge, applications for membership in the Insurance Department had to be in writing on forms furnished by the Grand Lodge. An applicant must have been in good physical health at the time of making application. Any misstatement relative to his age, physical condition, or family history rendered his beneficiary certificate void.

Every insured member was required to pay one insurance assessment monthly on or before the fifth day of each month. If the assessments collected were inadequate to pay claims against the department, the Grand Executive Committee could levy such additional assessments as might be necessary. An insured member was also required to maintain payment of his Grand and subordinate dues and assessments.

Benefits were payable on proof of death or total disability of an insured member. Under the laws then in effect, certificates of insurance for either $500.00 or $1,000.00 were issued. The monthly rates for the former ranged from 50c to 75c, depending on age; for the latter, from $1.00 to $1.50.

Applicants for insurance had to pass a rather unusual test. The constitution provided that the following table of weights would govern the acceptance of applicants for insurance, except when other causes appeared for the rejection of such applicants. Where the height of the applicant was greater than six feet, six pounds was added to the maximum weight for each additional inch:

HEIGHT			WEIGHT	
			Minimum	Maximum
5	feet		100 lbs.	150 lbs.
5	"	1 inch	102 "	156 "
5	"	2 "	105 "	162 "
5	"	3 "	108 "	168 "
5	"	4 "	112 "	175 "
5	"	5 "	116 "	182 "
5	"	6 "	120 "	188 "
5	"	7 "	124 "	195 "
5	"	8 "	128 "	202 "
5	"	9 "	132 "	210 "
5	"	10 "	136 "	216 "
5	"	11 "	142 "	222 "
6	"		148 "	228 "

The laws of the Insurance Department outlined in some detail the physical impairments that would be considered as a condition of total disability:

"At the death of an insured member in good standing his beneficiary shall receive the face value of his certificate. Should a member in good standing become totally disabled for life by accident, as hereinafter provided, he shall receive the face value of his certificate. Total disability shall consist of the loss of both legs, or both arms, or both eyes, or one leg and one arm. For the loss of one leg or one arm any insured member in good standing shall receive one-half of the face value of his certificate. When the hand is amputated above the wrist the arm will be considered lost, and when the foot is amputated above the ankle the leg will be considered lost.

Appendix A

"Claims for the loss of eyes shall not be paid until twelve months after the vision has been lost, except in cases where the eye balls are extracted from the head. Members who have but one eye when admitted to the insurance department can in no case recover more than one-half the amount of their certificate on account of total blindness."

The Insurance Department became bankrupt and had to be abandoned in 1913 when the assessments necessary to continue the payment of claims became so high that the members refused to pay them.

Earliest Record of a Lodge Meeting

Following is a newspaper account of a meeting on October 9, 1887, of the first subordinate lodge established by the Wilson organization:

"VOL. XV MARENGO NEWS NO. 25

DEMOPOLIS, MARENGO CO., ALABAMA

Thursday, October 13, 1887

MEETING OF RAILWAY ORDER OF TRACKMEN OF THE U. S.

October 9, 1887

"1st Resolution adopted and ordered spread on the minutes and copy of same to be printed in some leading paper and copy to be sent to Mr. J. M. Bridges, Supt., also one to Mr. J. Gallion, R. M.

"The meeting was called to order by the honorable President J. B. Panky. Opened with prayer and address of President.

"Gentlemen of the Railway Order of Trackmen:

"But a few short months have passed since our organization first assumed shape, and under the guidance of a kind Providence we have assembled this day to complete and perfect our order, which is destined in the near future to attract the attention and command the influence of trackmen throughout the length and breadth of every land over which a railroad bed is laid.

"I fail to find language sufficient to thank you for the honor done me in my election as president of this order, and should I fail to place before you the objects of our meeting in a clear and proper light, I earnestly trust you will overlook any shortcomings on my part, in explaining the worthy cause for which we are assembled.

"All grades and classes of railroad men have already formed organizations and meet annually to improve their constitutions and by-laws and promote the true interests of their respective orders. Yet all this time we, the trackmen, upon whom rests the gravest responsibility, are alone without an organization.

"I hope that every member present fully understands and appreciates the objects of this meeting, and that they likewise appreciate the kind courtesy shown us by the officials of the E.T.V. & Ga. R.R. Co. I heartily trust that from this day each and every member will take the necessary interest in furthering this noble work.

"God has permitted us to meet this day to conclude our organization, and I invoke in behalf of all future meetings His guidance and direction, and providential care over the growth of the order.

"The purpose of our meeting being to thoroughly establish the working of our order, this was successfully done, and we now stand thoroughly organized and ready to receive members. Any trackman desiring to join the order can get particulars and copy of constitution and by-laws by addressing the secretary, W. G. Self, Demopolis, Ala.

"We desire to return thanks to our supt. Mr. J. M. Bridges and Mr. Jo. Gallion, Road Master, for the favor granted which was appreciated by the order. We also desire to thank the citizens of Lauderdale for their kind and generous hospitality.

J. B. Panky, Pres.
W. G. Self, Secy."

(This was the editor's note):

"The Railway Order of Trackmen, the proceedings of a meeting of which was published today, is a new organization which will have its headquarters in Demopolis, and our citizens can well take an interest in its welfare. We wish it a rapid and prosperous growth."

ABSTRACT FROM BOOK OF RULES ISSUED TO EMPLOYES OF THE TALLAHASSEE, PENSACOLA AND GEORGIA RAILROAD, APRIL 3, 1858 (NOW A PART OF THE SEABOARD AIR LINE RAILROAD).

"All engines unprovided with lamps, running at night out of time, will be required to keep their dampers open to show a light.

"Rule 8—As a general rule when two trains meet between stations, the train nearest the turn out will run back. Any dispute as to which shall retire shall be settled by the conductors without any interference on the part of the engineers. This rule is required to be varied in favor of heaviest loaded train, if they meet near the center.

"Rule 12—Should a train run off or for any cause be stopped on the track at night, the red light must be instantly sent back to a safe distance to stop a train approaching in the rear. The green light will in like manner be sent forward to stop a train approaching in the front. A half mile each way from where the train is standing will be a safe distance. At that point a fire must be built in the middle of the track and a train hand stationed there who shall keep up the fire and the red or green lights burning.

"Rule 18—The spark catcher or chimney of an engine getting out of order so as to endanger the safety of the train, the conductor must put his train on the first turn out and return his engine to Tallahassee for repairs.

"Rule 17—The firemen will be in all cases used to assist in putting and taking out baggage and all other work which may be required by the conductor in charge.

"Rule 11—Overseers must not strike a negro with any other weapon than a switch except in defense of their person. Where a negro requires correction, his hands must be tied by the overseer and he will whip him with an ordinary switch or strap not to exceed 39 lashes at one time nor more than 60 for one offense in one day, unless ordered to do so by the supervisor in his presence.

"No. 15—The use of intoxicants by employes on repairs of the road is positively prohibited. Any overseer or other employe who keeps it at his shanty or uses it in any other way than when prescribed by a physician as medicine or who allows the negroes to keep or use it at the shanty or on the work will be fined or discharged.

"No. 19—No negroes must be allowed to bring or to have at the shanty any fresh meat or poultry, unless the overseer is satisfied he or she came by it honestly."

Appendix A

Certificate No. 3534 — CERTIFICATE OF MEMBERSHIP — Division No. 1.

Brotherhood of Railway Trackmen

OF AMERICA.

This Certifies, That W. Johnson, of Leanchoil, B.C., has been duly initiated into our beloved Brotherhood, and is an active member of Grand Division No. One and as such is entitled to all the rights, privileges and benefits according to the terms and specifications of the Constitution and Laws of the Order.

The holder of this Certificate is entitled to none of the benefits of the Insurance Department. In case of a desire to become a beneficiary member, the holder hereof will make application to the Insurance Department.

C. W. Johnson
MEMBER'S SIGNATURE.

IN WITNESS WHEREOF, I have affixed my official signature and attached the seal of the Order hereto at St. Louis, Mo., this eleventh day of January, 1900.

AN ... RE RENDERS THIS CERTIFICATE NULL AND VOID.

John T. Wilson
GRAND CHIEF

One of the early certificates of membership issued by the Brotherhood until 1902, when the dues-receipt or "working-card" system was adopted.

Appendix A

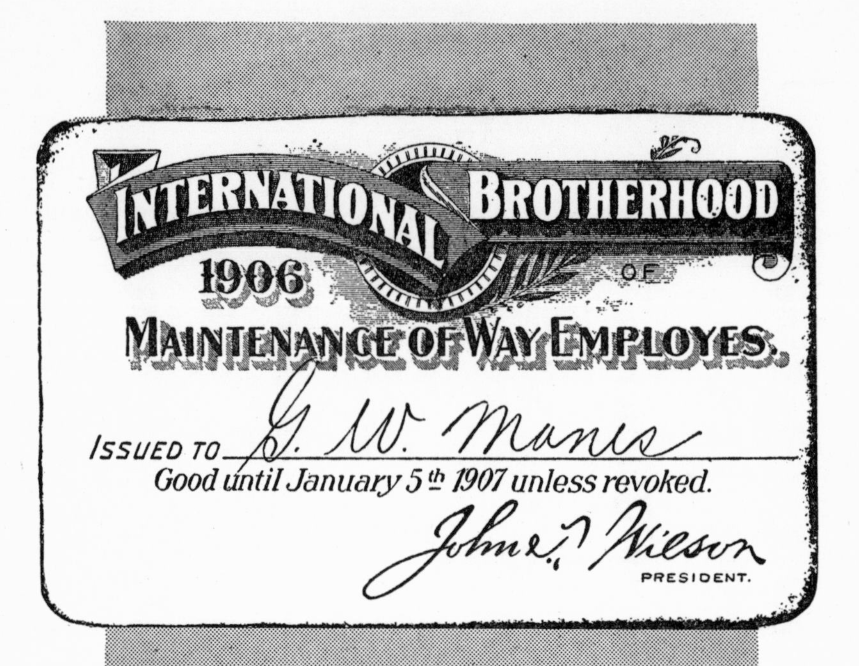

INTERNATIONAL BROTHERHOOD
1906
OF
MAINTENANCE OF WAY EMPLOYES.

ISSUED TO G. W. Manes

Good until January 5th 1907 unless revoked.

John T. Wilson
PRESIDENT.

Lodge No. One Certificate No. 52832

NOTICE

This card is not transferable. It must be signed in ink by the person to whom it is issued, who is entitled to fraternal courtesies. It is good only when countersigned by C. BOYLE, and expires on date named on its face.

Signed G. W. Manes

Countersigned: C. Boyle

No. A 6767

57

The form of dues receipt, commonly called a "working card," adopted by the 1902 Convention of the Brotherhood to replace the certificate of membership.

Appendix B

CHRONOLOGY OF DATES AND EVENTS

July, 1887—Brotherhood chartered under Alabama laws.

October 13, 1891—Amalgamation of Wilson and Pegg organizations.

1892—"The Foremen's Advance Advocate" began publication.

June 19, 1898—First chapter of the Ladies' Auxiliary formed.

1899—Amalgamation of American and Canadian organizations.

February, 1900—Affiliation of the Brotherhood with the American Federation of Labor.

June 10, 1901—First authorized strike (Maine Central Railroad).

June 17, 1901—The Canadian Pacific strike.

August 30, 1901—Successful termination of the Canadian Pacific strike.

June 1, 1902—Effective date of first agreement signed by the Brotherhood with a railway company (Canadian Pacific).

December, 1902 — Grand Lodge of the Ladies' Auxiliary formed.

February 7, 1908—Death of John T. Wilson.

March, 1913—Grand Lodge headquarters moved from St. Louis to Detroit.

September 11, 1914—The secession at the 1914 convention.

Appendix B

December 26, 1917—United States railroads placed under government control.

August, 1918—The reuniting of the two factions formed at the 1914 convention.

March 7, 1919—National agreement signed in Canada.

December 16, 1919—The effective date of the national agreement with the United States Railroad Administration.

March 1, 1920—Railroads in the United States returned to private ownership.

March 18, 1920—The resignation of President A. E. Barker.

1922—Wage reductions and the shopmen's strike (United States).

May, 1926—Passage of the Railway Labor Act (United States).

October, 1929—The great stock market crash.

January, 1932—The first formal national conferences between representatives of the railroads and the Brotherhoods in the United States.

June 21, 1934—Amended Railway Labor Act signed by the President.

June 27, 1934—Railroad Retirement Act of 1934 signed by President.

January 1, 1935—New Canadian National Contributory Pension Plan for railway workers became effective.

May 6, 1935—United States Supreme Court declared the Railroad Retirement Act of 1934 unconstitutional.

Appendix B

August 29, 1935—The President signed the Railroad Retirement Act of 1935 and the Carriers' Taxing Act of 1935.

May 21, 1936—Washington Job Protection Agreement signed.

1937—Golden jubilee celebration of the Brotherhood's founding.

February 18, 1937—Agreement signed by the Brotherhoods and the railroads in the United States leading to the Retirement Act of 1937.

August 1, 1937—Wage increase of 5c an hour (United States).

July 1, 1939—Railroad Unemployment Insurance Act became effective (United States).

October 10, 1940—Improvements in the Railroad Unemployment Insurance Act.

March 1, 1941—Minimum hourly rates of 33c and 36c established for railroad workers in the United States under the Wage-Hour Act.

December, 1941—Agreements signed granting wage increase and six days' vacation with pay (United States).

June 1, 1941—Cost-of-living bonus established for Canadian railway workers.

August 31, 1942—Minimum hourly wage of 40c established for railroad workers in the United States under the Wage-Hour Act.

January 17, 1944—Agreement signed granting wage increases (United States).

February 15, 1944—Cost-of-living bonus added to basic wage rates of Canadian rail workers.

Appendix B

October 21, 1944—National agreement signed providing improved overtime rules (United States).

March 1, 1944—Agreement signed granting a paid vacation of one week to Canadian rail workers.

July 31, 1944—Wage increase granted in Canada.

February 23, 1945 — Supplemental vacation agreement increased paid vacations in the United States to 12 days after 5 years' service.

January 1, 1946 — Wage increase of 16c an hour (United States).

May 22, 1946 — Additional wage increase of 2½c an hour (United States).

February 16, 1946—Wage increase of 2c an hour in Canada (3c, 4c, and 5c for section men in certain classified yards).

June 1, 1946—Additional wage increase of 8c an hour granted to Canadian rail workers.

July 31, 1946—Improvements made in Railroad Retirement Act. Railroad Unemployment Insurance Act amended to provide sickness benefits.

December 31, 1946—Death of E. E. Milliman.

September 1, 1947—Wage increase of 15½c an hour (United States).

January 9, 1948—Paid vacations of 6, 9, and 12 days granted (Canada).

March 1, 1948—Wage increase of 17c an hour for Canadian rail workers.

Appendix B

June 23, 1948—Railroad retirement and unemployment insurance systems improved (United States).

October 1, 1948—Wage increase of 7c an hour (United States).

September 1, 1949 — Forty-hour week established (United States).

May 15, 1950—Movement begun to stabilize maintenance of way employment (United States).

August 22, 1950—General railroad strike in Canada.

September 1, 1950—Wage increase of 7c an hour (Canada).

January 10, 1951—Union-shop amendment added to Railway Labor Act.

February 1, 1951—Wage increases of 12½c an hour plus an escalator clause gearing wages to the cost of living (United States).

February 1, 1951—First union-shop agreement signed by the Brotherhood in the United States.

April 30, 1951—Representation rights won on the Santa Fe System.

June 1, 1951—Forty-hour week became effective in Canada.

October 30, 1951—New international headquarters building dedicated.

October 30, 1951—Railroad Retirement Act liberalized.

February 14, 1952—Presidential Emergency Board recommended the negotiation of union-shop agreements.

August 29, 1952—Union-shop agreement signed with carriers in eastern region.

Appendix B

December 1, 1952—Improvement-factor wage increase of 4c an hour became effective (United States).

February 7, 1953—Wage increase of 7 per cent plus 7c an hour in Canada, effective September 1, 1952. Agreement reached providing for the check-off of union dues.

February 24, 1953—Agreement negotiated and wage increase obtained for extra gang laborers (Canada).

August 21, 1954—Agreement signed providing for a health and welfare plan, three weeks' paid vacation, and seven paid holidays each year (United States).

August 31, 1954—Liberalizing changes in railroad retirement and unemployment insurance systems (United States).

October 22, 1954—Conciliation Board recommended increased wages and improved rules for extra gang laborers (Canada).

November 19, 1954—Arbitrator's award granted five paid holidays and three weeks' vacation each year (Canada).

December 3, 1954—Escalator clause canceled and cost-of-living wage increases added to basic rates of pay (United States).

January 18, 1955—Health and welfare policy contract signed (United States).

Appendix C

CONVENTIONS OF GRAND LODGE

The records of the Brotherhood indicate that the first convention was held in July, 1887. With the exception of the meeting in October, 1891, at which time the Wilson and the Pegg organizations united, there is no definite record of the dates and places of the conventions held prior to 1893.

Conventions were held annually until 1896. From 1896 to 1914, conventions were held biennially. Thereafter, they were held triennally, except for the two special conventions in 1918 and the regular convention in 1919 scheduled by the special convention in Cincinnati, Ohio (1918).

1891—Meeting of the Wilson-Pegg amalgamation committees in St. Louis, Missouri, October 13 through 15, 1891.

1893—Convention held in the City of Atlanta, Georgia, beginning Monday, October 2, 1893.

1894—Convention held in the City of St. Louis, Missouri, October 1 through 4, 1894. Resolution passed that the conventions be held biennially.

1896—Convention held in the City of St. Louis, Missouri, October 5 through 8, 1896. First biennial convention.

1898—Convention held in the City of Macon, Georgia, December 5 through 7, 1898.

1900—Convention held in the City of St. Louis, Missouri, December 3 through 6, 1900.

1902—Convention held in the City of St. Louis, Missouri, December 1 through 4, 1902.

1904—Convention held in the City of St. Louis, Missouri, November 14 through 17, 1904.

1906—Convention held in the City of Toronto, Ontario, Canada, December 3 through 6, 1906.

Appendix C

1908—Convention held in the City of New Orleans, Louisiana, December 7 through 11, 1908.

1910—Convention held in the City of Boston, Massachusetts. September 5 through 12, 1910.

1912—Convention held in the City of St. Louis, Missouri, November 11 through 15, 1912.

1914—Convention held in the City of Winnipeg, Manitoba, Canada, September 7 through 16, 1914. At the Winnipeg Convention it was decided in the future to hold the conventions triennially instead of biennially.

1917—Convention held in the City of Detroit, Michigan, September 3 through 6, 1917.

1918—Two special conventions were held in 1918. The first in Detroit, Michigan, on August 12 and the second in Cincinnati, Ohio, August 15 through 22, 1918. By authority of the Cincinnati special convention, the next regular convention was scheduled to be held in the City of Detroit, Michigan in September, 1919.

1919—Convention held in the City of Detroit, Michigan, September 8 through 22, 1919.

1922—Convention held in the City of Detroit, Michigan, October 2 through 18, 1922.

1925—Convention held in the City of Detroit, Michigan, September 14 through 28, 1925.

1928—Convention held in the City of Detroit, Michigan, September 10 through 20, 1928.

1931—Convention held in the City of Toronto, Ontario, Canada, September 14 through 21, 1931.

Appendix C

1934—Convention held in the City of Detroit, Michigan, September 10 through 15, 1934.

1937—Convention held in the City of Detroit, Michigan, September 13 through 21, 1937.

1940—Convention held in the City of Quebec, Canada, July 15 through 23, 1940.

1943—Convention held in the City of Detroit, Michigan, July 19 through 24, 1943.

1946—Convention held in the City of Detroit, Michigan, July 15 through 20, 1946.

1949—Convention held in the City of Detroit, Michigan, June 20 through 25, 1949.

1952—Convention held in the City of Montreal, Quebec, Canada, June 16 through 23, 1952.

Appendix D

ROSTER OF PAST AND PRESENT GRAND LODGE OFFICERS

(Early records incomplete.)

Grand Lodge Presidents

Name	Years	Name	Years
John T. Wilson	1887-1908	E. F. Grable	1920-1922
A. B. Lowe	1908-1914	F. H. Fljozdal	1922-1940
T. H. Gerrey	1914	E. E. Milliman	1940-1946
A. E. Barker	1914-1920	T. C. Carroll	1947-

Note: Following the death of President Milliman on December 31, 1946, Secretary-Treasurer A. Shoemake served as acting Grand Lodge President until the election of President Carroll on February 14, 1947.

Grand Lodge Secretary-Treasurers

Name	Years	Name	Years
M. O'Dowd	1891-1893	W. Allen	1893-1894
J. R. Ice	1894-1896		

(Position abolished in 1896. President John T. Wilson assumed duties from 1896 to 1902.)

Name	Years	Name	Years
C. Boyle	1902-1907	*S. J. Pegg	1907-1914 1920-1922
*Alexander Gibb	1912-1914	George Seal	1914-1920
E. E. Milliman	1922-1940	A. Shoemake	1940-

* S. J. Pegg served as Grand Secretary and Alexander Gibb as Grand Treasurer from 1912 to 1914.

Note: Vice President T. L. Jones served as acting Grand Lodge Secretary-Treasurer from January 4 to February 14, 1947.

Grand Lodge Vice Presidents

Name	Years	Name	Years
P. R. Bridgemen	1891-1894	George B. Jenness	1910-1914
D. W. Cash	1894	Henry Irwin	1910-1918
J. R. Ice	1896-1898	T. H. Gerrey	1912-1914 1918-1919
J. F. Craiglow	1898	W. B. Nichols	1914-1917
W. C. Cain	1898	W. V. Turnbull	1918-1940
J. W. Davenport	1898-1904 1906-1908	O. Folland	1918-1919
A. B. Lowe	1900-1908	F. H. Fljozdal	1918-1919
W. W. Haygood	1900-1904	C. R. Patten	1918-1919
W. S. Powell	1904-1906 1908-1914	E. F. Grable	1918-1920
W. F. McAbee	1904-1906	D. Stroud	1918-1922
A. F. Stout	1906-1912 1922-1928	Alexander Gibb	1919-1920
M. J. Powers	1908-1918 1919-1922	G. H. Flynt	1919-1922
J. F. Davis	1908-1910	S. J. Pegg	1919-1920
E. G. Gashel	1909-1910	G. H. Planten	1919-1922
H. A. Vurpia	1909-1917	J. B. Malloy	1919-1922
John Cotter	1909-1910	M. D. Barker	1919-1922
		J. C. Smock	1919-1922
		William Robson	1919-1922
		W. D. Roberts	1919-1922

Appendix D

Name	Years
J. J. Farnan	1919-1922
A. L. Lynch	1920-1921
F. C. Gassman	1920-1925 1928-1935
J. O. Raley	1920-1922
M. J. Cadigan	1921-1925
C. E. Crook	1922-1949
H. Hemenway	1925-1928
T. C. Carroll	1925-1947
John E. Perry	1928
J. H. Myers	1928-1934
Thos. F. Holleran	1934-
M. Duncan	1935-1943
T. L. Jones	1940-
E. J. Hopcraft	1940-1943
J. J. O'Grady	1940-1952
George Hudson	1943-
W. Aspinall	1943-
J. H. Hadley	1947-
L. Vogland	1949-
W. K. McKee	1952-1955

Grand Lodge Executive Board Members

Note: Prior to 1908 the Grand President or a Grand Vice President served as chairman of the Executive Committee. For a time, the Executive Committee was called an "Advisory Board" and consisted of elected members of the Board and the Grand President and Grand Vice Presidents.

Name	Years
S. J. Pegg	1891-1892
W. W. Allen	1891-1892
R. H. Coxe	1891-1894
W. F. McAbee	1891-1893 1894-1900
James H. Elkins	1891-1892
James H. Jackson	1892-1893
D. W. Cash	1893-1894
P. F. McAneney	1893-1894
R. B. Phayer	1893-1896
Patrick Joyce	1894-1896
J. D. Jeffords	1894
J. C. Lambert	1895-1908
James Beggan	1896-1898
S. E. Hawes	1896-1908
J. A. Bouger	1898
John Hendrickson	1900
C. Boyle	1900-1902
J. S. Eastman	1900-1908
R. Ferguson	1902-1907
W. H. Noyes	1907-1913
Henry Irwin	1908-1909
J. E. Smith	1908-1914
G. H. Flynt	1908-1912 1918-1919
T. J. O'Donnell	1908-1912
C. E. Crook	1918-1919
L. I. Kennedy	1918-1920
W. Robson	1918-1919
A. L. Lynch	1919-1920
F. C. Gassman	1919-1920
Patrick Woods	1919-1922
A. M. Everett	1920-1921
John Hall	1920-1922
E. L. Hardy	1920-1921
John J. O'Grady	1920-1922
J. J. Roach	1921-1922
E. L. Enke	1921-1922
E. E. Clark	1922-1925
George Seal	1910-1914
Lawrence Lewis	1912-1913
Lucian Brown	1912-1917
W. V. Turnbull	1913-1918
W. B. Nichols	1913-1914
F. H. Fljozdal	1914-1918
William Dorey	1914-1920
Oliver Folland	1917-1918
T. C. Carroll	1922-1925
J. E. Waggoner	1922-1925
J. S. Moorhead	1922-1925
E. J. Hopcraft	1922-1940
Frank M. Sillik	1925-1934
W. O. Beaver	1925-1928
John F. Towle	1925-1951
George H. Davis	1925-1949
M. Duncan	1928-1935
Louis Vogland	1934-1949
T. J. Finneran	1935-1937
R. H. Smith	1937-1943
William Jewkes	1940-1946
H. H. Reddick	1943-1951
William Crampton	1946-1952
M. C. Plunk	1949-
J. P. Wilson	1949-
R. Freccia	1951-
L. E. Rhyne	1951-1952
C. L. Lambert	1952-
J. A. Huneault	1952-

Appendix D

Directors of Statistics and Research

L. E. Keller	1922-1947	F. L. Noakes	1947-

Roster of Editors or Associate Editors of the "Advocate" and the "Journal"

M. O'Dowd	1892-1893	Alexander Gibb	1912-1914
W. W. Allen	1893-1894	F. Finnson	1914-1919 1922-1940
J. R. Ice	1894-1896		
John T. Wilson	1896-1902	Charles P. Howard	1919-1922
J. E. Mulkey	1902-1910	Thomas R. Downie	1941-1947
S. J. Pegg	1910-1912	E. J. Plondke	1947-

Note: Under the current laws of the Brotherhood, the President is also the Editor of the "Journal."

ROSTER OF PAST AND PRESENT GRAND LODGE OFFICERS—LADIES' AUXILIARY

Grand Lodge Presidents

Mrs. Alice C. Mulkey	1902-1909	Mrs. Josie Berg	1928-1934
Mrs. Cora B. Smith	1910-1917	Mrs. Edna Keyes	1934-1937
Mrs. May G. Downey	1922-1925	Mrs. B. H. Miller	1937-1952
Mrs. Charles Albert	1925-1928	Mrs. Francis T. Brennan	1952-

Grand Lodge Secretary-Treasurers

Mrs. George B. Jenness	1910-1915	Mrs. Edith A. Betts	1931-1940
Mrs. I. P. Steel	1915-1917	Mrs. G. E. Vance	1949-1952
Mrs. C. E. Hardiman	1922-1928	Mrs. B. A. Daun	1952-
Mrs. Louis Vogland	1928-1931 1940-1949		

Appendix E

EMPLOYMENT AND EARNINGS—SIXTEEN* MAINTENANCE OF WAY CLASSES

CLASS I RAILROADS IN THE UNITED STATES
1921 - 1953

Year	Number of Employes	Average Annual Earnings	Average Straight Time Hourly Earnings
1921**	386,805	$ 514.34	$ .414
1922	365,082	996.39	.395
1923	402,243	1,044.06	.402
1924	389,251	1,025.01	.407
1925	389,114	1,038.39	.409
1926	414,208	1,046.33	.410
1927	416,680	1,047.33	.413
1928	395,957	1,050.70	.416
1929	405,152	1,062.73	.419
1930	343,474	1,041.69	.427
1931	273,260	987.05	.432
1932	216,946	824.14	.392
1933	199,782	818.90	.384
1934	208,038	883.86	.392
1935	205,679	966.08	.422
1936	223,945	1,020.02	.422
1937	228,845	1,070.40	.445
1938	186,440	1,135.63	.476
1939	200,686	1,140.43	.479
1940	205,182	1,164.52	.483
1941	231,752	1,288.72	.520
1942	257,624	1,533.14	.587
1943	267,348	1,918.43	.664
1944	286,403	1,961.53	.683
1945	292,532	1,936.28	.683
1946	256,748	2,205.79	.863
1947	255,416	2,358.80	.925
1948	256,060	2,670.55	1.046
1949	224,067	2,762.62	1.159
1950	226,994	2,802.24	1.309
1951	237,944	3,180.52	1.476
1952	228,411	3.322.87	1.556
1953	225,430	3.369.61	1.592

** For six months ended December 31, 1921.
SOURCE: Annual M-300, Interstate Commerce Commission.

* Classification and Interstate Commerce Commission Reporting Division Number: Bridge and Building Gang Foremen, 29; Bridge and Building Carpenters, 30; Bridge and Building Iron Workers, 31; Bridge and Building Painters, 32; Masons, Bricklayers, Plasterers and Plumbers, 33; Maintenance of Way and Structures Helpers and Apprentices, 34; Portable Steam Equipment Operators, 35; Portable Steam Equipment Operators Helpers, 36; Pumping Equipment Operators, 37; Gang Foremen (Extra Gang and Work Train Laborers), 38; Gang or Section Foremen, 40; Extra Gang Men, 41; Section Men, 42; Maintenance of Way Laborers (other than track and roadway), 43; Bridge Operators and Helpers, 102; Crossing and Bridge Flagmen and Gatemen, 103.

Appendix E

EMPLOYMENT AND EARNINGS—THIRTEEN* MAINTENANCE OF WAY CLASSES**

STEAM RAILWAYS OF CANADA
1926 - 1953

Year	Average Number of Employes	Average Annual Earnings	Average Hourly Earnings
1926	32,073	$1,130.29	$ .449
1927	33,042	1,185.57	.468
1928	33,674	1,200.32	.470
1929	33,360	1,228.70	.482
1930	31,204	1,245.55	.492
1931	29,140	1,210.02	.492
1932	26,193	1,123.04	.462
1933	24,758	1,085.19	.445
1934	26,355	1,021.37	.420
1935	26,193	1,088.11	.444
1936	27,259	1,095.36	.447
1937	25,808	1,150.65	.464
1938	24,472	1,210.78	.494
1939	24,614	1,218.66	.498
1940	24,766	1,238.85	.499
1941	26,600	1,313.69	.532
1942	27,621	1,471.16	.537
1943	29,602	1,518.90	.591
1944	29,740	1,816.18	.715
1945	30,374	1,673.87	.672
1946	29,677	1,828.22	.742
1947	29,618	1,940.82	.783
1948	30,491	2,324.10	.925
1949	30,947	2,363.81	.948
1950	30,846	2,387.74	.975
1951	31,995	2,608.88	1.145
1952	32,972	2,666.15	1.251
1953	39,895	2,834.69	1.309

** Twelve Classes—1926-1952. Thirteen Classes in 1953. Agreement covering Extra Gang Laborers became effective in 1953.

SOURCE: Railway Transport, Part II, (formerly Statistics of Steam Railways) Dominion Bureau of Statistics.

* Classification and Dominion Bureau of Statistics Division Number: Bridge and Building Department Foremen, 9; Carpenters and Bridgemen, 10; Blacksmiths, Pipefitters, Plumbers, Tinsmiths and Pump Repairers, 11; Masons, Bricklayers, Plasterers and Painters, 12; Bridge and Building Department Helpers and Apprentices, 13; Pile Driver, Ditching, Hoist and Steam Shovel Employes, 15; Pumpmen, 16; Extra Gang and Snow Plough Foremen, 17; Section Foremen, 19; Section Men, 20; Labourers, 21; Drawbridge Operators, 62; Signalmen or Watchmen at Crossings, non-interlocked, 63.

Appendix F

EMPLOYMENT TREND—TOTAL EMPLOYES AND MAINTENANCE OF WAY EMPLOYES

CLASS I RAILROADS IN THE UNITED STATES
1921-1954

Year	Total Railroad Employes[1]	Index	Average No. of M of W Employes[2]	Index	Percentage of M of W Employes to Total Employes
1921*	1,659,513	100.0	386,805	100.0	23.3
1922	1,626.834	98.0	365,082	94.4	22.4
1923	1,857,674	111.9	402,243	104.0	21.7
1924	1,751,362	105.5	389,251	100.6	22.2
1925	1,744,311	105.1	389,114	100.6	22.3
1926	1,779,275	107.2	414,208	107.1	23.3
1927	1,735,105	104.6	416,680	107.7	24.0
1928	1,656,411	99.8	395,957	102.4	23.9
1929	1,660,850	100.1	405,152	104.7	24.4
1930	1,487,839	89.7	343,474	88.8	23.1
1931	1,258,719	75.9	273,260	70.7	21.7
1932	1,031,703	62.2	216,946	56.1	21.0
1933	971,196	58.5	199,782	51.7	20.6
1934	1,007,702	60.7	208,038	53.8	20.6
1935	994,371	59.9	205,679	53.2	20.7
1936	1,065,624	64.2	223,945	57.9	21.0
1937	1,114,663	67.2	228,845	59.2	20.5
1938	939,171	56.6	186,440	48.2	19.9
1939	987,675	59.5	200,686	51.9	20.3
1940	1,026,848	61.9	205,182	53.1	20.0
1941	1,139,925	68.7	231,752	60.0	20.3
1942	1,270,687	76.6	257,624	66.6	20.3
1943	1,355,114	81.7	267,348	69.1	19.7
1944	1,414,776	85.3	286,403	74.0	20.2
1945	1,419,505	85.5	292,532	75.6	20.6
1946	1,359,263	81.9	256,748	66.4	18.9
1947	1,351,863	81.5	255,416	66.0	18.9
1948	1,326,597	79.9	256,060	66.2	19.3
1949	1,192,019	71.8	224,067	57.9	18.8
1950	1,220,401	73.5	226,994	58.7	18.6
1951	1,275,744	76.9	237,944	61.5	18.7
1952	1,226,421	73.9	228,411	59.1	18.6
1953	1,206,312	72.7	225,430	58.3	18.7
1954	1,064,434	64.1	184,743	47.8	17.4

[1] Average of twelve monthly counts.
[2] Sixteen Classes.
* For six months ending December 31, 1921.
SOURCE: Statistics of Steam Railways in the United States, Interstate Commerce Commission.

Appendix F

EMPLOYMENT TREND—TOTAL EMPLOYES AND MAINTENANCE OF WAY EMPLOYES

STEAM RAILWAYS OF CANADA
1926 - 1953

Year	Average No. of Employes	Index	Average No. of M of W Employes[1]	Index	Percentage of M of W Employes to Total Employes
1926	174,266	100.0	32,073	100.0	18.4
1927	176,338	101.2	33,042	103.0	18.7
1928	187,710	107.7	33,674	105.0	17.9
1929	187,846	107.8	33,360	104.0	17.8
1930	174,485	100.1	31,204	97.3	17.9
1931	154,569	88.7	29,140	90.9	18.9
1932	132,678	76.1	26,193	81.7	19.7
1933	121,923	70.0	24,758	77.2	20.3
1934	127,326	73.1	26,355	82.2	20.7
1935	127,526	73.2	26,193	81.7	20.5
1936	132,781	76.2	27,259	85.0	20.5
1937	133,467	76.6	25,808	80.5	19.3
1938	127,747	73.3	24,472	76.3	19.2
1939	129,362	74.2	24,614	76.7	19.0
1940	135,700	77.9	24,766	77.2	18.3
1941	148,746	85.4	26,600	82.9	17.9
1942	157,740	90.5	27,621	86.1	17.5
1943	169,663	97.4	29,602	92.3	17.5
1944	175,095	100.5	29,740	92.7	17.0
1945	180,603	103.6	30,374	94.7	16.8
1946	180,383	103.5	29,677	92.5	16.5
1947	184,415	105.8	29,618	92.3	16.1
1948	189,963	109.0	30,491	95.1	16.1
1949	192,366	110.4	30,947	96.5	16.1
1950	190,385	109.2	30,846	96.2	16.2
1951	204,025	117.1	31,995	99.8	15.7
1952	214,143	122.9	32,972	102.8	15.4
1953	211,951	121.6	39,895	124.4	18.8

[1] Twelve Classes—1926-1952. Thirteen Classes in 1953. Agreement covering Extra Gang Labourers became effective in 1953.

SOURCE: Railway Transport, Part II, (formerly Statistics of Steam Railways) Dominion Bureau of Statistics.

Appendix G

ANNUAL EXPENDITURES FOR MAINTENANCE OF WAY
AND STRUCTURES WORK EQUIPMENT
UNITED STATES AND CANADA
1937-1953

Year	Units	Expenditure
1937	3,310	$ 5,000,000
1938	1,376	2,180,000
1939	3,547	6,000,000
1940	5,414	7,250,000
1941	8,007	10,500,000
1942	7,612	10,270,000
1943	8,507	12,300,000
1944	9,984	14,400,000
1945	11,733	17,500,000
1946	9,939	15,400,000
1947	9,500	19,100,000
1948	9,300	18,700,000
1949	8,700	17,500,000
1950	8,700	18,270,000
1951	9,700	19,500,000
1952	8,000	20,700,000
1953	9,500	16,500,000

SOURCE: Railway Age.

Index

J

K

L

M

N

S